# *HEARTFELT*

# HEARTFELT

*Supping Bovril from the Devil's Cup*

## Aidan Smith

**Birlinn**

First published in Great Britain in 2005 by
Birlinn Ltd

West Newington House
10 Newington Road
Edinburgh
EH9 1QS

www.birlinn.co.uk

ISBN 10: 1 84158 422 3
ISBN 13: 978 1 84158 422 5

British Library Cataloguing-in-Publication Data
A catalogue record for this book
is available on request from the British Library

Typeset by Hewer Text UK Ltd, Edinburgh
Printed and bound by Thomson Litho, East Kilbride

## PREFACE

If you're looking for a book about infiltrating a gang of football hooligans, where the writer spends so long with a bunch of radges that he can't or doesn't want to come back out the other side, then put this one down. If you don't know what a radge is, put this one down. All I have done, as a Hibs fan, is spend a season trying to follow Edinburgh rivals Hearts.

It wasn't my idea. 'Do you fancy writing a book?' said Stan, my agent, during the desolate, football-free summer months. 'Yes please,' I said, anticipating a commission about the greatness of Hibs which would grow into a 24-volume masterwork bound in handsome leatherette with display-case option that no self-respecting supporter, of whatever persuasion, could possibly do without.

I would of course die shortly after finishing vol 23, and the magnum opus would be completed from beermat scribblings dutifully collected from my Hibs pubs, Robbie's and the Windsor Buffet, by my grieving widow, the supermodel Tyra Banks. Posthumous cult-classic status was guaranteed.

'Er, not quite,' said Stan, who then suggested the radical, bonkers alternative.

So Stan is the first to receive thanks, closely followed by Neville Moir and the rest of the staff at Birlinn who bought the idea. Colin McLear, editor, played a quiet game at the back.

At *The Scotsman*, I am indebted to Donald Walker, the Sports Editor, and his deputy, Graham Bean. If they didn't let me write a column of football blethers every Saturday, and let Hibs hog it, keep the ball down near the corner-flag, then this book would never have happened, not for me anyway.

My proper job is at *Scotland On Sunday*, writing about what you might call showbiz but what we refer to as the arts, and I fear that over the course of the season some Hearts references might have slipped into my copy. To Fiona Leith, the Arts Editor, I apologise for that, and am also grateful to her for the time off.

Many friends and colleagues have supported me, supporting Hearts, and in those dark days at the beginning, Simon Pia, Rab McNeil, Magnus Llewellin, Richard Neville, Alan Pattullo, Douglas Smith, Steven Rafferty, Scott Douglas, David Begg and Ivan Middleton all offered valuable advice and encouragement. In Australia, one of my oldest friends, John Fraser, and a long-lost cousin, Douglas Harrower, cheered me on from afar, the former a fanatical Hibby, the latter a rabid Jambo.

I did not tell anyone in a blazer at Tynecastle I was writing this book and so don't have to offer up a formal thank-you to Hearts. I paid to get in, I did not get a 'lift over', although Carol in the club shop made sure my new best Jambo mates and I got tickets for the big games. Lots of fans let me into their little Jambo lives and the book could not have been written without them. Joint top of the league in this respect are Billy and Ricky, not their real names, but they were absolute stars.

Thanks, too, to Lucy Tucker who started out providing technical support but as the season reached its conclusion, assumed a pivotal role, like the central midfielder from whom all good things emanate. We're a team now.

And now the end is near (I've followed Hearts from Perth to Paisley). This book is for my sisters, Wendy and Belinda, and my brother, Sean, and is dedicated to the memory of my parents.

# *AUGUST*

### 14 August. Opening Day

A scorching hot day, fans in short-sleeves, many sporting this-year's-model replica strips, lots of them hand-in-hand with their sons. The boys are skipping – they're too young to know the hurt caused by football – but even the dads have a spring in their step. It's the first home game of a new season and optimism abounds. Past failures are forgotten, hope springs eternal, dreams begin anew, *let's go round again, baby we'll turn back the hands of time*. And the shuffling mass of XX-Large polyester fairly crackles and shimmers in the sun.

Admittedly, the dreams can be dead by the end of August, after three straight defeats that include a tanking by your hated local rivals. But there is nothing quite like the shiny, scrubbed, clean-pants expectancy of the opening day. As a boy, yearning for the new season, I counted the sleeps like it was the build-up to Christmas. I checked the pools forecasts . . . week after week of Wogga Wogga Wanderers in the Australian Leagues then . . . uh-oh, what's this? . . . Glentoran vs Dundee! Forres Mechanics vs Partick Thistle! Pre-season tours of Ireland and the Highlands were a sure sign that football – real, proper Scottish football – wasn't far away.

Real, proper Scottish football is not what it was. Only two teams, Celtic and Rangers, can realistically win the Premier League but still fans of the others pledge themselves to their clubs with season tickets, the complete, club-crested wardrobe and a conveyor belt of accessories (including the cuddly toys). And a loyalty that borders on lunacy.

It's an impressive sight, punters in motion. The crowd surges towards the stadium and swells in number every time a side-street links up to the main drag. We pass a chip shop, then a church, then a crossroads where three routes syphon more of the faithful into the throng. Everyone is united in purpose: they're going to the match. Except for a wee woman who's chosen this moment to wheel a pram in the opposite direction, cursing as she pushes against the tide.

It's a scenario I know well; I've been down this road many times. But this particular road is Edinburgh's Gorgie Road and everyone else here is a Jambo, the Saturday name for the Jam Tarts, Hearts, whose Sunday name is Heart of Midlothian. I follow hated city rivals Hibs, Hibernian. I am a Hibby, my team are the Hibees.

'If you hate the fuckin' Hibees clap your hands' chant the Jambos.

I'm the only fuckin' Hibee here and I feel physically sick. For I am about to sup Bovril from the Devil's cup.

A man can change his house, job, car, religion, political affiliations, socks and even his wife, but his football team is supposed to be one of life's constants. Could he, though, for an experiment swap sides for a season? Could he support the other lot, the dreaded enemy from the far side? And would the experience teach him anything about football, loyalty and, most of all, himself?

I am a Hibs fan, my father was a Hibs fan. We followed our team all over the land. We stood on the same terrace steps, then later, sat in the same seats, come rain, hail or relegation. As my school results show, I've sometimes cared for Hibs a bit too much. And dad, who enjoyed a rich and varied life, once cancelled dinner with Julie Christie because it clashed with a Hibs European tie. When he died, his closest friends wore green-and-white scarves to the funeral.

We were Hibees through and through. My little brother, however, believes dad took a dark, dark secret to the grave: that deep down, when all was said and done, *at the end of the day, Brian,* Faither was a Hearts fan. Is this my real heritage?

Today, opening the 2004–2005 season, Hearts are playing Aberdeen. There have been seasons past when I've kicked off a football year at Tynecastle, or as Hibbys prefer it, Swinecastle. I've even seen a Hearts-Aberdeen curtain-raiser before, at the start of the 1978–79 campaign when the Scottish public was still deep in the throes of a monster hangover following the national team's disastrous World Cup in Argentina. Some would claim we've never got over Cordoba. Unlike the perms of Alan Rough, Asa Hartford and Derek Johnstone, the bad memories have never grown out. Unlike the little yellow go-faster pills in Willie Johnston's hand, held up to the glare of the TV lights, they've never melted away.

At Tynecastle that August, and doubtless all across the land, fans were in a murderous mood. If oor fitba's pride was not fully restored within 90 minutes, somebody was going to get it. Today, they actually have a prime candidate for a lynching: a Hibby swimming against the synthetic maroon tide, while trying vainly to pass himself off as one of them.

An overactive imagination is a dangerous thing. And today, coming from a safe, sheltered, thoroughly *drippy* middle-class background, and never having been in a proper fight in my life, mine is in serious danger of combusting. Everyone else is walking to the stadium, minding their own business, or talking about *Big Brother*, or the opera at the Edinburgh Festival the night before (joke), but I'm pretty sure they're all mere seconds away from identifying the imposter in their midst. I'm absolutely convinced I couldn't be more conspicuous if I was sporting Roughie's ludicrous bubble-perm, 26 years out of date, or wearing a Hibs shirt and singing a Hibs song, such as that socially-perceptive terrace favourite, 'In your Gorgie slums'.

It's not the fact that, almost every week in a national newspaper column, I profess my love for Hibs, and that these dribblings are accompanied by my mug-shot. It's not that which makes me assume I've already been spotted, clocked, metaphorically measured for a wooden box. Even without this damning evidence, I'm sure they can tell I'm a Hibs fan. They can just tell. After all, I know, just by looking at them, that they're Hearts fans.

And those Jambos that I've just overtaken on the outside, the ones nattering about *Big Brother*, the televised social-experiment game-show which this year will eventually be won by a man who's been transformed into a woman, Nadia Almada . . . do these Jambos know they are participants in a similar experiment where one of their number has a shocking identity secret of his own and that 'Nadia' re-arranged spells 'Aidan'?

Gorgie Road, which starts off as Dalry Road, is a long, grinding route into the Wild West of Edinburgh. Tynecastle's closest counter-attractions are, in no particular order: a cemetery, a bingo hall and . . . that's it, really. An establishment calling itself Raffles would seem to have absolutely no connection with the famous old colonial hotel in Singapore. It's a hairdresser's, and there are an incredible 15 of them bunched tighter than a bubble-perm on the walk to the ground. International Barber . . . New Visage . . . George & Jim. Competition among the crimpers must be fierce, involving much flouncing and sulking. There are shops all along this beat, and tenements above. From first-storey windows, old-timers watch the crowd pass, doubtless remembering when the Tynecastle attendance was four times this number.

I pass the programme-sellers at the Ardmillan junction – £2.50 each; they're called 'magazines' now – then Gorgie City Farm where the cock, disorientated by its urban existence, crows just before kick-off, then . . . eyes fixed on the road, shoulders tensing up . . . quicken my pace as I reach Robertson's, a Hearts pub, *the* Hearts pub, and the kind of establishment where, in legend and especially in that fevered imagination, a request for a mineral water will silence the metaphorical piano-player in the corner, silence the whole seething rabble.

At last, the stadium. I join the queue, not for the away end, where among the Aberdeen lot I could feel safe, or safer, but the main body of the kirk, the Hearts stand that many times during Derbies I've greeted with a cheery, two-fingered wave. Everyone is in good humour, and I'm hoping no-one tries to engage me in small talk about the form of Paul Hartley, previously an ill-starred midfielder at Hibs, because I might not be able to resist asking: 'Don't you mean Pauline?'

At the turnstiles, I notice the price above the entrance – £18. That's two quid cheaper than an equivalent match at Easter Road, so much as today might pain me, and in lots of different ways, I console myself that it won't hurt me in the pocket. But when I reach the gate the attendant doesn't have change of a £20 note. Her supervisor has been informed, but as I wait for my measly two quid, she ushers the rest of the queue through. As they squeeze past me, cheerfully informing the attendant they're happy to pay more if it will guarantee Hearts' future, it must be crashingly obvious, if it wasn't before, that I'm not One Of Them. Eventually, my pathetic two quid arrives and the turnstile clicks to grant me entry into Tynecastle. It is like the sound of a rifle being cocked.

My head buried in Hearts manager Craig Levein's welcome message in the match programme, I reach the top of the steps just in time to hear the stadium announcer urge the faithful: 'MAKE SOME NOISE!' This is his big, match-day moment, his 'Stairway To Heaven', his 'Son Of My Father', Chicory Tip's best-known song being, in its way, as anthemic as Led Zep's, and I can't quite believe I'm going to have to suffer it right the way through to the following May. But on this day, with the match already under way, I can't find my seat. Someone is sitting in it. Too scared to do the job myself, I ask a steward to move the squatter. He says I'll have to find a senior steward for that task. As we debate the problem, at the mouth of my own Stairway To Hell, we're blocking the view of fans behind us and now they're out of their seats, shouting. One man, of an age that suggests he's long retired from his Jambo-style job, has leapt to his feet to lead the protests. Now the supporters behind him are telling the old git to sit down.

Great. Various members of the Tynecastle staff already have me down as a cheapskate and a yellowbelly and, if I haven't quite started a riot in the Wheatfield Stand, I've certainly made an enemy of a sizeable number of its season-ticket holders before the first home match of 2004–05 is five minutes old. My T-shirt is dripping with sweat.

I mustn't do anything else to upset them. I must cheer loudly for Hearts, and abuse the opposition with cartoon venom. But *can* I do these things? A great goal is a great goal, and instinctively as a Hibs fan, appreciative of the finer things in life, and especially football as an art form, I've applauded them when scored against my team. But a *Hearts* goal?

My best hope today is that the match is abandoned. But for what reason? Bad football stops play? Bad municipal maroon colour scheme stops play? Bad fan fashion-sense stops play? It's not going to happen. This game still has 80 minutes to run and they're going to be seen out. My second best hope, then, is that I'm not required to acknowledge a Hearts goal.

It's a brilliantly sunny afternoon and I'm reminded of *The Perfect Storm*, Sebastian Junger's thrilling book, and the clinical descriptions of 'painless and easy' deaths by drowning.

'Like falling about in a green field in early summer,' reports a doctor in the *Edinburgh Medical Journal* in 1892.

Am I undergoing a *before*-death experience, the end of football as I – a Hibby – know it, under a blazing sun? One more aimlessly-lumped high ball as viewed from my maroon plastic pop-up seat, one more demonstration of how perspiration holds sway here over inspiration, and I might start to think so.

For most of the Jambos in the crowd of around 14,000, this is the first competitive match of the new season after a summer when the sumptuous deedle-dawdle of the Czech Republic's Pavel Nedved and Portugal's Cristiano Ronaldo thrilled Euro 2004's armchair audience. Spoiled by this skills carnival, you might have thought they would be more demanding of their team – no matter that Scottish football has regressed since Argentina and the national side no longer get invited to the big soccer extravaganzas.

Apparently not.

'It's a battle,' says the man behind me.

'Aye,' agrees his friend, 'a *right* battle.'

And there's relish in their voices rather than reproach. This is typical opening-day fayre: spurious excitement and lots of playing to the gallery with soap-melodrama lunges for hopelessly-overhit passes. Oohs and aahs are louder and last longer because fans are just happy to have football back, to have their Saturdays blocked off for another nine months, to have an excuse not to accompany their wives or girlfriends to soulless, out-of-town shopping centres, that they'll pretty much accept any old tosh on the pitch.

Once, at Easter Road, we accepted Paul Tosh, a member of manager Jim Duffy's radical, bonkers vision of football-team-as-circus. There was Jimmy Boco (rhymes with Coco), John 'Yogi' Hughes, an Icelandic goalie who was really a basketball player ('Like a drunk trying to catch a balloon,' conceded Duffy eventually) and Chic 'Chico' Charnley, a semi-mythical trick-cyclist of a footballer who could score goals from the halfway line and disarm intruders at training when they were intent on settling arguments with swords. But although we led the league during the first few weeks of 1997–98, the clown-smiles were wiped off our faces when Hearts won the derby.

Aah, the derby. I could write a whole book on it. I could write seven books on the most famous Hibs defeat of Hearts there's ever been. But right now I'm struggling to get to the end of this match report. To quote David Byrne, Dumbarton fan and chief Talking Heid: 'This is not my beautiful house.' And Hearts – huffing and puffing in their new kit, not much different from the old one apart from the pigeon-shite epaulettes – they're not my beautiful team.

They are, however, the so-called third force in Scotland. Every season, Celtic and Rangers slug it out for the main prizes. Then they clear off and, like hyenas after a big-cat slaying or looters after a hurricane, the rest of us scrabble around in the dirt for what's been left behind. This might result in a day out at Hampden, possibly even winning the CIS Cup, but this devalued and thoroughly diddy trophy doesn't qualify you for Europe anymore and Hearts fans, flexing their capital-city superiority, nickname it the Come In Second Cup. The sure way of getting into the UEFA Cup is to finish third in the SPL and for the last two seasons, Hearts have been the third men in Scotland.

On this showing, their third way involves tons of physical presence, a mean defence, a right-up-your-arse midfield, a ginor-mous Dutch tree of a striker called Mark de Vries who's injured today, a coach in Levein who doesn't take any snash from the SFA, referees or other managers who bleat about aggressive tactics, and a support who seem perfectly happy with win-ugly football and don't want it any other way.

I do, I'm a Hibs fan, and, aesthetes that we are, we crave football played with flair. We don't just crave it, we hunch up the collars of our Noel Coward smoking jackets, tighten our Oscar Wilde cravats, flick our Dorothy Parker cigarette holders on the heads of the fans in front of us and pine for it, like Algernon Charles Swinburne would a randy monkey. Then we demand of the nearest Rock Steady bouncer: 'Peel me a grape!' Hearts have fans, Hibs have aficionados.

I can't claim recently that Hibs have been especially beautiful: until last season, they scudded about under the long-ball terror-reign of Bobby Williamson, a coach who never 'got' Hibs, or the expectations of their fans. When we complained about the poor quality of football on offer, he blurted: 'If you want entertainment, go to the cinema.' At last, the wretched Williamson – somewhat less than sylph-like, I called him Mr Bobby – has gone, to Plymouth Argyle. But his replacement, Tony Mowbray, is a rookie boss who was ploddingly unsophisticated as a central defender and has been absent from the Scottish scene since his time with Celtic. He hardly seems the most inspiring choice and many Hibbys think he's been got in on the cheap.

If he had spies here today Mowbray might conclude that to achieve third place you have to play the third way, the joyless Jambos way. Celtic have dominated in Scotland without their kitman needing to order a shirt smaller than size 44ins chest and Rangers are now copying their muscle-pumped template. Similarly, Hearts have a system which isn't broke, so is not likely to be fixed anytime soon. I don't know, maybe flair should go the way of flares. It's so long since I saw Hibs play with any that I've almost forgotten what it looks like. So if my team continue with the agricultural approach under Mowbray, maybe it's better that I don't watch them this season. After all, they've just decided to 'modify' the classic strip, changing from white shorts to green ones. Sacrilege.

Maybe it's best that I come here, to Tynecastle, and, with Scottish football in such a peeky state, adopt the role of the martyr, the masochist, and wear a maroon shirt because it's not that much different from a hair shirt. Maybe it's best that I become a glory-hunter, like so many who follow the sport these days. Can third place be termed glorious? Close your eyes, and maybe it can. Yes, shut them tight, excellent idea.

The game passes in a blur – a month-long blur. And finally it's over. I can go home. My first match as a wannabe Jambo has made my head spin and my stomach lurch. Nobody put a foot on the ball. Nobody passed it along the ground. Nobody scored a goal. And nobody in the crowd, if they're brutally honest, left Tynecastle believing that association football, Scottish-style, is on the brink of a bright and shiny tomorrow. It's going to be more of the frantic, blundering present.

And nobody died. I got out alive, even though, one game in, I'm spotted by Neil, an old Jambo mate from school. 'What are you doing here?' he says. I try to pass off my attendance with some guff about this being the only game in town on such a nice afternoon but I know he doesn't believe me. Fans from the rival sides of this football divide – any football divide – just don't watch the other lot anymore. I ask Neil what he thinks of the way Hearts play. 'We're boring,' comes the reply. Well, he said it. But he doesn't seem unduly perturbed by this. Hearts are the best of the rest, after all.

I jog most of the way home, stopping only to check the Hibs score in a TV shop window: a 2–1 win at Motherwell. It's safe to say that my debut as a fan of Heart of Midlothian FC was not entirely transcendental. I don't think I can do this. In fact, I know I can't. I know why, I understand why – absolutely. For you to understand, you need to be aware of the depth of feeling I have for Hibs, and the petty, perverse, playground-formed, increasingly embarrassing, character-stunting, girlfriend-disillusioning, social status-impairing but entirely reasonable and completely justified loathing I have of the other lot.

The security number for my mobile phone is 7–0, 7–0 after the most famous Hibs win over Hearts in my fantime. Same with my phone at work. You can only gain access to my email if you first type in the password 'seven'. I wanted 7–0, 7–0 for my Sky TV account but the company said I couldn't use the same digit twice, and only under protest did I agree to change it to 7–0, 6–2, taking in the second most memorable tanking of our great Edinburgh rivals. My bankcard number I won't tell you but you can probably guess which digit figures most prominently.

I am still living my life – indeed can only gain entry to the various functions of my life – by use of child-like codes. Honestly, you'd think I was a member of the Secret Seven or something. When I die, there are instructions in my will for equal amounts of my ashes to be deposited at the sites of the Seven Wonders of the World. Actually, that last bit is a lie. They've to be scattered at Easter Road.

I know I'm not unique in my perversity; in all two-team cities, grown men with serious jobs, wives, families, mortgages and pension plans support their team as if still wearing short trousers. In Manchester, fans of City and United do it and even in cities which have slipped off the football map such as Bristol, followers of City and Rovers still do it. In Buenos Aires, the lunatics who pledge allegiance in blood to Boca Juniors and River Plate do it, except that in the Argentinian capital, insurance companies don't pay out on football-related shootings and will only settle claims of football-related kidnappings if torture is involved. Because being tortured by rival supporters, being forced to, I don't know, support the other lot for a whole season and then write a book about the experience, that would be a fate worse than death, wouldn't it?

It surprises some people, however, that fans of Hibs and Hearts behave in this way, too. Edinburgh – Embra – is known the world over for many things: its Castle and its history, including the put-that-in-your-pipe boast of being the birthplace of the Enlightenment; the seven hills on which it's built and endow it with such stunning vistas (there were eight until the famous Easter Road slope was levelled); the Festival, when everyone with a story to tell and a scam to sell squeezes it to bursting-point; the New Town and the order and civility of those classical Georgian crescents; a great literary tradition stretching from Sir Walter Scott, who wrote *The Heart Of Midlothian*, to Irvine Welsh, who's managed to namecheck Hibs in just about every book, and all told more than 500 novels have used the city as a backdrop; Jenners, which will sell you a fur coat, Morningside, where you will wear it without knickers; more lawyers than you can shake an exocet missile at; the time-honoured 'You'll have had your tea' welcome extended to its many visitors . . . but it's a bonnie place and so what if it knows it?

And somewhere near the bottom of Edinburgh's claims to fame, down in the relegation area just above the city's reputation as the former AIDS capital of Europe, are its football teams. Isn't it just too refined, too *polite*, a place to get excited about *fewtball*? Not so.

Not so at all.

It's said of Edinburgh, usually by Glaswegians, that when two of its citizens meet, the first question after the introductions is: 'Which school did you go to?' This kind of exchange, chin jutting, buttocks firmly clenched, may have happened once or twice – perhaps over cocktails in Moray Place, grandest of those crescents, before the Advocates' Ball – and it may well say something about Edinburgh's preoccupations with status and class. But I don't hold with that school of thought, possibly because my school was the kind whose high rating in any education-performance leagues would be dependent on there being categories for the most head lice, teenage pregnancies and gang-fights involving heavy use of ox-blood, yellow-laced, 22-eye Doc Martens. At my alma mater, the first question, the one that could save you from, or lead to, a stiff kicking, was: 'Which team do you support?' For me and my kind, as teenagers in the 1970s, the only order that mattered was your team finishing higher up the league than the hated rivals.

My memory might be playing tricks, but in the 1970s, the answer to the 'Which team . . . ?' question amid 12 simultaneous games of 17-a-side with a tennis ball in the playground – and I would imagine, in the non-fee-paying, determinedly keelie schools right across Edinburgh – was either 'Hibs' or 'Hearts'. There might have been the odd lad who favoured Glasgow's Old Firm. Back then, I like to think they did this because of some long-established family connection rather than simply because they were the biggest clubs and tended to win just about everything. Mostly, however, you were Hibs or you were Hearts.

If you loved one team . . . obsessed about them, dreamed about them, felt-penned the club crest and their name in bubble-letterings on cludgie walls and the grey gas-mask bags from the Army & Navy Store that my Hibs-oriented droogs and I – this was the *Clockwork Orange* era – used as satchels . . . then it followed that you despised the other lot. You wanted them to lose, all the time, every game.

And now? Well, I'm older, wiser and regarded as house-trained enough to occasionally get invited to dinner parties. But I'd still want Hearts to be beaten by Fallujah Athletic. No, I'd want them to be beaten, heavily, by Fallujah Athletic *and* Basra Academical. And I snigger like the stupid schoolboy I undoubtedly was every time I see my nickname for their manager in print – Craig Latrine.

In the 1970s, in the long, interminable gaps between Derbies – and in those days there were only two per season, none at all when one of the Edinburgh teams were relegated – you'd spend the lunch-hour and most of the (for keelies) pointless lessons such as Latin and Religious Education engaged in a phoney war with your rival fan about who had the best ground, the more informative match programme, or boasted the more crucial playlist of glam-rock choons.

**Essential Top 10:**
*David Bowie – 'Drive-In Saturday'*
*Roxy Music – 'Pyjamarama'*
*T. Rex – 'Get It On'*
*Alice Cooper – 'Elected'*
*Mott The Hoople – 'Roll Away The Stone'*
*Slade – 'Coz I Luv You'*
*Chicory Tip – 'Son Of My Father'*

*Gary Glitter – 'Rock 'N' Roll Part 2'*
*Sweet – 'Ballroom Blitz'*
*Cockney Rebel – 'Mr Soft'*
*(On the bench: Wizzard – 'Angel Fingers')*

**Reserve 10 (Non-Glam But Still Vital):**
*Hawkwind – 'Silver Machine'*
*Python Lee Jackson – 'In A Broken Dream'*
*10CC – 'Rubber Bullets'*
*Family – 'Burlesque'*
*Medicine Head – 'One And One Is One'*
*The Strawbs – 'Lay Down'*
*Argent – 'Hold Your Head Up'*
*Focus – 'Sylvia'*
*Free – 'Wishing Well'*
*David Essex – 'Rock On'*
*(On the bench: Geordie – 'All Because Of You')*

Heart of Midlothian were actually founded first, in 1874, and took their name from a dancehall off the Canongate in Edinburgh's Old Town, which in turn had taken its name from the Tolbooth jail. There are two theories. The first is that a group of lads were causing a public nuisance by playing football outside the dancehall and ordered by the local authorities to take their ball to the green expanse of Meadows. The second is they were simply hanging around the street-corners; they didn't start playing football until a policeman suggested it. I believe the latter theory as it says a lot about Hearts – the polis involvement, the ball as an afterthought.

Hibs came along the following year. The first major club in Scotland formed out of the immigrant Irish community, they were instituted at a meeting of the Young Men's Catholic Association but initially they struggled to gain admission to the Scottish Football Assocation as this was for 'Scotchmen' only.

The YMCA – not to be confused with the YMCA where you can get yourself clean, have a good meal, and do what your body feels – had their offices in St Mary's Street not far from the dancehall or the 'Heart of Midlothian' stone marking the site of the jail in the cobbles of the Royal Mile which today Jambos spit on for luck and Hibbys just gob at. The two teams played each other for the first time on Christmas Day, 1875, on the East Meadows, Hearts winning 1–0.

I was at school when both clubs celebrated their centenaries. Even maths-class dunderheids like me could tot up that in 100 years, Hearts had won more trophies than Hibs, including six in six seasons (two league championships) between 1954 and 1960.

But Hibs could lay claim to a number of firsts and we memorised them like those momentous dates chanted at us by our history teacher, 'Big Som'. First British team in Europe. First in Scotland to get floodlights, undersoil heating, shirt sponsorship, an electronic scoreboard. The latter was a truly crappy contraption, more state-of-the-dark than state-of-the-art, which was perched above the Cowshed at Easter Road and, when it was working, flashed up Etch-A-Sketch-style football 'action' and this occasional epistle: 'GOA . . . !' Oh, how we gloated.

And now? Do we still go in for that my-team's-better-than-yours juvenilia? Well, yes. Especially at dinner parties.

Hibs fans were thrilled by the story a few years ago about the discovery of a Brazilian football encyclopedia dating from the 1950s. Within its pages, the book acknowledged the brilliance of Hibs' Famous Five forward line of Gordon Smith, Bobby Johnstone, Lawrie Reilly, Eddie Turnbull and Willie Ormond who brought their Brylcreemed, baggy-shorted, buccaneering style of play to South America when pre-season tours were considered downright decadent. Well, that settles it, we agreed. That confirms beyond any shadow of a doubt that Hibs were instrumental in the development of the greatest footballing exhibition of my fantime – the stream-of-consciousness soccer of Jarzinho, Gerson, Tostao, Pele and Rivelino which won Brazil the 1970 World Cup.

Of course, as we've reached the age we are now, the half-time of life, we prosecute the case for Hibs' superiority over Hearts with subtlety, wit and a stramash of pop-culture references. For instance, Hibs aren't just the coolest team in Edinburgh, they're the coolest on all of Planet Football.

The next time you watch the film of fanatical Hibby Irvine Welsh's *Trainspotting*, and you come to the scene where the hero Renton, played by Ewan McGregor, locks himself away with a year's supply of tomato soup in order to go cold turkey and wean himself off smack, freeze-frame the moment where he's lying on his bed and study the poster on the wall. It's Hibs' Scottish League Cup-winning team of 1972, caricatured by Harry Gilzean of the *Edinburgh Evening News*, and while the movie had to ditch most of the Easter Road references in the original text, Welsh ensured this definitive evocation of a splendid Hibs side survived.

Apart from Welsh, who refers to his heroes as 'the cats in emerald green', Hibs can field a complete team of famous fans, including brilliant speccy skiffle twins The Proclaimers, brilliant dour actor-hunk Dougray Scott, brilliant sulky ging-er rock-chick Shirley Manson . . . and, well, the fallen daytime telly presenter John Leslie has a certain dangerous outcast intrigue about him now, doesn't he? Then there's another popster, Finlay Quaye. And, er, um . . . Fish?

Hearts? You could count their celebrity supporters on the fingers of one foot. Ronnie Corbett is always quoted but, despite being small enough to still qualify for a lift-over, the diminutive comedy giant is never seen at Tynecastle. Not unless that's him inside the mascot outfit.

Yes. *Hearts have a mascot.* Hibs, it goes without saying, don't. If any further proof were needed to demonstrate that Hibs are cool, super-cool, and Hearts are irredeemably naff, then it's contained in the fact that they allow a sweaty galoot in a foam animal-suit to cavort around the pitch before games.

Another example of the gulf in real, genuine *class* is that while Craig Levein wears a baseball cap, his opposite number at Easter Road, Tony Mowbray, does not. Mowbray's predecessor, Bobby Williamson – Mr Bobby – did favour the ned headgear but his tenure as coach was an aberration and an abomination. He spewed a *House Party* Gunk-Tank of crap football over Easter Road, in outright defiance of club philosophy. What a balloon; he didn't appreciate that Hibs are like Celtic, Ipswich Town and West Ham United in belonging to grand old traditions of playing a passing game with panache; Hearts are not so fussy.

Hibs have a better club song, for while *Hearts, Hearts, Glorious Hearts* is a waltz, *Glory, Glory To The Hibees* is a rap. OK, not an actual hip-hop track, but it does contain the names of the Famous Five – 'Smith! Johnstone! Reilly! Turnbull! Ormond!' – shouted out at the end in a vaguely MC style. Scares the Wu-Tang Clan shitless every time.

Hearts also *look* old-fashioned and it's all in the socks. Like the black of Newcastle United, a dark colour on the calves gives teams a dour, plodding, *ancient* appearance. Billy Connolly talks of wee, bauchly, almost square-shaped Glasgow wifies wearing fat coats. Well, the Hearts players wear fat socks.

The *Big Brother* age has made pop-psychologists of us all. We're also weekend-sociologists and like to think we can spot the difference between us – Hibs – and them. Thirty-odd years ago, the differences were easier to detect: Hibs fans sang songs about the IRA; Hearts the UDA. Celtic and Rangers were more clearly defined as Catholic and Protestant clubs, and still are. But at the height of the Troubles in Northern Ireland, Hibbys and Jambos hitched onto the Old Firm hordes' sheepskin collars and first-generation parka hoods. And we all chanted rubbish about a religious divide we didn't understand.

Now, so the theory goes, we're all supposed to be part of the same big, amorphous, homogenous, football mass, boiling under the same crappy clubwear, munching the same lukewarm pies, and the differences barely exist and therefore hardly matter. You're one or the other but here's the thing: you could be either.

Rubbish. Absolute rubbish. It takes a keen eye to discern the differences, but they're there all right. For instance, Hearts fans would maintain that they are *the* Edinburgh club, Edinburgh's *only* club. 'Come on, the Edinburgh team!' is a cry heard at Tynecastle, asserting Hearts' status as the capital outfit, the establishment team, who stand ramrod-straight on the ramparts of Edinburgh Castle and scoff and sneer at the serfs using a boar's head for a football down in Leith.

Before boundary changes, and before Edinburgh swallowed it up, Leith was a separate place. It gave Scotland a great port, also a great tongue-twister: 'The Leith police dismisseth us.' Originally, Hibs drew much of their support from the area, and they still do today, although this middle-class boy used to journey to Easter Road from Great King Street, a very uptown address.

I started going to football with my father who, among other things, was a broadcaster and a playwright. Many of my dad's friends and associates were bohemian types, painters, poets, musicians, and most were Hibs fans. Painters like John Bellany and Sandy Moffat didn't, as far as I know, come from long family traditions of Hibbys, but must have gravitated towards Easter Road – I liked to think – because Hibs were the more aesthetically-pleasing team. Maybe Moffat saw romance in the colour green; maybe Bellany saw it in Hibs' connection with the old seafaring community of Leith, he being a fisherman's son from Port Seton, a few miles down the Firth of Forth in East Lothian. Whatever the reasons, I told my teenaged self, eager to establish yet more proof of Hibs' superiority, artists knew great art when they saw it.

But a key element of Hibs' appeal is that while they know they play the better football, they are not by nature a superior club. Hibs have always been the underdogs in Edinburgh, and there are many fans for whom this is all the romance that's needed. Hearts, on the other hand, like to lord it over Hibs; their fans also refer to Hibs as 'the wee team' and the stadium announcer uses this terminology when reading out the full-time scores. An equivalent put-down, putting Hearts in their place, has never been part of the Easter Road vocabulary, even at times when that place has been a whole division below.

In 1990, Hearts tried to kill off Hibs. The then Tynecastle

chairman Wallace Mercer spoke of a 'merger' and the sum of the Edinburgh clubs being greater than the parts, but this was a hostile bid with the clear aim of wiping Hibs off the face of the earth. We would have become 'Hearts incorporating Hibs' in much the same way that, in the world of comics, it was '*The Hotspur* incorporating *The Hornet*' and before too long we would have fallen off the masthead altogether. It is impossible to imagine a scenario where those roles would be reversed. Hibs would not try to devour Hearts because they simply don't have the same tip about themselves.

So where does this idea of superiority come from? Well, Hearts, as I say, are the establishment club. I know a lot of policemen who are Hearts fans. I have a hunch a lot of bank managers are Hearts fans. I strongly suspect that a lot of taxi drivers, that master race of motorists, are Hearts fans. And the two Hearts fans in my office with whom I regularly engage in full and frank exchange of football views are both public school-educated. Nothing wrong with any of that, nothing at all.

Hibs, though, are the team of the outsider and the hopeless dreamer, the incurable romantic. But we do not suffer from an inferiority complex; we do not feel squashed down by Hearts.

'I think of most Hearts fans as being drapers,' says fellow Hibs fan Martin.

'Hearts fans all live in bungalows in Corstorphine and Davidson's Mains; they have funny wee Jambo moustaches and wear funny wee Jambo jerkins and they really are a bunch of bloody boring bastards,' adds Simon, another fully paid-up member of the Hibee Nation.

'Quite a lot of them will be old-skool, working-class Tories,' reckons David, a one-time Labourite and all-time Hibby.

If Hearts were a sexual position, they'd be the missionary, once a month, twice on birthdays. Hibs, on the other hand, would be whatever they call the impossible, only-in-the-movies routine where the woman locks her legs round the man's waist while he stands, supporting her back with one hand, caressing her cheek with the other, looking completely heroic. Do Hibbys believe themselves superior after all and have I just contradicted myself? So what? C'mon the Hibees.

Hearts are conservative. They are convention addicts and tradition junkies. This makes them stuffy and dour, the roundheads to Hibs' sexy cavaliers. The differences between the clubs are so obvious they can be seen from space. That's the way it is, always has been, always will be. And always should be.

The more things change, in this town, in this life, the more things stay the same. It's 30 years since Hibbys and Jambos fired taunts back and forth across my school quad. And now? The taunting still goes on. As we get older we need football even more. It's just about the only area of life where you can be totally irresponsible and act like a kid all over again. And I would contend the rivalry is important to Edinburgh, much more so than 30 years ago.

This city has changed a lot since I started watching football. Take Princes Street: it used to be the greatest one-sided street in the world, with the northerly aspect crammed with shops of character that were very Edinburgh. Now it's like any other high street, any cloned main drag, except the bored, gum-chewing shoe-store girls in Edinburgh have a better view – the Castle – on slow days than their counterparts in the Slough and Reading branches.

New housing is made of brick, rather than traditional stone. It pops up everywhere, to meet demand from relocating office workers, Edinburgh consistently finishing high up those 'Most desirable places to live . . .' polls. Gap sites never stay empty for long, churches with falling attendances are constantly under threat from developers, and all my old childhood play spaces have long been engulfed by new estates featuring lots of exterior wood styling totally unsuitable for the 'You'll have had your summer' Edinburgh weather.

And those developers would love to get their hands on Tynecastle and Easter Road, creating yet more accommodation for incomers who don't support Hibs or Hearts, while the clubs would end up playing their football – possibly together – in a location far from their core communities, in a featureless stadium that looked like a branch of Plumb Center.

An estimated 25 per cent of the New Town is English. Welcome Toby, welcome Tristan, welcome one and all. The English like Embra's civility and some of them make it more civilised still – frightfully-awfully so. But the pubs of my 'hood, Stockbridge, are full of Sassenachs in chunky, zippered knitwear, with ridiculously beautiful girlfriends, all hair and teeth, draped round them as they cheer on Chelski and The Arse and, really, Edinburgh could be anywhere.

As a result, it's us, the upholders of the great local football antagonism, who give Embra a large part of its individuality. The only way you can properly assert your Edinburgh-ness, indeed your Scottishness, in the capital city is to declare: 'I am a Hibs fan.'

Or (this with a squeaky, high-pitched voice): 'I am a Hearts fan.'


### 21 August. Hearts 3, Kilmarnock 0

I have decided against getting a season ticket for Tynecastle because, whatever the stadium, being stuck next to 100 per cent bams from August to May and first kick to last is no fun. By moving around I can hopefully pick up on subtly different variations on the 'Get intae thum!' credo and come to understand Jambo culture – Jamboness – more than I do now, which is not at all. And if I can minimise the risk of getting my head stoved in, bonus . . .

So this week, immediately after bumping into John, another old Jambo chum – this is a small city, especially when you've lived in it all your life – who turns out to be as suspicious of my Tynecastle presence as Neil at the first home game of the season, I take a seat high up in the Wheatfield Stand . . . high enough to see over the other side and out across the city, my city . . . so why don't I recognise it?

Edinburgh Castle looks boxy, almost square, as if built by Jerry Constructions Ltd. There's a big industrial chimney that situationist japesters from the Edinburgh Festival Fringe must have erected the previous night because I've never seen it before. And the conference centre, a newish addition to the cityscape, appears to have a dry ski-slope on its roof. Hearts fans definitely do see the world differently from the rest of us.

Football too. There's no displeasing some people. The play is rugged and ragged. The ball needs a protection order. The ball needs a re-familiarisation course so it can get to know the turf again. Real Madrid put their trust in *galacticos*, but the SPL have cornered the market in *gallumphicos*, and quite a few of them are on display here.

Some Dadaist conspirators on the Fringe have contrived this excuse for a football match. Hibs fans wouldn't put up with such bilge but the Jambos don't seem to mind. Then Hearts score, and the 'MAKE SOME NOISE!' DJ plays a burst of 'Cum On Feel The Noize', and I leap to my feet. No, no, you don't understand, I'm acclaiming the song. I've always been a fan of Slade. 'Coz I Luv You' was the first single I bought and I used to have a Dave Hill haircut – yes, the one clipped high on the forehead as if in readiness for frontal lobotomy.

Not counting cup-ties, this is shaping up to be Hearts' 18th last game at their historic Tynecastle home. A perverse statistic, I know, but one that is surely being mined of all significance by most of the Jambos present on another prickly-heat afternoon. Hearts are chronically in debt. Last month, the chairman, George Foulkes, announced the sale of the ground to the property developer Cala Homes. The debt is £19 million, the sale will bring the club a minimum of £20.5 million, and in a strictly business sense, that's a good deal. But in a strictly football sense . . . ?

The Save Our Hearts campaigners were leafleting the crowd before kick-off. Note their name, it's not Save Tynecastle, they obviously believe this isn't just about their 118-year-old ground: the club's very existence is at stake. SOH is run from a shop in Gorgie Road; buy a mug or a ruler and help the cause.

During the match, there are frequent angry chants directed at the chief executive, Chris Robinson, who many hold directly responsible for Hearts' financial meltdown. Robinson made his money in catering, so perfectly understandably is nicknamed 'Pieman'. The most popular anti-Robinson taunt is 'Pieman, Pieman, get tae fuck.' And after the final whistle, a placard-wielding mob will gather at the stadium entrance to ram home their point and polis on horseback will have to be despatched to quell an angry scene. Despite SOH pleas that all protests should be peaceful, Robinson has previously been attacked and had his home targeted.

It is not the purpose of this book to investigate how Hearts got into this monumental pickle. In Scottish football right now, Hearts' story and their plight are far from unique. Neither can the book be a plea from the *Hearts*; I'm not one of them. But a plea from the *heart* about tradition, the preserving of, is easy.

I – big breath – love Tynecastle. I may find its views of Edinburgh disorientating, and I certainly find its occupants in maroon difficult to be around within the context of a football match as I understand the concept. But this is a great little ground. On good days, or rather on bad days, it's a bearpit. The stands are high-raked and tight to the pitch. They loom over the grass in a thuggish way and I have some sympathy for the grass. If I was confronted in the same manner by a group of shaven-headed Jambos, I am sure I would be terrified. But as a spectator, the proximity to the action, the feeling that the whole crowd is wrapped inside one big three-quarter-length quilted polyester football-manager-style dugout coat, is exciting.

Contrast this, however, with being forced to play home games in a rugby stadium only a sixth-full. This is the grim prospect facing Hearts right now. As of next season, they would lodge at Murrayfield, the home of Scottish rugby, half a mile away, and while an average gate of 11,000 rattles around in a 67,500-seater ground, the wrecking ball would be getting tore into Tynecastle. Eventually, says Robinson, Hearts would have a new stadium of their own. But there are many who fear that by then, irreparable damage will have been done – to the club, its support and a way of life.

Your home is your home. Both Tynecastle and Easter Road are at roughly the same stage of development – that is, the money ran out before the last stand could be knocked down and rebuilt, leaving both grounds looking lop-sided. But fans would rather have this gap-toothed resemblance to Plug of the *Bash Street Kids* than be uprooted from their communities.

There are few grounds left in Scotland like Tynecastle, hugging up this tight to ordinary, everyday life, commerce and hairdressing. It's jammed against the back greens of tenements on the north side of Gorgie Road. Across the street, before the Gorgie Stand went up, the top storeys afforded excellent views of the pitch. A Jambo could turn his favourite chair to the window and watch the match in his string vest. Luxury! But he and his type are still close to God: Gorgie Parish Church's próximity to such a large, regular assembly of folk surely cannot be matched by any other Scottish kirk.

Last summer, a plan to make Hibs and Hearts share a new stadium united both sets of supporters in condemnation. The proposal would have moved the clubs to Straiton, which is actually in Midlothian, and thus would have left Scotland's capital without any top-grade football for the first time in the history of the game. Fans could have waved across the motorway to the ex-supporters who now spend their Saturdays sitting glumly in their cars at Ikea, while their wives divert the *leezure* pounds in the household budget into amassing monster-sized collections of cushions and tiny photo-frames. But watching football there would have been a thoroughly soulless experience, devoid of life, tradition, a sense of belonging, with a Weatherspoons wind-tunnel failing pathetically to meet match-day pub-banter needs. In *The Scotsman*, I campaigned against the dismal scheme all summer long, and the idea was eventually abandoned.

Today, Hearts score twice more against Killie, including a first for the club by new striker Ramon Pereira, a Michael Bolton haircut-double from Spain via Kirkcaldy. Thankfully the support quickly becomes fat and lazy on the delirium of it all so, when the ball squirts from under the feet of opposing players and out of play, no-one hears me shout: 'Hibs throw!' No-one hears me because they've got far more important matters on their minds. I'm kidding myself – and rather fancying myself – if I really think they're bothered about my presence when the future of their football club is at stake.

I leave early, convinced there's nothing to this undercover nonsense. As I dive down the stairs I hear one Jambo say to his pal: 'There's that cunt Aidan Smith.'

### My Top 10 Recurring Nightmares

1. *I get beaten up by Jambos dressed head-to-toe (and, never forget, they only have three per foot) in Jambowear.*
2. *Hearts win something.*
3. *I wake up with a Hearts tattoo on my backside with no memory of how I got it.*
4. *No, it's on my tadger.*
5. *I forget key Hibs facts, such as the most important one: we're the football team and they're not.*
6. *I'm not allowed back into Easter Road, banned for ever.*
7. *The tattoo is on my forehead and it says: 'I'm a Jambo girl, in a Jamboworld.'*
8. *Hibs play their best football for 30 years and I miss it (aye, right).*
9. *Hibs win the Scottish Cup for the first time in 103 years (nae chance).*
10. *I become a Jambo, a total scarf-twirler (there's more chance of 9 happening; 8 too)*

I mean, I expected to be spotted, but hoped it wouldn't happen quite so soon. I'm not an investigative journalist or *MacIntyre Undercover* or even dear, old Fyfe Robertson under a bushy ginger beard and a baffled expression. In *The Scotsman*, I wear my Hibs on my sleeve, but like to think I portray football in broad strokes, that fans of all persuasions can relate to my grumps about crummy pies, kiss-the-badge chancers, and the supreme vanity of David – I call him Derek, because that's how he was introduced to America on a promo tour there – Beckham. Some hope. This lot don't like my Hibbyness. Well, I say to myself, when I'm sufficiently far enough away from Tynecastle, and after I find out that Hibs have suffered an entirely predictable 4–1 humping from Rangers at Ibrox . . . I don't like their Jamboness.

On reflection, my mother wasn't a virtuoso at knitting and sewing; most women of her generation were highly proficient at both. Between making the tea – two sittings: mince and tatties for the four kids, *coq au vin* for her and my father – and a spot of shocking-for-its-time adult drama involving an exhaustive search for the G-spot on the G-Plan in the BBC's *Play For Today*, she would conjoin two determinedly different sisters in matching frocks, plain and purl my brother itchy, blood circulation-imperilling poloneck jumpers and, on her trusty Singer, fashion Dad groovy purple safari suits that were the envy of Alan Whicker.

Me, I got tartan knee patches on my turned-up Levi's for that brief moment in the 1970s when the plaid was cool, immediately prior to the toerag pomp of the Bay City Rollers. And a few years before that, I got a green-and-white scarf.

Celtic were my first love. In 1967 they became the first British team to win the European Cup; the old man told me this was a tremendous achievement so it seemed only reasonable that I become a fan.

I can't actually remember watching a game on TV before Lisbon, and I certainly didn't see a match in the raw. Sometimes I wonder just what it was I was doing for those first ten years of my life. (It's just come back to me . . . I was a spy. Or rather, I had all the gear – Secret Sam briefcase which could fire bullets and see round corners; Dinky Toy version of James Bond's Aston Martin with working tyre-slashers; membership card for *The Man From U.N.C.L.E.* Fan Club – I was just waiting for the right mission).

Anyway, it was the Lisbon Lions – Tommy Gemmell, socks round his ankles, falsers in the back of the net, shimmying like a drunk with the ball before that wonder goal; Bertie Auld, cavorting on the pitch in a gangster's trilby; Billy McNeill setting a new Euro record for snatch weightlifting by hoisting aloft that unfeasibly large trophy – who turned me on to football. After that

I begged my father to take me to a game, and my mum to knit me that scarf.

Because we lived in Edinburgh, and Glasgow, to a boy, was a million miles away, the first games I attended were Hibs and Hearts matches. My very first was a Hibs game, against Clyde on August 19, 1967, in the Scottish League Cup, when it used to kick off with groups, rather like the European Champions' League does now (all similarities end there). After that Faither and his laddie went week about to Easter Road and Tynecastle.

I still got bored in those early days. I fidgeted and fiddled with the soor plooms in my pocket and flicked through my collection of American Civil War bubblegum cards and thrilled at the ones where soldiers and horses were impaled on wooden spikes. Then I counted up my Confederate banknotes which I would try to pass off as legal tender, in a bid to obtain yet more cards. And I missed entire passages of play while following, with a keen eye, the half-time scoreboard operator's slow trudge round the perimeter of the pitch.

The operators were fascinating, and so were the corrugated-iron constructions, the size of small houses perched on stilts, from which they issued this vital information. Old mobile phones look funny now, because of their bulk. But they've got nothing on the half-time boxes, gargantuan when you seriously scrutinised the information they imparted, follies that stand comparison with those of Ancient Rome – and as a boy with a healthy interest in facts, stats and, of course, dimensions, I couldn't help noticing that the Easter Road box was considerably bigger than the Tynecastle one.

Size isn't everything, of course. There were other reasons why I eventually favoured Hibs over Hearts. At that time there wasn't much between the teams, football-wise, so a lad had to apply a far more scientific methodology to the business of choosing a club.

I'm sure colour came into it – must have done. I'm sure I must have viewed maroon as synonymous with winter in my part of Scotland in the late 1960s and early 1970s – dank, dreich, dismal, and some other words/phrases beginning with d . . . ah, yes, duffel-coats that were all fusty after being hurried through the slushy streets by your Auntie Jean for the bumper yuletide treat of the pantomime.

The boring, bloody panto, where no expense would be spared on special effects, all to tee up jokes that the Acme Christmas Cracker Company would reject for being too crummy. For instance, Stanley Baxter and Ronnie Corbett as the Ugly Sisters, being winched down onto the stage in a hot-air balloon, their basket full of antlers, all so that Corbett could quip: 'These are for the Hearts – they could do with a few points.'

And I would sit there, bored out of my tiny skull, duffel-coat steaming, in a theatre honking from all the other sturdy wet wool lying like dead fish on bare thighs. With the benefit of hindsight, and Hibsight, I reckon I must have thought: a maroon corporation bus brought me to this place, and if I half-shut my eyes, the curtains of the proscenium arch are maroon as well. Then after all the camp, it will be back into the damp, to wait for another maroon corporation bus to take me home. Maroon, I must have thought, is bad.

Green was different. I would like to believe that I associated it with summer, especially the summers that came a few years later. And even though football isn't played in summertime, even though these summers were spent 100 miles away from Edinburgh, in the Mearns: countryside, seaside, bumper editions of your favourite comics, bicycling adventures to the next village, scouring rockpools for crabs, fishing for podleys off a harbour wall, raiding pea-fields, battering golf balls into the North Sea with a taped-up mashie niblick, chasing butterflies, chasing what Val Doonican called the bright, elusive butterfly of love, fastening reef knots but desperately wishing you were unhooking bras, circuses and funfairs, strawberry-picking and tattie-howking to pay for dodgem rides and bottles of American Cream Soda – two straws – for local lassies prepared to let a city boy go a bit further with them. That was green.

In other words, the eternal sunshine of the spotty 13-year-old's mind. I would love to think that for all these blissful sun-kissed reasons, I chose Hibs over Hearts.

Did football matters influence the decision – at all? Hibs, in the late 1960s, seemed to have more flamboyant players in Pat Stanton, Peter Cormack and especially Peter Marinello, but I cannot pretend that I was aware of Marinello's status as Scotland's George Best, or that I remember the screams from the girls who commandeered the terrace wall when he sprinted down the right wing. Or the song they sang, 'They call him Marinello . . .', to the tune of Donovan's *Mellow Yellow*.

But perhaps, subliminally, I *was* influenced by this. From those days, I can't recall a single Hearts player you'd term sexy, not that the word was bandied about in football circles back then. Alan Anderson was a big, cloggy centre-half. Ernie Winchester was a big, cloggy centre-forward. Doubtless this was something to do with the sock-shinpad combo of the time: the pads were thick, as thick as cans of India Pale Ale, and as we've already established, maroon is a *fat* colour. Supermodels don't wear maroon. In the cult comedy flick *Zoolander*, Ben Stiller flitting between his catwalk looks – Blue Steel, Magnum, Ferrari, Le Tigra – never wears maroon.

And of course, in the late 1960s, in my memory at least, it was always sunny at Easter Road – no matter that The Proclaimers' anthem *Sunshine On Leith* wouldn't be played before every match at Easter Road for another quarter of a century – and rainy at Tynecastle. The rain over Gorgie continued unabated for a full three years until, with the proceeds of my paper round, I bought my first pair of Levi's. Again, in my less-than-total recall, the Hibs star who strode through the western saloon swing-doors of Jean Machine in Edinburgh's Rose Street as I handed over my £3.75 for these tremendous trousers was Alex Cropley, but as his cunning and bravery wasn't yet thrilling Easter Road it couldn't have been him. What is certain is that the journey Faither and I took to Tynecastle involved crossing a building site on foot, and in the relentless Gorgie rain, my Levi's got caked in mud. After that, it had to be Easter Road on a permanent basis.

Except I've forgotten one thing; something I've never admitted before. I wasn't one of the 'in crowd' at my secondary school but desperately wanted to be. The top guys – the bad yins – had the best gear, the longest hair, properly darkening moustaches (rather than bumfluff touched up with boot polish) and self-consciously slouched around the playground carrying the correct progressive albums by John Kongos and Curved Air. Even greater respect was bestowed on the lad who turned up for one of the lunchtime games clutching a boxfresh pair of Adidas 2000 boots. *Complete with screw-in studs!* None of us had ever seen screw-ins before, so the held-breath huddle which formed round him as he produced a spanner to remove them for the tarmac was akin to grunting cavemen watching the first non-square wheel being fitted.

This time the memory isn't playing tricks, and I'm not being revisionist: the lad with the 2000s was a Hibs fan, and so were all the boys with the John Kongos LPs. I wanted to be like them. Sure, I wanted to preserve my Levi's. And my relationship with my mother, who had knitted me my green-and-white scarf. But a big part of my decision to choose Hibs over Hearts was about wanting to be accepted, by the right kind of wrong role-model, some of whom would end up in prison, one of whom would die of a heroin overdose.

A couple of years later, around the time of the great Turnbull's Tornadoes team at Easter Road, I knew I'd made the correct choice. Sometimes it's small, frivolous things – a football strip's colour scheme, association with Ronnie Corbett (bad), association with the kind of semi-mythical delinquent who would get me an introduction to the beautiful, wafty, first-out-of-trainer-bra, first-into-kinky-boots, second-year hippy-chick chemistry-class pin-up Geraldine Cruikshank (good, very good) – that influence the big, character-forming decisions. For the unwitting part she played in this, I could kiss my Auntie Jean. I'd even go back to the panto. And that joke about Hearts needing a few points, well, I realise now that it's a classic, the kind on which a country's entire tradition of live theatrical entertainment is based.

But one thing has always intrigued me. Faither, although he was permanently by my side through the best football years of my life, didn't try to sway me towards Easter Road. I chose Hibs and he went with it. It intrigues my younger brother Sean even more.

'Because Dad was a Hearts fan,' he says.

### 28 August. Motherwell 2, Hearts 0

I don't go to Fir Park; away games are a different holdall of smelly jockstraps and I'm just not ready for them. Being outed so quickly has unnerved me. At away matches, fans think they're big and brave for having ventured to a strange town and they look around to see who else has made it; I would have been far too conspicuous. So I sit at home in front on the TV and wait for the results to pop up on what used to be called the viddy-printer.

Hearts suffer their first defeat of the season, and in his frustration, Craig Levein ends up in hospital after punching a tactics board. The most intriguing aspect of this story is the existence of a tactics board; what do Hearts need one of them for? And despite the urgings of my regular Hibs posse, I don't go to Easter Road either. This must have been an emotional day for Hibbys. The death of Gordon Smith, the third member of the Famous Five to pass away, was being marked by a minute's silence, the opening of a memorial exhibition at the ground and a parade of former team-mates at the clubs where the Gay Gordon – old-skool meaning – won Scottish League Championship medals: Hibs, opponents Dundee – and Hearts.

Presumably all of this overshadowed the match, which was just as well, with Hibs tossing away a three-goal lead in a 4–4 draw. This vindicates my decision not to go, even though the Dundee manager Jim Duffy says that for a spell – which included an exquisite goal direct from a free-kick from the extravagantly-talented young striker Derek Riordan – Hibs played like Brazil. *Aye, right.* I dismiss his remark as bunk. I boot it right out of the stadium-in-my-mind, straight into the car park.

**31 August**

Where is Lithuania? The question must be challenging the grey matter of some Jambos today as they wake up to the news that a Lithuanian banker wants to buy their club. The second question belongs back in Dreamland: 'Could this Vladimir Whatsisnov be our Roman Abramovich?'

Vladimir Romanov is actually no stranger to the Scottish football scene, having previously sounded out Dundee, Dundee Utd and Dunfermline with a view to investing in the SPL. Hearts of course have agreed to flog Tynecastle, although the contract includes Groucho Marx's sanity clause, allowing them to pull out at any time over the next four months. Chairman George Foulkes said at the time of the deal: 'As a long shot there is also the possibility of our own Abramovich who comes in to help us.'

*Our own Abramovich*. What club wouldn't want one of them, and to be money-drenched like Chelski? Even Hearts, despite previous big investment deals turning to dust? *Especially* Hearts, more like. 'The club's financial position is desperate,' reports *The Scotsman*.

For the benefit of Jambos, *The Armchair Diplomat On Europe* lists Lithuania as the largest of the Baltic States, population: 3,608,000. In the box marked 'known for', it gets 'being a troublemaker'. It gained independence from the Soviet Union in 1990 but a nuclear plant built to the same design as Chernobyl was a creepy parting gift. Stalin World is possibly the world's oddest theme park and there's a statue of Frank Zappa in the capital, Vilnius. 'The most backward of the Baltics,' reports *The Armchair Diplomat*, and almost inevitably there's a problem with organised crime.

But little is known about Romanov; in photographs his hair is blow-dried and his smile freeze-dried. He's not as super-rich as Abramovich, so maybe Jambos shouldn't be playing Fantasy Football in their heads just yet. In truth, there's a bit of anxiety about him. And how daft must he be to want to invest in *Scottish* football?

'He's like some guy at a disco when the DJ announces he's about to play the last record,' says my friend David. 'Those other clubs have given him the knockback, so he's prowling a dancefloor that's reeking of smoke, stale beer and Desperation by Yves Saint Laurent, and suddenly, with the song dying and everyone drifting towards the coat-check, he's left with the old slapper in the corner – Hearts.'

# SEPTEMBER

**4 September. Hearts 3, Hibs 1**

This doesn't matter. Course it doesn't. It's not an all-singing, all-dancing derby, but the Festival Cup, a challenge match instituted the previous season as fitba's contribution to Edinburgh's world-famous cultural clamjamphrie. And it's because this is not a proper derby that I'm not properly crapping it.

Because the game doesn't matter, I turn up late, complete with a Festival-sized hangover, the result of lingering in the Assembly Rooms Bar until 3am and really believing I had a chance of getting off with the comedy sex thimble, Lucy Porter. And although I missed the build-up, I bet MC Tynie broke with tradition and did not urge the crowd to 'MAKE A KERFUFFLE!' because this match is *so* inconsequential.

Since it doesn't count, I go to the away end. I can't sit in one of the home stands, not when it's Hibs who are the opposition, even in thoroughly meaningless matches like this one.

Hearts score. Doesn't matter. They score again. See how we're all lounging around, stretching out across the empty seats, soaking up the sun, chatting and laughing, like we're straw-boatered, candy-stripe blazered, gilded youth from an E.M. Forster telly drama – see how much we *just don't care*? Then Hibs pull one back. Uh-oh . . . then Hearts, who've fielded a strong side while Hibs play mostly second-stringers, bring on their towering striker Mark de Vries in time for a corner-kick and he clinches a Jambo victory with his first touch.

At the final whistle, Hearts celebrate like they've won the World Cup, the Nobel Peace Prize and, yes, *Screen Test with Michael Rodd – Champion of Champions*.

Baseball cap at a haughty angle, Craig Levein justifies these wild excesses on the grounds that the previous month, when Hibs won the equally worthless East Of Scotland Shield, the other piddly local contest in which the Edinburgh clubs are the sole competitors, they made a big fuss.

See, told you this one mattered. *All* Derbies do. And maybe they matter more now because 14 years ago, they almost ended for good.

Wallace Mercer – visionary or enemy of tradition? When, as chairman of Hearts, Mercer tried to buy Hibs, he spoke of a united Edinburgh team finally capable of taking on, and beating, the Old Firm. But the audacious plan only succeeded in uniting both sets of fans against him. Mercer suffered death threats, he was sent bullets through the post, and bricks were hurled through his living-room window. His family needed police protection and every morning his car had to be checked for bombs. In 2000, on the tenth anniversary of his big idea, he admitted: 'With the benefit of hindsight, perhaps it could have been handled slightly differently.'

But Mercer was a breath of fresh air when he first appeared on the Scottish football scene. For the sports hack, he was a gift. Previously, chairmen could be summed up in just two words: 'No com-*ment*'. Here was a man who liked to talk, and who had interesting, intelligent things to say. He spoke of fans as 'customers', and we all murmured approval; clubs had been ripping off the paying punter for yonks.

But when news of the bid broke, those customers could not share his view of football as business. When Wallace *Merger* said it was his duty to his shareholders to bid for the Easter Road club, the campaign group Hands Off Hibs swung into action. In describing football in strictly business terms, Merger never mentioned tradition, history and certainly not sentiment – you can't factor it into a balance-sheet – so the customers turned back into fans, The Proclaimers' 'Sunshine On Leith' was installed as the campaign anthem, and Mercer's dream went kaput.

'The grimy romance . . . the conflicting sentiments which football provokes – the great Waldo tends to founder when he strays into such territory,' remarked *Scotland On Sunday*.

'I won the argument but lost the battle,' Mercer reflected.

His plan had its backers. A *Sunday Times* opinion-piece in 1990 argued that for decades in Edinburgh, 'tradition has survived at the expense of achievement' and called on the clubs to team up.

But there would have been no guarantees that a joint effort would have offered Celtic and Rangers double the challenge that the best-performing Hibs or Hearts could muster. Some Hibbys and Jambos would never have darkened the doors of a merged Edinburgh club.

In trying to weaken the ties that bind, Mercer has actually made them stronger. Last year's shared-ground proposal – if it had involved redeveloping Meadowbank, scene of Edinburgh's two Commonwealth Games – might have gained approval but for Mercer's bombastic vision. A spectacular luncher, to whom the normal match-day greeting is 'Who ate all the foie gras?', he bit off more than he could chew in 1990.

No matter, he's ensured that every derby is tasty, that they *all* matter.


## 12 September. Hearts 0, Rangers 0

In my professional life I have impersonated a Klingon and a Butlin's Redcoat. Journalism isn't just about writing stories, you know. Sometimes you have to go undercover, and do remarkable things, in order to *get* the stories.

This was my time at the tartan tabloid, the *Daily Record*, my circus years, where in relentless pursuit of . . . well, not so much the truth, more a byline, to keep the tally high and avoid getting the sack, I also infiltrated a nudist camp (twice) and, in advance of the release of the *Trainspotting* movie, squeezed into a five-sizes-too-small anorak and bottle-bottom specs from Oxfam (clothing budget: must not exceed £10) and stood on a railway platform to try to imagine the life of a real choo-choo checker, the kind of berk who absolutely did not feature in the film.

The circus years included a stint as an actual clown, also the role of a prisoner in a rat-infested jail in a television costume-drama. That dank, festering cell, with the only respite being the occasional glimpse in silhouette of fellow con Alex Kingston's gloriously heaving bosom as eponymous heroine *Moll Flanders*, was truly the heart of darkness.

But what about the Hearts of darkness? I don't go to this game because it's Hearts, mocked by Hibbys as Rangers' Wee Team, the Cousins of William, the Apprentice Boys' apprentices, against The Real Thing. As such it would be way beyond my talents as a master-of-disguise. It's bad enough when Hibs are playing one of these sides; Hearts and Rangers are the meanest fixtures in the calendar for a Hibby. Hearts *versus* Rangers, therefore, would be double-trouble, the two teams to whom a Hibby is most ideologically opposed, which would increase the risk of me being fingered to, um, let's see . . . 100 per cent.

I don't think I would be able to control myself. Three seconds would be all I could last, then I'd have to shout something: at the brutish teams and the brutish fans. Er, who am I trying to kid? I'd be quaking in my Adidas Chile '62 trainers from first whistle to last.

I think I must have been the last boy of my generation in Edinburgh to be allowed to see Rangers for real. I grew up watching football at the height of the Irish Troubles, when fans of Glasgow's Big Two were viewed as wild, hairy, lawless and – until the Criminal Justice (Scotland) Act 1980 came into force – partial to lugging a slab of 24 cans of Double Diamond per man onto the terraces and drinking it before half-time.

My father barred me from Rangers games and my mother took a similarly tough stance on *Psycho*. I was only permitted to stay up late to watch it on TV, long after everyone else in my school had seen it, ho-hummed about it, and moved on. As a direct consequence of both bans, I've convinced myself that at the time I was the last boy in the world still dressed in short trousers. But Mum and Dad's over-protectiveness only half-worked. In 30 years I've managed to conquer my fears surrounding Alfred Hitchcock's horror classic and that's all.

Because I have had less exposure to Rangers and *Psycho* than the rest of my generation, I get them confused. I remember the excitable playground chatter and feeling so incredibly left out of things. '. . . And did you see that bit when that guy falls backwards down the stairs after gettin' plunged?' Was that Martin Balsam's last moments in the movie, or a bit of bovver involving the Bridgeton Derry Boys? In those days, it could have been either.

So how 'Rangers' are Hearts? I attempt to seek some answers by watching the game on the crap Sultana sports-channel in a Jambo boozer. I'm not going to a bar in Bandit Country, not yet anyway, and certainly not Robertson's, the hell-pub. The closest thing the New Town has to a Jambo hostelry is Clark's, a traditional howff with maroon livery although it could also be a St Bernard's bar. There's a display case devoted to the old Edinburgh team, waxed-moustached winners of the Scottish Cup in 1895. Clark's is popular with lawyers, councillors and other professional disreputables because it's been left untouched by the blondewood-table revolution and the genial host, Big Davie, displays a couple of photos of the 1998 Cup-winning Jambos with quiet pride.

The cameras don't focus on the stands overmuch but, even so, it's obvious the Union Jacks are out in force at the away end, the Rangers masses clearly proud to call themselves brutish. And what of the Jambos? They flaunt Union Jacks to wind up Hibs and Celtic fans but such tactics today would surely be applauded by the Huns, and are the Jambos keen to gain that kind of approval from, as the terrace-song puts it, a bunch of smelly weegies?

When do pro-Embra feelings of municipal superiority override those of sectarianism? I don't understand how Jambos can direct the chant about squealers and dealers and nicked hubcaps at Rangers fans and mean it when, against Celtic, some of them have been known to whip off their Hearts shirts to reveal Rangers ones underneath. And what do Jambos think of the fact that both Old Firm teams have souvenir shops in the centre of Scotland's capital and Hearts and Hibs do not? And what do they think of the fact that both Old Firm teams would drop the rest of the SPL like a Double Diamond can full of pee if another league would have them? Hearts fans would seem to have a strange relationship with the red, white and blue.

Today, from the safety of the pub, I watch as the home crowd produce Saltires in defiance of all the Union flags, the Red Hand of Ulster and the orange strips. But it's not a big gesture so the Huns don't feel the need to sing the English rugby anthem, 'Swing Low, Sweet Chariot', which is their usual response at Easter Road when they want to niggle a team with Catholic Irish roots, who are nevertheless more Scottish than Celtic, but are also based in rugger-oriented Edinburgh.

Come on, keep up. Rangers are pretty uncomplicated. Fans of every other club in Scotland hate them and their supporters glory in this, in the song that goes: 'No-one likes us, we don't care.' Hearts are probably included in that 'every other club' category, but nonetheless there are aspects of Jamboness I just don't get, nor if truth be told, want to get.

I'm probably going to have to go to a Hearts-Rangers game at some point; I'm certainly going to have to go to more Hearts matches. It's no good me sitting in a pub in the New Town and feeling the kind of things which, if I was at Tynecastle, would expose me as a Hibby more obviously than if I was wearing a green-and-white fedora. I even venture to utter them today: 'What a crap game – it's like one of those lowbrow bullet-fests starring Jean-Claude Van Damme!'

It is a horrible, hackit match, but Hearts get a deserved point by standing up to Rangers. There's a bit of a pagger between the players at the end, but Hearts' beefcake striker, Jean-Claude de Vries, doesn't concede ground to Gers' Jean-Alain Boumsong.

Craig Levein is a hard, hard man. While playing for Hearts, he was once banned for 14 games for a punch which left his victim with a broken nose and two black eyes. The game was a friendly, the other player was team-mate Graham Hogg. Levein has created a hard, hard team in his own image, because *that's the way (uh-huh, uh-huh) he likes it,* but also because this seems to be the way to take on the Old Firm, to match them in the grunting department. It isn't a formula conceived in the football heavens but Hearts' tight grip of third place would suggest he's not wrong, and while it ain't pretty, some grudging respect is due to them today.

**'Son Of My Father' – Chicory Tip**
*'Mama said to me we gotta have your life run right*
*Off you go to school where you can learn the rules there right*
*Be just like your dad lad*
*Followin' the same tradition*
*Never go astray and stay an honest lovin' son.'*

My mum used to buy the birthday cards in our family, and she also signed them from her and my dad. If the old man was still alive, and I was so minded, I could probably have him done retrospectively for serious neglect. But this was a different time, the New Dad hadn't been invented, the multi-million pound parenting guidebook industry was still a forest somewhere, and the kids, the mucky kids, fed Spam or spanked, or if they were really unlucky, both . . . they didn't know any different.

Dad did scribble on one card, however, and although I no longer have it, the inscription remains vivid in my mind. The picture sequence was of the preoccupations of a teenager and how, even though the lad had embarked on the first tentative steps on the journey from boy to man, paternal wisdom still had its uses.

One of the pictures was football-themed, its message concerned the need to keep believing, and at the bottom Faither had scribbled: 'And they will win the cup!'

The word 'will' was underlined three times. In green ink.

My dad took me to the football. This is important: *my dad took me to the football.* He did other things for me, but if this had been all he did, it would have been enough. 'Gonna gie's a lift over, mister?' Scruffy urchins would ask him this as we queued to get in. 'Sorry, son,' he'd say, 'I've got one of my own.' And for those first few years of fanhood I was hoisted over the turnstiles for free. Later he paid me in, bought me match programmes and once I'd settled on Hibs, and home matches were no longer enough to satisfy the Hibby habit, he drove me to away games too.

It was at the football, at half-time at Easter Road and following our team on their travels in the Saab Estate, that father and son bonded, although once again, bonding is not what we would have called it, back in the unreconstructed 1970s. (Henry Cooper may have passed over to Kevin Keegan for those commercials for Brut, but they weren't in the showers together and he didn't actually hand him the soap-on-a-rope – no way).

Dad: 'Big crowd in.'

Me: 'Uhuh.'

Dad: 'How's school?'

Me: 'S'ok.'

Dad: 'How's the girlfriend?'

Me: 'Chucked me.' (This was Alison Donald, the luscious, pouting, fabulously top-heavy redhead who caused me to do something I'd never done before and not since: leave a football match before the end in pursuit of love, and a great match, too – Hibs vs Leeds Utd, 1973 UEFA Cup).

Dad (after long pause): 'Bought any new LPs?'

Me: 'Saving up for the new Yes one, it's a triple.'

Dad: 'So how do you think Hibs will get on today?'

Me: 'Well, a lot depends on whether Alan Gordon is fit; he's got a late test on his knee. He causes Billy McNeill problems in the air and I think Caesar's days must be numbered. Gordon's scored with a header the last two times we've played Celtic at Parkhead but, of course, we've yet to see Hibs win here. Celtic are a team in transition, but even though the surviving Lisbon Lions are starting to resemble zoo lions – you know, a bit mangy, dull repetitive behaviour – those oh-so-familiar moves of theirs are still too canny and cute for the likes of Hibs, who seem to turn up in Glasgow timorously resigned to their fate. When is this mouse ever going to roar? There never seems to be any gameplan. They haven't even worked out what, as condemned men, they'd want as a last request. It's just *pathetic . . .*'

Or something like that. But I was not left mentally scarred by the lack of deep and meaningful, Faither-Laddie chat. In fact, I considered myself well adjusted because Dad and I had football to talk about, compared with those decidedly odd boys who didn't like it. I, of course, was completely obsessed with football and I sometimes wonder if my father ever thought to himself: 'My God, I've created a monster!' I mean, he got me into football, tutored me in the finer points, but did he really mean for it to consume me, for Hibs to take over my life?

At a crucial age, when I should have been knuckling down to my studies, he despaired of me. I distinctly remember a Saturday lunchtime – *Grandstand*, *Football Focus* with Sam Leitch – and Dad's astonishment that three or four years on from the 1969 Celtic-Hibs Scottish League Cup Final, I could not only remember a Bobby Lennox goal, but was able to anticipate every pass in the lead-up play. 'Why can't you swot like that for your bloody maths?' he would groan.

Bloody maths was not Dad's thing either. His game was words. He started out in newspapers, finished there, too. Between times he was a BBC Scotland producer for 25 years and among scores of programmes, mainly arts-oriented, was a late-night chat show called *Saturday Round About Sunday*, where Tommy Gemmell would describe how, in the heat of Old Firm battle, in the midst of the glaur, he lost a contact lens and arch-rival Willie Henderson found it. But I was proudest of a documentary marking the 1973 centenary of the Scottish Football Association called *Bring Your Own Ball* in which he interviewed tartan totems of the game such as Matt Busby and Bill Shankly. A few years ago, a clip from the programme turned up on the box, and I got quite a fright to hear the old man, off camera, and by then off planet and perched, serene and seen-it-all in that great grandstand in the sky, ask Jock Stein: 'Are you a disciplinarian?'

My father's name was W. Gordon Smith and he was known as Gordon, like the Famous Five winger, to whom he also bore a slight resemblance – same jet-black hair and long face. Dad loved his namesake, and thought him the finest player he'd ever seen. I have a picture of him and my mum in their amateur-dramatics days in fancy-dress outfits made entirely from newspaper and he's supposed to be Archbishop Makarios of Greece. His tie is an *Edinburgh Evening News* backpage headline: 'Gay Gordon Up For Cup'. This was before I entered the world and therefore some years before I started tugging at his coat urging him to take me to see Hibs, but these seemed like important details to a junior Hibby *obsessionista*.

In truth I think Dad swung both ways back then. I remember him telling me that it was common for young men of the 1950s to do this, to go weekabout to Hibs and Hearts. Both had great teams, the greatest in their respective histories. Hibs had the Famous Five, Hearts the Terrible Trio of Alfie Conn, Willie Bauld and Jimmy Wardhaugh. Outstanding forward lines who brought success and silverware to Edinburgh. When he and my mum were courting, she went to the football, too.

Back in the words arena Dad also wrote books and plays, among the latter several box-office stormers for the Edinburgh Festival Fringe starring Russell Hunter, best-remembered by telly detective fans as Lonely, the manky informant of Edward Woodward's *Callan*. In the programme notes for each production, Dad described himself as an 'incorrigible, ineluctable [and some other clever word beginning with "in" which I've sadly forgotten] Hibs supporter'. I didn't doubt this; we were cheering on the Hibees home and away every week. But my brother, always the contrary one, asking the awkward questions, preparing from the age of seven for a future career in law, was unconvinced. 'So if Grandad Smith was a cobbler in Gorgie Road,' Sean was fond of saying, 'then it stands to reason that Dad is, underneath it all, a Jambo.'

Like all big brothers, I ignored the provocative pipsqueak prosecutor. Dad was a snuff addict. He wore his silver hair down to his shoulders. He had an exotic taste in motorised transport, such as a Riley with runnerboards and a Lotus racing car, Formula 3-grade I think, in which he gave me a lift to school, freeze-framing the entire playground in gawpy wonder. None of these things was the style thumbprint of a Jambo.

Dad and I followed Hibs and that was that. A football travel guide given away by Texaco when you bought enough of their petrol helped us find the grounds in towns like Airdrie to which even the old man, a proud Scot, was a stranger. Then on the journey home we'd listen to *Take The Floor*, the Radio Scotland country dance music show, which in my memory, was always transmitted from a ceilidh at the Memorial Hall, Laurencekirk, or somesuch bacchanalian hellhole of the Mearns, and hosted by 'Mistress Stewart'.

Dad was a renaissance man as far as I was concerned, but he wasn't above the odd bit of Hibby hero-worship. I discovered this when I was rooting around in his study and, bored with the 'tasteful' nudie shots in *Amateur Photographer*, the nearest thing he had to a porn stash, I found his diary and an entry in which he enthused about the 'Ally Shuffle' – the deceptive deedle-dawdle of dead-eyed striker Ally MacLeod, the best player in Hibs manager Eddie Turnbull's second-phase 1970s team.

On match-days when Hibs were playing away and I was desperate to go but my father was working – and being too scared to take a supporters' bus – my mother substituted as chauffeur. She lovingly covered that Texaco guide in protective plastic. She knitted that green-and-white scarf, of course. And she was on the terraces of Falkirk's old Brockville ground with me to witness Alex Ferguson panel Pat Stanton. The headbutt was just about Fergie's last act as a useless centre-forward; the great Paddy was actually a good friend of his.

Dad and I soldiered on through the mostly lean 1980s for our club. Enthusiasm was waning, though, and so was his eyesight. I took over the driving for night games, such as Scotland's World Cup qualifier against Spain en route to the 1986 Finals. I don't know how much he saw of the archetypal arse-swivel by Kenny Dalglish before the goal that crowned a thrilling Hampden night;

not much probably. Like the same Fergie in the dugout at Man U, he became the last man in the immediate vicinity to acknowledge goals being scored, but football wouldn't have been the same without him, and when he stopped going for good in the early 1990s, I did too.

Dad died in 1996. Visiting him in Edinburgh's Western General Hospital during his final days, I tried a few times to thank him for being my father. 'Thanks for leading such an interesting life and letting us watch,' I'd say. 'And thanks for taking me to see the Hibs.' But the morphine had zonked him like a Kenny Burns slide-tackle and I never got a response, so I'd end up just sitting by his bedside, holding his hand, squeezing my initials in morse code, something he taught me as a boy, when we'd go in search of monkey puzzle trees or some other fantastical quest. Dot-dash, dot-dot-dot . . .

Then on what would be his last day, I was travelling in the hospital lift when I spotted a nifty piece of graffiti: 'Still no cups in Gorgie'. The elevator doors were metal and the legend had been carved with a penknife or − 1970s throwback − the kind of steel-comb bad girls used to smuggle into discos for badder boys. Such was the effort required, the letters with curves were gouged with right-angles. Clearly this was the work of a true Hibby fanatic.

I went straight to Dad's bed and told him about this great revelation. First, nothing. Then, a smile I can see still. Two years later, in 1998, Hearts would win the Scottish Cup. But so what? Dad was a Hibs fan. And if I ever need reminding of this, I go to the Scottish National Portrait Gallery where a painting of him by his artist-friend Sandy Moffat hangs in the cafe. He's wearing − naturally − a safari suit crafted by my mum, and in the pocket . . . for ages Sandy didn't know what to put there, but it had to be something which summed Faither up . . . I can see the proof: a Hibs match programme.

Dot-dash, dot-dot-dot . . .

## Get To Know Your Team

I think I can put faces to the Hearts names now, but to further aid recognition, I've decided to give the players handles of my choosing . . .

Craig Gordon – The boy-goalie. I'm sure he'd like Flash as a nickname, but it doesn't go with the look, which is scared, especially when required to cope with a cross. Who else is scared of crosses? Well, there's Dracula . . . got it: The Young Count.

Robbie Neilson – Bearded backwoodsman on the right of the defence. Lumberjack. ('He cuts down trees, he wears high heels, suspenders and a bra . . .').

Steven Pressley – The captain. Everyone else calls him Elvis so for me it's Lisa-Marie.

Andy Webster – Lisa-Marie's central-defensive bum-chum is from Arbroath, home of the smokie, the Scottish delicacy of smoked haddock. The pub-rockers, Smokie, had a hit with *Living Next Door To Alice*, therefore Alice.

Alan Maybury – The Irish left-back is a good friend of relentless chart-botherers Westlife, once memorably dubbed 'shiny-faced close-harmony bastards' by *The Guardian* who also called them 'pan-faced donkeys' for good measure. A scan of the Westlife songbook threw up – and I do mean threw up – their cover of Barry Manilow's 'Mandy' but I like Maybury's hard, urgent style, so instead he's Barry, which still isn't very masculine, but what the heck.

Phil Stamp – 'Stampy' is the chant of choice but it's too obvious and unironic for such a pie grunter in the midfield . . . how about Pirouette or, better still, Pas des Bas?

Paul Hartley – The team's only true creative force, a one-time Hibs slug who's turned into a Jambo butterfly. But a too-coiffeured playmaker, so sorry, I can't resist: it's Pauline.

Patrick Kisnorbo – The Jambos' top *gallumphico*. I have great difficulty pronouncing the Aussie midfield enforcer's name. Bearing in mind his nationality, he'll be Kookaburra.

Kevin McKenna – This play-anywhere guy is Canadian, and I've heard shouts of 'Moose' aimed in his direction. I feel I've overdone the girls' names so I'm rejecting Celine, as in his prow-nosed countrywoman La Dion, in favour of All Trades, as in Jack of, master-of-none.

Neil MacFarlane – Holding midfielder. What a horrible term. Did the 1970 Brazil team have one of them? I don't think so. I need something deeply ironic for MacFarlane, who looks a bit like Art Garfunkel and is receding in more than just hairline. Walter Kidd, a plucky Jambo trier in the 1980s, was known as 'Zico' . . . MacFarlane is unusually tall for the midfield . . . my favourite unusually tall midfielder is . . . Socrates.

Jamie McAllister – Bought by Hearts purely out of gratitude for scoring the cup final goal which stopped Hibs winning the only silverware up for grabs for either Edinburgh club these past few years. Done nothing so far on the left flank, living on a memory – Dine-Out.

Dennis Wyness – Hunched, haunted, non-scoring striker. Dennis, *Why?*

Mark de Vries – Talismanic frontman from the Netherlands, size of a tree, often injured, therefore Dutch Elm Disease, Elmer for short. Or: Elmer Fudd?

Ramon Pereira – Is there a Michael Bolton song which could do the trick for the similarly-barneted striker? A chant of 'Ramon, Ramon' to the tune of Gary Glitter's 'I'm The Leader Of The Gang (I Am)' is already running but the Spaniard doesn't play enough to deserve his own song. At this rate his appearances will turn out to be seasonal, so how about Ferrero Roche?

Joe Hamill – Hamster. Looks like one.

Graeme Weir – Weeble. Ditto.


## 16 September. Hearts 3, SC Braga 1

I'm struggling. For a month now I've been trying to look at the world through maroon-tinted spectacles and I'm struggling. Hearts are not my team and, let's face it, they never will be. Football, as a

Hibs fan, was at best a joyous affair and at worst a grand day out with my mates: eating, drinking, toasting our good fortune at having been teenagers in the early 1970s and . . . what's the score again? Ach, who cares.

Now I watch a team I hate and I do it alone.

I had hoped to be able to entice some pals along to Hearts' first Uefa Cup tie of the season but none of them fancied it. I have to go to the game, obviously – *tragically* – but I was mildly intrigued to find out if captains in Euro competition still exchange pennants. In this age of cheap travel, foreign bars and restaurants on every street-corner, and foreign players in every dressing-room, it seems an old-fashioned custom when in a strange land, like wearing socks with sandals.

You certainly never hear 'pennant' used in other contexts any-more, and maybe no longer even this one. Euro competition has a language of its own, but it seems to be dying out. 'Dossiers' compiled on 'spying missions' to see the opposition in action are probably old technology as well, belonging to Old Europe. Catch them quick, then, before they disappear for good.

There's also the curiosity value of tonight's venue: it's Murray-field, the home of Scottish rugby. Murrayfield with its clock, famous meeting-place for Barboured hordes on foot. The car park, famous rendezvous point for the Barboured convoy in Range-Rovers. The schoolboys' enclosure, gathering place for the next generation of masters-of-the-universe, turned out awfie nice, without a single headlouse between them. One day, these boys will host tailgate picnics, just like their paters. But all of this is alien to Jambos.

Because their pitch doesn't appear to meet the specifications of those batty banana-curvature assessors of Europe, Hearts must play all their Uefa Cup ties this season at Murrayfield. Because they're chronically skint, the plan is that Murrayfield hosts all their matches next season and beyond, while Tynecastle is sold and flats are built on the site. Result: debt cleared, tradition lost, but . . . club saved?

Hibbys might smirk at the thought of Hearts in a rugby ground. At last that bunch of cloggers re-locate to their natural habitat! But you'd have to have a heart of stone and a soul of pie-filling not to feel some sympathy for them. It could be your team forced to shack up with some rugger-buggers, it could be mine.

Murrayfield is too big for Hearts' needs, too big for rugby's too, and while a decent-sized crowd – almost 19,000 – have gathered for this first-round, first-leg tie, you can imagine how echoey and desolate the place would be for a CIS Cup game against Albion Rovers on a rotten Tuesday night in December.

Tonight is pretty foul anyway, one for the Barbours, but football fans favour the manager's dugout coat. Well, some do. On the evidence of the season thus far, there's a higher take-up of the dugout coat in Gorgie than in Leith. Fan fashion is rubbish now. Clubs sell you a complete wardrobe, and many fans buy the lot. Thirty years ago, clubs only sold you strips, but you didn't wear them to matches . . .

*The well-dressed fan, circa 1973:*

*Ben Sherman checked shirt, button-down collar. Fair Isle-patterned jumper (the collar points of the shirt stayed under the jersey, but – this was important – the back of it was displayed in full, so that its mysterious third button could confirm it as a Ben Sherman). Or, alternatively, College V. Or tank-top. Plus . . . Levi Sta-Prest trousers, uncreaseable, unsinkable, worn with a turn-up and – you were right, Faither, they are great shoes – brogues.*

*A classic look, which changed to a short-sleeved Simon shirt in the summer and was augmented by a Crombie or first-generation parka during the winter months. Most of the gear could be got from the splendid Cowan Tailoring in Leith Street, outfitters by appointment to the 1970s Edinburgh street-gangs, the Young Leith Team, the Young Mental Drylaw, the Clery Jungle, the Niddrie Terror, etc. Boot-boy chronicler Richard Allen's follow-up to his novel* Skinhead *identified the attire as 'suedehead'; I was allowed elements of the ensemble but not the whole get-up, and in any case would almost certainly have been too chicken to wear it complete.*

The stewarding at Murrayfield is atrocious. Even allowing for the fact this is a new experience for everyone – team, fans, security – we're all staggering about, searching in vain for the cash gate. This week there was infiltration at the very heart of state and nation by Batmans and bampots and it's been easier to gain access to Buckingham Palace and the Houses of Parliament than Murrayfield. 'I'm no' coming back, definitely no',' mutters the old-timer behind me. I'm ten seconds away from giving up the game as a bad joke myself when finally I find a way in.

I'm hungry and food comes before football, especially when it's the Jambos, particularly since it's Euro competition and I'm jealous of the fact I'm not seeing Hibs. I miss the pennant-exchange and join another long queue at the grub-trucks. The rugger menu is bigger than its football equivalent, but only serves to tease and tantalise when I finally reach the head of the line. 'There's nae venison burgers the night,' says the harassed serving wifie, standing below a board detailing the exotic fayre. 'And the wild boar's aff as well.'

The game has started, but high up on the walkways, lots of fans are still running around, trying to locate the right entrance. It's like a mass break-out, or a break-in, and the toilets are no less disorientating for football folk because here loo paper is provided.

The stadium bowl is huge, the grass is long, and during the first half hour the Hearts players seem as befuddled as the fans. But no-one is more confused than me: who should I support tonight?

Hearts, because they're representing Edinburgh, Scotland, or the opposition because I'm a Hibby? The opposition – from Portugal's religious capital; their ground being the one blasted out of rock that featured in Euro 2004 – are difficult to love in their pale-yellow kit, quite the worst I've seen. But so are Hearts as they blunder about the Murrayfield undergrowth, bumping into Japanese soldiers still fighting the Second World War.

'Show a bit of imagination!' is the cry from a few rows back. Oh really? And how would *you* know what that was, being as you are a Hearts poltroon? I'm warming up an especially vicious piece of abuse – who shall get it? . . . Paul Hartley, *Pauline* . . . when the same player scores with a half-volley of casual arrogance.

The crowd goes berserk. Everyone twirls their scarf (it's a Jambo thing). They all love Murrayfield now. And, more than that they love the fact Hearts are in Europe and Hibs are not. 'Stand up, if you hate Hibees . . .' Everyone around me is on their feet; I stay in my seat. It's like a boat is capsized and I've found the only airhole but the water is closing in around me. If I'm not going to stand, I must say something. 'Not bad goal, eh?' The lad next to me smiles a toothless smile. 'Fuckin' barrie!'

**25 September. Hearts 1, Inverness Caley Thistle 0**
Through most of the 1980s, and what seemed like the next five centuries as well, Hibs never beat Hearts. For 22 games, Hearts held the city bragging rights in their little fleshy hands. And now, after that Euro win, they have the Braga-ing rights as well.

Hearts didn't win all 22 but there were more than a few tankings in that grim sequence, and much of the Jambos' supremacy was down to a stunted, tubby goal-hanger called John Robertson. He scored a record 27 derby goals against Hibs, and at the peak of his gonk powers, his reputation went before him. Successive Hibs defences wet their breeks at the merest glimpse of his name on the teamsheet. We could be leading 3–0 with five minutes to go and he'd score a hat-trick, the final goal bouncing off his considerable arse as he bent over to tie a bootlace.

'It's not over 'til the fat striker scores,' he once famously declared. And Hibs fans hated him, although we couldn't absolutely despise him. Deep down, under all those folds, Robbo was a Hibby, or at least had been one in boyhood.

He could have become a Hibs player, he could have become Hibs manager, but instead he's taken Inverness Caley Thistle into the SPL, a first for a teuchter team. Some typical bampotery by the beaks in charge of oor fitba at the SFA means they're having to rent Aberdeen's Pittodrie for their home matches, meaning in effect that all games are away ones. I forget how Caley Thistle are supposed to have contravened the rulebook. An insufficient number of shiny brass buttons on team blazers? Something like that . . . Nevertheless, on this dull autumn afternoon, a decent number of the

Highland capital's perfect pronouncers have made it down the A9, including a couple of lusty drummers.

I'm in the lower level of the Wheatfield Stand, five rows from the pitch, near enough to be able to inspect Andy Webster's ludicrous DIY streaked haircut and also sufficiently close to spot the smirk on Caley Thistle defender Stuart McCaffrey's face when his every touch on the ball is greeted with cries of 'Hibs wanker!'

Some fans like to monitor the movements of players who once turned out for rival clubs. No former association is too vague – I don't even remember McCaffrey playing for Hibs – or can ever be forgiven. At Easter Road, a mate, Neil, has earned the nickname 'Jambowatch' for his tireless tracking of tenuous Tynecastle ties, and this encourages him to claim he trained under the Nazi hunter and Holocaust conscience, Simon Wiesenthal.

It's just as well there are counter-attractions today because the game is dire. Paul Hartley scores early – a delicate chip on the run that wafts into the Snekky net on a zephyr of Harmony hairspray from his feathercut; the second smart strike by the player in as many games – and Hearts sit on the lead. Phil Stamp – Pas des Bas – just squats on it. I have another go at some Jambo interaction.

'Rubbish game, eh?'

A grunt from the lad alongside me in the white away top.

'Too few teams,' I say, 'too many meaningless matches, too little to play for if you're not one of the Old Firm, too expensive, too many counter-attractions like tax forms and Tom Cruise films where there's always got to be one scene where he runs – that's the story of Scottish football.'

Another grunt. I'm talking too much. It's like we're watching a Marx Bros film, infinitely preferable to a Tom Cruise one, apart from the obligatory romantic interludes, usually involving a song, which were always the cue for my brother Sean and I to natter, quickly turning to arguing, then a fight on the living-room floor, much to the annoyance of our sisters, while waiting for Groucho, Chico and Harpo to return. Oh, that Hearts were fielding that classic midfield trio today.

At half-time, MC Tynie mildly endears himself to me by dusting down Eddie And The Hot Rods' 'Do Anything You Wanna Do', a song I've not heard since I pretended to be a punk (just like the Rods). There's a penalty shoot-out in aid of Alzheimer's Scotland – 62,000 Scots suffer from dementia, according to the man at the mike. And when, without wishing to make light of a serious condition, Patrick Kisnorbo – Kookaburra – under no pressure, and with no opponent near him, passes it straight out of play, I feel like I make it 62,001. But no-one else seems to mind. They've got bigger fish to fry; they're hoping to make a Portuguese stew out of SC Braga. So they sing the Hearts version of 'My Way':

> *And now the end is near*
> *We've followed Hearts from Perth to Paisley*
> *We've travelled far, by bus and car*
> *And other times, we've went by railway*
> *We've been, to Aberdeen*
> *We hate the Hibs, they make us spew up*
> *So make a noise you Gorgie boys*
> *We're going to Europe*

[Oh there's more . . .]

> *To see, HMFC*
> *We'll even dig, the Channel Tunnel*
> *When we're afloat, on some big boat*
> *We'll tie our scarves around the funnel*
> *We have no cares, for other players*
> *Like Rossi, Boniek or Tardelli*
> *When we're overseas, the Hibs will be*
> *In Portobelly*

In this communal feelgood moment, the fans behind me suddenly become charitable to Dennis Wyness. When he falls over in an attempt to control the ball with no-one near him, they laugh, when they might previously have gone spare. In honour of the homecoming hero in the away dugout, they polish up an old chant: 'Who put the ball in the Hibees net – Johnny Robertson.' This is the kind of generosity of spirit towards the opposition you only get from fans when their team is winning. It's one of football's Hamlet moments – the cigar, not the Shakespeare – and of course today it's been brought on by a Harmony moment.

A couple of rows back, Robbo's presence is the cue for more reminiscing, which throws up a fairly illuminating answer to that age-old question: how Hun-oriented are Hearts?

Jambo (re-assessing ex-Tynie favourites): 'Aye but Neil McCann went off and joined Rangers.'

Mrs Jambo: 'That's rich coming from you with the Red Hand of Ulster tattooed on your arm.'

Jambo: 'Ah ken, but Rangers don't have a monopoly on that.'

Walking home I find myself singing the Rods' hymn to youthful struggle with identity, and the line 'I'm sure I must be someone/ Now I'm gonna find out who' is soon being recited on repeat.

### 27 September

Hibs won 1–0 at Aberdeen on Saturday and I catch up with the highlights on *Scotsport SPL*. The winning goal is a piece of stunning, pick-that-out nonchalance from a player, who – if Hibs were Brazil – would be called Derek Riordaninho. But they're not Brazil, of course they're not.

### 30 September. SC Braga 2, Hearts 2

Robbie's is one of my favourite Hibs boozers: halfway down Leith Walk, wooden floor, clubbing posters, plenty familiar faces, all sharp features, a conspiratorial but friendly ambience which earns the pub this recommendation from the guidebook *Scotland The Best!*: 'More rough than smooth, but with the footy on the box, a pint and a packet of Hula Hoops, this is a bar to savour life.'

At just gone 6 pm the place is full. Most seem to have come straight from work: a few in suits, but many in paint-spattered jeans and mud-caked boots. There's a bloke in a City of Edinburgh Council T-shirt and another in a Plumb Center jumper.

And they're all Hibbys, here to cheer on the Portuguese? Well, no. It starts as a murmur, tests the water with a cry of 'Jam Tarts!', builds in confidence . . . 'Get in there!' . . . then breaks into wild cheering at the first of a blundering brace from Mark de Vries – Elmer Fudd. Jambos in Leith, going radge.

The game is being piped into Robbie's courtesy of the Sultana channel, but there's a moment midway through the first half when the action freezes. Some of Sultana's standby music fills the pub. Is that really Level 42? It is, you know. Everyone looks at the still pix, and tries to avoid twitching an arm to the throbbing bass lines, twanged, like Mark King, high up the chest.

Coverage resumes and I can't help noticing that the Hearts players, in peely-wally close-up, are all wearing yellow wristbands. These are cyclist Lance Armstrong's anti-cancer bracelets and his 'Livestrong' message has been picked up by the footballer-ponce, The Painted Fool himself, Derek Beckham. The Jambos don't usually have a stubby finger on the pulse, but they've got in early with the bands, and have a Euro stage on which to wear them. Bastards. So I convince myself that in their case, the bands are the kind signifying entitlement to a senior citizens' aqua-aerobics session at the local Dalry Public Baths.

And there they are at the final whistle, hugging each other in the centre-circle and celebrating their passage into the new-style group sections of the UEFA Cup. Yeah, yeah, very good. Now can we switch over to UK Tin? There's an old episode of *Peak Practice* I want to see . . .

# OCTOBER

**1 October**

I have lived in Edinburgh all my life. It's probably because I share the city with Jambos that I believe that in essence we're millions of miles apart; that Hibs are from Mars, Hearts from Uranus.

For a Hibs fan who's gone away, though, does distance from Gorgie hordes lend them a perverse kind of enchantment? The furthest-flung Hibby I know is John, who emigrated to Sydney to work in publishing and now writes plays. Our dads were great mates, our families used to meet up every New Year's Day and – bonding the pair of us until the day we die – we were at the 7–0 game together.

I email John to tell him about my strange season and within minutes he writes back:

*Too true Jambos are different from us. As befitting a team in green, Hibbys gaze to exotic lands, the far horizons. Jambos look at flock wallpaper. At Easter Road, from the Famous Five Stand, you see Arthur's Seat and the high ground of Edinburgh which has fascinated invader and historian alike for a millennium. From the West Stand your vantage is green fields, on the horizon the Bass Rock and Firth of Forth, the trading hub of Embra going back to Norse and Hanseatic times.*

*From all sides of Tynecastle you look at . . . other Jambos. There's the odd pie stand, the grim upper floors of dirt-caked tenements filled with Jambos and their black-and-white tellys, and that's your lot.*

*How else shall we know Jambos? It's not quite true that they all work for the Post Office, it only seems that way. Embra is of course a prosperous city, so both teams have their supporters at financial institutions such as Standard Death. But the Hibbys will be in the boardroom; they're also the product developers, the writers, the thinkers. Jambos are identified by their business cards, and the term 'assistant'.*

*In most work sectors, Hibbys are in possession of the interesting jobs. At the casino, the croupier will be a Hibby, the doorman in the drookit cape will be a Jambo. I don't know the name of the assistant zookeeper at the elephant cage at Edinburgh Zoo but I could tell you which team he supports.*

*My father was of course a polisman – a Jambo job if there ever was one – and a Tynecastle regular in his younger days. However, as he matured, and started admiring the great Hibs team of the 1970s, he progressed up the Lothian and Borders force. By the time he agreed to take me to see Hibs play the mighty Juventus – I refused to be fobbed off with Hearts vs Airdrie – he'd won the Queen's Police Medal and made it to Deputy Commandant of the Police Training College in Scotland. If only he'd wised up earlier, he could have landed the top job.*

*The happiest I ever saw the old boy at a football match was when the Jambos gubbed Lokomotiv Leipzig 5–1. That was the game where I suddenly discovered a passion for Erik Honecker's model state.*

*Good luck at the Dalry sub-post office*
*John*

### 3 October. Hearts 0, Livingston 0

I've been a bad boy. Yesterday afternoon, I skived off to watch Hibs. Because of their Euro exploits, Hearts' game against Livi had been switched to the Sunday – and with my big experiment still at the 'early doors' stage, as Ron Atkinson would say, I decided that a wee trip to Dunfermline to see the boys wouldn't do anyone any harm. I was wrong. It left me crushed.

Smirking Hibby mates had been telling me that they'd been

playing well, deserving a draw with Celtic and beating Aberdeen at Pittodrie with a routine screamer from Derek Riordan, the most talented young player to emerge at Easter Road for ages. Hibs didn't win yesterday, their game finished 1–1, and according to some of the pals I've deserted, this was one of their poorer performances – but I was entranced. I saw them play more passes on the ground in one game than I've seen Hearts do in half a dozen, and every one of them was despatched with a white, silver or gold boot. Very appropriate. Hearts, as you would expect, have resisted the fad for sexy footwear, sticking dourly to black. This suits them, too.

The average age of the current Hibs side is eight. All right, I'm exaggerating, but most are kids. Some broke into the first team the previous season under Bobby Williamson, but Mr Bobby made them play a harshly-disciplined, bed-with-no-supper style completely reliant on the long ball, the big hoof. For these urchins, this was the equivalent of being sent up chimneys before 18th-century social reform.

What a contrast under Tony Mowbray. At the start of this season, many sniggered at his appointment. They laughed when he promised that Hibs would play a passing game. They guffawed when he said he'd use even more kids than Mr Bobby, because that was all he had at his disposal. But his bold plan is working. For Hibs, Mowbray has truly been the football version of Lord Shaftesbury, freeing the club from tot-tyranny. He's intelligent, keen to probe his players' minds He's articulate, booting the traditional post-match cliché high into Row Z. A rounded man, then, as opposed to Mr Bobby, who was merely round.

Presumably using a reward system involving bags of sweets and sleepovers with their mates, Mowbray has got his young bucks playing with a scampering exuberance. The midfield that Mr Bobby bypassed has been crucially helmed by a languid Frenchman called Guillaume Beuzelin who, this being Scotland, has been nicknamed 'Boozy'. All over the rest of the park, striplings and skelfs and skinnymalinks not old enough to have seen Hibs slam five goals past

Dino Zoff, or lose to Montrose and Arbroath either, run wild and free.

The Hibs kids are a boy band. They're a street gang. They're a comic strip. They're Ocean Terminal mall-rats. They're an Urban Outfitter's window display. They're the queue for the Candy Bar on a night when it's 'Breezers £1, Wonderbras get in free'. They're the queue for a *Hollyoaks* audition. They're *Brat Camp*-Comes-To-Leith. They're a commercial for Clearasil or Dorrito's or a teen chatline or some ultra-performance styling gel with super-extra hold. Ah yes, the Hibs haircuts. Were they a band, 100 Haircuts would be the name. But am I watching Tony Mowbray's Hibs or Toni&Guy's Sunday team? Tragically, because of my absenteeism, I can't tell the haircuts apart: to these un-tutored eyes one peroxide, streaked mullet looks the same as any other. I confuse Dean Shiels with Steven Fletcher, Fletcher with Sam Morrow, Morrow with Limahl from Kajagoogoo, Limahl with Pat Sharp the twerpish DJ and Sharp with the spookiest of the zombie urchins from *The Village Of The Damned*. And the reason I don't know the Hibs haircuts? Because I've been too busy watching the Jambo beards.

This Easter Road side have always *looked* pretty groovy but the players who came through last season often flattered to deceive. Now, with the addition of a few more youngsters, and the influence of Mowbray's serene paternalistic tutelage, they're playing football to match those exotic plumages, and it was a chilling thought indeed, as my train chugged back over the Forth Bridge to Edinburgh, that the next time I would see my team would be at Tynecastle in three weeks' time, with me sitting among the Jambos.

So, it's Gorgie once more. The determinedly non-fabulous Hearts, *again*. Somewhat predictably, after their European exertions, the Jambos are a bit knackered for the visit of Livi, Lothian neighbours from the new toon. Somewhat predictably, after spoiling myself at Dunf, I'm bored out of my skull. And I'm not the only one; the place is dead. It's so quiet you could hear a pie drop. The yellow-band fad has spread to the stands and, to amuse myself, I try to count the fans wearing them.

The man next to me is playing with his; the bands rate as jewellery and, as a Scottish terracing archetype, he might be thinking them too feminine. 'Pretty quiet today,' I venture. 'Aye, Hearts fans are a fickle bunch,' he says. 'But they should never have closed Section N.'

This is the part of the old main stand closest to the away end where the ultras among the Hearts support stood from first whistle to last and sang nasty songs, but at least they sang. 'Some of them were Nazis,' says the band-man, 'but fitba cannae be too picky if it wants grounds to have atmosphere.'

Generally, you could argue that since the advent of the all-seated stadium, singing at football grounds has gone the way of variety, music hall and vaudeville. But there are degrees of non-singing and in Scotland it seems to work in inverse proportion to the size of the crowd and the level of success. Once, at Parkhead, grimly waiting for the procession of Celtic goals against Hibs, my friend Rab and I were deafened by a hideous crunching sound. 'What the hell was that?' asked Rab. 'Is the ground about to cave in on us?' It transpired that high up in the stand the length of the pitch away from us, someone had just opened a packet of crisps. Monster Munch, if I'm not mistaken.

You've never heard 50,000 people make less noise than at Parkhead when one of the SPL's cannon-fodder teams are in town. Unless you're at Ibrox, of course, because it's even quieter there. And maybe Tynecastle in the wake of Hearts' he-man display as the third force in the SPL, is getting a bit presumptuous on relative success. Wins against this kind of opposition are expected as a matter of course. There's no need to sing to help the team achieve that end.

From a purely selfish point of view I'm grateful for this. If the real Hearts fans aren't singing, it means I don't have to either.

**4 October**

Inspired by that Hibs–Hearts juxtaposition just there, some more differences . . .

1. Hibs are back-heeling the ball over your head and catching it on your neck. Hearts are a game of long-bangers, played to the death.

2. Hibs are the matador, slaying with panache. Hearts are the abattoir-man, dragging the beast to the local slaughterhouse at Chesser.

3. Hibs are a novel by Michael Houellebecq, the cannae-keep-it-in-his-culottes French author of *Atomised* and *Platform*. Hearts are something chunky and embossed and stultifyingly coy where, at the crucial moment, the action cuts straight to the morning-after with the proverbial shafts of sunlight streaming through the bedroom window, larks twittering.

4. Hearts stopped developing at the sixth stage of man. Hibs, as they so brilliantly demonstrated on January 1, 1973, got to seven.

5. 'Ah,' says my brother Sean, 'but have you considered the deconstructionist's perspective? Hibs are represented as being *completely different* from Hearts, but they only exist by virtue of defining themselves *against* Hearts. In other words, they *depend* on Hearts. As Jacques Derrida, who knew about such matters, once put it: "To be *un* Hibby you have to first acknowledge *ton* Jamboness." '


**16 October. Celtic 3, Hearts 0**

On the taxi ride across Glasgow to my first away match, the cabbie asks: 'If you could blame wan man for what's wrang with Scottish fitba, whae would it be?'

Don't know, I say.

'It's goat tae be Graeme Souness, naw?'

This has been a grim week for the national team – defeat by Norway and a draw with Moldova in the qualifiers for the 2006 World Cup – and it's prompted much soul-searching, navel-gazing, breast-beating, heart-wringing (if not quite throat-slitting) about the state of the game. It was my cabbie's view that Souness's Rangers revolution, with other clubs following his example of stuffing his team with imports at the expense of local talent, had stifled the game's development for a generation. He's a Rangers fan, and although I think the wan-man verdict harsh, there's something in his argument.

We're back to league business today, though, and what better place to forget about Scotland's woes than Celtic Park? 'They're all bastardin' Irish,' mutters a Jambo outside the ground. 'All the way here on the bus I never heard one Scottish accent.' And half an hour later, with Hearts well on the way to a perfunctory Parkhead humping, I will hear the same voice, same moan: 'Fuckin' chancers exploiting your "poor Irish" roots for your fuckin' worldwide rebel brand. Fuck yez!'

Relationships between the Old Firm and the rest of Scottish football have deteriorated in recent years. If Celtic were to win the European Cup now, it's unlikely they could count on the country-wide good feeling experienced in 1967. I cheered Rangers all the way to the penultimate of the inaugural Champions' League in 1992–93 but they can go and stuff themselves if they think I'm doing that again.

How has it come to this? One of the reasons is that the rest of Scottish football do not view Celtic and Rangers as especially Scottish. The Irish Tricolour flies at Celtic Park, the Union Jack at Ibrox. The Catholic and Protestant traditions of these clubs have never been subliminal, emphasised only through code. But you might have thought the end of the Irish Troubles would have cooled temperatures among the hodden masses. Not a bit.

The old songs of hate still boom out, and maybe a reason for this is that football has become safe and a bit soft. Certainly these revamped grounds amplify them more. Under massive stadia re-development, the stands have soared into the sky. In the all-seated era, the Old Firm have courted corporates, professional fans, middle-class fans. Safe and snug in – at Parkhead at least – heated seats, these fans don't sing. So the old-skool seem to bellow even louder, to remind newcomers of tradition, to emphasise that Celtic have always been a grand old team to play for . . . that some were following, following Rangers back in the days when crowds of just 10,000 rattled around inside Ibrox and John McDonald was appealing for penalties for slipping on the soap in the dressing-room. And they sing their songs of hate to ram this point home: 'We were here first, ya bass.'

Not particularly Scottish, then, and also, not wanting to play in Scotland anymore. The Old Firm are desperate to switch leagues, preferably down south, but so far, England has proved curiously resistant to Celtic and Rangers' lumpy football and the lumpen hordes who truly believe themselves God's chosen people, as selected by different Gods, obviously. So, reluctantly, they're forced to remain in the SPL, where they're currently about as welcome as the husband caught cheating but who continues to live in the family home.

The husband is by far the dominant one in the relationship, he makes the most money and gives the relationship – the league – what little status it has. So as a result the spurned other party is in a quandary. Should she boot out the dirty, rotten cheat for not loving Scotland anymore? But if she did that, could she survive by herself?

At Parkhead today, I can't decide. Celtic cruise to a 3–0 lead, it's another no-contest, another example of how much they've out-grown the rest of Scottish football. Two of the goals are scored by on-loan players, Henri Camara and Juninho. In the Brazilian's case, Celtic can afford to fork out a weekly wage – £35,000 – that's more than the combined first-team salary of many clubs in the SPL. It's my first instinct to say, yes, the Old Firm should bugger off.

But, despite the nasty songs, I still think of the Old Firm as more or less Scottish. Long before Glasgow's Big Two started routinely cherry-picking from other SPL teams – another reason for everyone else to despise them – Celtic won that 1967 European Cup with a side – all bar Bobby Lennox – drawn from a twelve-mile radius around Parkhead.

And, despite the heavily Irish-accented chant of 'Churry-o, churry-o' as some Jambos leave early, a day out at Celtic's home is still a vivid Scottish footballing experience, and one I'd be sorry to lose. Because I haven't come to Glasgow by road, I miss out on an encounter with the junior car-valet service. The transaction goes like this: a gang of toerags approach you and ask: 'Watch your motor mister?' You agree. If you don't, they turn themselves into the junior haw-haw-tight-git-tyre-removal service and when you return to your car it's propped up on bricks. I've missed that, but all the other Parkhead staples seem to be present and correct.

A man in white winklepickers with lethal points who isn't in fancy-dress; he put them on this morning without thinking because this is Glasgow, the flashest city in the world . . . lots and lots of priests . . . lots and lots of plumbing millionaires . . . a walking-wounded with the purplest face I've ever seen . . . swankers with hair in ponytails and coats on their backs that shout, 'Feel the material, by the way', and tanned trophy-bauchles on their shoulders – and who bellow into their mobiles until they stop to greet one another like mobster-brothers. Five times the size of a Tynecastle crowd, Parkhead is, effortlessly, five times as dramatic in its local colour and extremes. There's a greater devotion here, and some of it even concerns football.

On days like this Glasgow is a big, big city and Edinburgh simply isn't in the same league. It's also a football city, and while I can make a case for Edinburgh being one too, it cannot really compete with its rowdy, rumbustious neighbour in the west. That's another reason we don't like Glasgow and its football teams: jealousy. Football is the only arena in which Edinburgh feels inferior to Glasgow.

So today the Jambos goad the Hooped hordes with stuff about Glasgow's slums and also this little ditty:

> *Who shagged all the boys?*
> *Who shagged all the boys?*
> *Celtic Boys' Club, Celtic Boys' Club*
> *Who shagged all the boys?*

That's quite tame, though. A nervous glance over my shoulder confirms that some of the Hearts ultras are in this afternoon; the Union Jacks are flying high. Every ten minutes or so, an arm is pushed up a back and the Strathclyde Polis make another arrest. One is bundled down the stairwell for this little address to Celtic's black defender, Bobo Balde: 'Fuck off, ya coon fuck!' I find out later that 15 were chucked out for sectarian chanting and racist abuse as part of a planned operation targeting far-right lunkheads.

The 'away end' at Parkhead is a bit of a misnomer; it's more of an 'away gully', a narrow corridor of seats at one corner of the stadium with poor sight-lines rendered even worse if, like me, you're stuck right down at the pitch, trying to catch a glimpse of the action between the big, big Strathclyde arses of the security detail in this big, big football city.

And what am I doing as Celtic win this game with ease, with Hearts playing ultra-defensively, with only Graeme Weir weebling around up front? Away games are different. At Tynecastle, mostly, I can mind my own business, and not cheer if I don't want to (and I don't). But on the road, in a confined space, if you just sit there, you stand out. So I shout for the refereeing decisions you just never get at Parkhead if you're a fan of one of the SPL's plankton-teams, and at the end I affect an air of gnarly defiance.

There's a long walk back to the city centre, past the parked cars with the scruffy tykes standing proud on the pavement, waiting for their reward. I thought about my last car journey back from Parkhead: Rab and I were in the company of his Celtic friends, with one of them driving. If this had been our car, we would have quickly turned on the radio to check the rest of the scores. That day, the trip was completed in silence because, of course, no other games can impact on the Old Firm, far less hurt them. And then I thought about the conversation the previous night in the pub after work with Dan, a Celtic-supporting friend, who told me he was going to today's game but admitted he couldn't remember who the champs were playing.

Yes, Celtic should go, and take Rangers with them.

## 21 October. Feyenoord 3, Hearts 0

I feel like the shoebomber. On this plane, flight XLA7138, I'm the only one with the ulterior motive. And even though I'm doing my best to appear normal and Jambo-like, I can't help feeling they know exactly what I'm about. What must the security boys be thinking? Will the fact I'm concealing Hibs affiliations about my person cause the bleeper to go off?

A little bit of history is created at Edinburgh Airport at 5.45am as the cry of 'Haw, fat boy!' and – I kid you not – five Jambos turn round. No, that's not the notable thing, it's this: Hearts are representing Scotland in the first of the new group matches for the UEFA Cup and, away to Ruud Gullit's Feyenoord, this is the queue for the flight to the opening match. Then, after check-in, at a minute after 6am, the bevvying starts.

At the bar, a Jambo with 'Hearts – The Edinburgh Team' tattooed on one arm is explaining the niceties of relationship trust to a friend while fielding drinks orders from the rest of his gang. 'Lager, Davie? Aye, well you've kind o' *goat* tae let her go to Newcastle for a hen night if she's cool about you coming on this trip . . . two lager, hen . . . John, Malky? . . . four lager . . . what you dinnae ken winnae hurt you . . . five lager . . . it's called reverse psychology . . . six lager . . . the power'll then be back with you: that's the moment you say you want tae try a threesome . . . seven lager, pet, and a Tia Maria.' (OK, I made the seventh lager up).

Hearts On Tour, and I've sneaked a seat on the Jambo jet although, slightly worryingly, I don't have a ticket for the match. Hearts have qualified for Europe more times than Hibs in recent years so their fans must be seasoned campaigners, expert packers who forget nothing, with a knack for putting together that just-right travel attire. So let's wipe the last of the sleep from our eyes and check them out: there are some wives and girlfriends on this trip but it's mostly guys. Guys with spammy haircuts and sovvy rings. Guys in Hearts strips, different vintages. Guys in kilts, but only a few of them, because this is a Jambo trip, and they wear the plaid with Timberlands or other rugged bootwear. Whatever happened to the classic tartan accessories of Adidas Sambas and dirty white towelling socks?

Hanging about the departure lounge, I'm starting to spot Jambos from previous games, such as the bloke who found Celtic's Oirishness so offensive at Parkhead and is still complaining about the ref from that match. Since then he's acquired a wristband; the yellow peril spreads. When *will* that Dalry Public Baths swim-sesh be over? But if I can spot them, do they recognise me? My paranoia is increasing and, as we queue up to board the plane, my right leg starts to shake. The guards must be thinking I have a detonator strapped to it. Or a Hibs scarf.

I sit next to Simon and we get talking. He's a hairdresser, and I'm thinking, he wouldn't want cabin-supervisor Gervaise announcing *that* over the speaker-system on this flight, so we've both got something to hide. Any famous clients? 'I once cut Elvis's hair [Lisa-Marie, the captain]. It used to be just horrendous and his gaffer came with him to make sure he got a fringe. But the cut I gave him, it was a complete bawbag. Next game against Rangers he was Man of the Match and interviewed on the telly. I was mortified.'

We discuss other Jambo haircuts. Dave McPherson – organiser of this trip through his sports management company – used to play encumbered by a style Simon calls a 'rucksack'. From further back, Johnny Haynes was one of the first players to be sponsored by Brylcreem. 'I'm setting up my own salon and he's offered to help promote it. But that's not the direction I'm headed,' says Simon.

Simon is actually headed into darkest Leith for this venture; so what does he think of Hibs? 'I don't hate them. I've got respect for them but I absolutely love beating them. I must admit, though, that Hibs are probably the cooler team. Dougray Scott's a fan and when he flicked the Vs at us at a derby that was probably the most frustrated I've felt as a Jambo. And then there's The Proclaimers. I'd *love* them to be Hearts fans. At weddings, when their songs get played, you just have to keep your head down.'

Simon seems like a good lad, and is almost definitely the only person on this flight who's uttered the word 'metrosexual'. Edinburgh is a metrosexual city, he says, or it tries to be, but if a hairdresser walked into the terror-pub Robertson's on a Friday night he would not come out laughing. And a Hibby . . . ?

It's hard being a football-loving hairstylist, he says, and difficult to get banter going in his profession. 'I reckon the number of hairdressers who like football is only one in 300,' he says. Remembering my assignment for *The Scotsman* requiring me to get a baldy on the Channel 4 reality show *The Salon*, I have to agree. The programme's star was a flamboyant, temperamental, hissy-fitting, permanentally-having-a-bad-haircut-day Brazilian blow-dry queen called Ricardo, and I had a hunch he was the only man from down Rio way who didn't like football. He confirmed he'd been to the Maracana Stadium just once and had hated it – 'Ooo, too noisy!'

Later on this trip, though, I will meet Dougie, who turns out to be yet another Jambo crimper. Maybe Hearts are the only true metrosexual football team. But this doesn't explain why the players' haircuts are so naff. As Simon would put it, complete bawbags, the lot of them. Like Simon, Dougie's made the trip with his girlfriend; by the end both couples will be laden with shopping bags.

In Amsterdam's Schipol Airport, waiting to pass through customs, I get talking to Fred, manager of a West Lothian heating and ventilation company who's going to the game with his 19-year-old son. Fred is a professional Eurofan, to the extent he hitches onto the coat-tails of other clubs' continental excursions.

'Although I'm a Hearts man, I love foreign cities and the crack you get on a football trip,' he says. 'I was in Seville with Celtic and got photographed in the Hoops. When I turned up in Braga with the Hearts, the guys were like: "What fuckin' top ye gonna wear the night, ya wee cunt?"'

Fred is like Alan Whicker when he reels off his soccer sojourns with Celtic and with Rangers. Hibs?

'Yer kiddin'. I draw the line there.'

Worst country for football?

'Italy. The cops herd you about like cattle and the fans spit and piss on you.'

But Amsterdam is one of Fred's favourite cities and, in a display of swank – like lighting up a cigar with a €10 note, or a photo of Donald Ford – but also of Jambo generosity, he gives me his spare ticket.

Alastair, on the trip with his grandson and the lad's pal, runs a coach firm and can go all the way back to 1958 against Standard Liege as a Jambo in Europe. He saw Willie Bauld play but rates Dave Mackay the all-time best in maroon. Grandpa is wearing white slipperette-type trainers on his feet, confirming the novelist Gordon Burn's observation in his book *The North of England home service* that all men, of whatever age, now dress like they're 19.

I'm envious of the Jambos being so inter-continental, and so pan-generational with it. Euro football wasn't really geared up for fans travelling abroad when Dad and I welcomed the likes of Sporting Lisbon and Locomotiv Leipzig to Leith. The only time I've seen Hibs abroad was in 1989, against FC Liege. I travelled to Belgium by bus and before the coach had left the East End of Princes Street, the lad across the aisle from me had puked into a poly bag.

I'm in the centre of Amsterdam now, and this trip is shaping up as much more pleasurable. Forgetting for now that it's Hearts I'm here to see, this is the home of total fitba so: respect. As a Hibs fan, I feel proud to be in the HQ of a leading practitioner of the beautiful *geme* and, hang on, I recognise these snug little lanes . . . ah yes, the Red Light District. It's just gone midday, and the girls are already perched in their windows, but they're eating. One Amazonian in zingy purple bra and pants is munching on a hotdog. Well, if you're working, if you're going to be on your back all day, you can't do it on an empty stomach. Call me old-fashioned, though . . . doesn't it detract from the romance?

I *am* old-fashioned, because the Jambos are piling inside. Close to the Sex Palace which shows XXX flicks, a flag draped from a first-floor bedroom at the Heart of Amsterdam Hotel proclaims: 'Drylaw Jambos'. The Red Light District is being turned maroon.

How do I feel? Like I'm getting a day out in Amsterdam, on a sunny autumn day. With an hour or so to kill before the bus leaves for Rotterdam, I stop off in a bar for a beer . . . then another, this one's playing Van Der Graaf Generator, prog-rockers of fond, Falmer-looned memory . . . hey, remember *Van Der Valk*, TV's top cracker of canal crime? Feeling pretty relaxed now . . . then:

'You're a journalist, aye?'

I wouldn't say this bloke's cold stare is threatening, not yet, but it is insistent. 'You write that Hibby guff, don't ye?'

Shit.

I've been talking to a Jambo about Vladimir Romanov and he's just finishing saying how he's suspicious of the Lithuanian's motives but the club are so desperate they'll probably *have* to do business with him, when I'm rumbled by his mate. I do something stupid; I try to deny I'm the Hibby guff-writer. But my accuser has got me, and the other Jambos standing nearby – half a dozen of them – have got me too. What now? They're closing ranks. They're going to want to know what I'm doing here.

Then one of them says: 'Are you the guy who calls Colin Murdock, "Stinker"?' It's a fair cop, that *is* my nickname for the Hibs centre-half, a nod to radio comedy legend Richard Murdoch but also a reference to how rubbish the baldy tube is.

'We love that,' says my new best friend, the peace-broker. 'And you hate Celtic and Rangers as much as we do.'

A pause, it goes on for ages.

'Guys, he's OK.'

Saved, by a mutual disaffection for the Old Firm.

But the near-thing has put me on edge. On the journey to the match – under police escort – I elect to sit behind the driver. It's the bad yins up the back in time-honoured tradition and right away they start up the songs:

> *We've got Bobby, Bobby, Bobby, Bobby Prentice*
> *On the wing*
> *On the wing*

*His name is Drew Busby*
*The cock o' the north*
*He drinks all your whisky*
*And Newcastle Brown*
*The Gorgie Boys are in town*
*Na na na . . . na-na-na-na-na . . .*

*He's here, he's there, he's every fuckin' where*
*Kenny Aird, Kenny Aird*

I remember these players. I went to Hearts matches when they were in their pomp. Me and my dad. I mean, we were thoroughly thirled to Hibs, but a game was a game. Do you guys know any other golden oldies?

*Hullo, hullo, we are the Gorgie Boys*
*Hullo, hullo, you'll know us by our noise*
*Up to our knees in Fenian blood, surrender or you'll die*
*Oh we are the Gorgie Billy Boys*

Can't say that was ever one of my favourites. I try to avoid eye contact. 'Look out the window,' I tell myself, 'count the windmills, try and spot the mice, the little mice with clogs on.' The journey through low-slung countryside seems to go on forever until, finally, the stadium looms. It's big and round and the police presence is massive as we're shepherded into our designated area – a pen surrounded by high fencing – and I'm reminded of Fred's remark about fans being treated like cattle. In such conditions is it any wonder supporters react badly?

Some Jambos spot a couple of Dutch lads on a bridge above us and give them abuse, about how if it wasn't for the Brits in WW2, they'd be Krauts. Never mind what Basil Fawlty says: do mention the war, mention it all the time, it's just about all we've got left. And some more Dutch fans, older, academic-looking, peer at us through round, wire-framed specs and shake their heads.

Jambo, to pleasant, patient girl at food kiosk: 'If I don't get 20 Regal, you're gettin' banged.' She understands, of course, and sniggers in a way he finds completely unnerving. The Jambos aren't causing the Dutch to run for the hills, or what passes for them here, so they turn on their oldest foes. The simplest Jambo logic, the one they understand best, is this: Hearts are in Europe, Hibs aren't. Well, apart from the spy in the camp, the fly in the fondue.

> *The last time Hibs won a trophy*
> *Noah built an ark of wood*
> *On the way back to town*
> *Their horse and cart broke down*
> *And the cup it got stolen by Robin Hood.*

Such a keen sense of history these Jambos . . .

> *Your cupboards are bare*
> *You've no silverware*
> *103 in a row*

And, as they would see it, social awareness . . .

> *Hibs are gay*
> *Fuck the Pope and the IRA*

And . . .

> *He's got Aids and can't get rid of it*
> *He's a Fenian bastard*

I can shout encouragement for Hearts tonight because my usual stance – wishing them to lose, all the time – has altered, possibly under the threat of being outed again, *definitely* because of this . . . but these songs are difficult to sing. So I laugh along with a girly titter. In the nick of time the game starts, and we can all concentrate on what's happening on the pitch . . . apart from the Jambo sitting on my right who spends the entire 90 minutes threatening the Feyenoord fan directly across from him, through the clear-plastic wall separating the two factions. He does this silently, by drawing a finger across his neck in imitation of a knife.

The match takes an age to pass and I try desperately to appear invisible. I'm such a scaredy-cat. Although being rumbled didn't result in a sore face, it has knocked my confidence, especially as I'm so far from home. Then the Jambo with the imaginary blade starts up a song and turns towards me with enough of a scowl to suggest that I should accompany him for one of his favourite ditties. So I sing it. I sing: 'Are you watching, Hibee scum?'

Hearts are well beaten. And I'm in such a hurry to exit the stadium and get back on the bus that I take a wrong turning. I end up on the train platform, and have to run the gauntlet through a tunnel of Jambos. Uh-oh . . . someone tries to trip me . . . here we go . . . and then I spot Fred, the ventilation tycoon. I've never been so happy to see a tubby wee bloke in a maroon strip in my life and I greet him like a long-lost friend. 'How's it goin' big man?' he says. 'Crap result, eh? Never mind, wait 'til I tell you about my day in Amsterdam.'

It appears that not only did Fred provide me with a ticket for the game, he also gifted his laddie with one to adulthood. They'd had a nice meal, big, juicy steaks, and Fred was feeling right at home in another foreign city and thinking he'd like to pass on some of this Euro perspective to his son. So they went to a brothel. Together. Fred paid for the boy and there they were, father and son, in the boudoir together. Never having been in such a compromising situation with his old man before, not really wanting to think about his old man having sex, in the same room as he was about to engage in the business of doing pleasure, the plaintive voice rang out: 'Fuck's sake, Dad, turn your back!'

## 23 October

My life began in 1973. Well, it actually began in 1957, but '73 was my big year, the year I properly grew into my long trousers. And if I remember right, the big boy's breeks were blue-and-grey checked Oxford Bags from C&A.

This was the year, after a few false starts, that Roxy Music's *For Your Pleasure* album properly got me into rock music. This was the year, after reading by rote for O-level English, that Martin Amis's *The Rachel Papers* properly got me into fiction. This was the year, too, that I got my first proper girlfriend. And this was the year that Hibs beat Hearts 7–0.

The game has assumed mythical status among Hibs fans who were in the sell-out 36,000 crowd at Tynecastle that New Year's Day, and also those who weren't but claim to have been there, and those who missed it but are still trying to do a *Zelig*, and like Woody Allen's great-moments-in-history gatecrasher, transport themselves to that dull, cold, utterly glistening afternoon, and squeeze in up the back.

I *was* there. I've got the programme *and* the ticket stub. I can half-shut my eyes and summon up the dog-eared photo-memory album containing a shot of *the exact colour of the sky beyond the packed terraces of the School End*. Hearts could have been three up before Hibs began the blizzard of goals which would shoot them to the top of the old First Division. Hearts were 5–0 down at half-time and my Uncle Don, bless him, felt moved to offer these words of encouragement to his son: 'Don't worry, Johnny, Hearts will bring on Cammy Fraser in the second half, you wait and see.'

It was an epochal result, inspiring wild abandon. Dad decided there and then to give up the fags. A month later, he took up snuff. The most embarrassed I've been in my football life were those moments, when other fans would nudge each other and point at the old man as he spooned another load from the whalebone box onto his wrist in readiness for a big snort. But so what? He was there with me for 7–0.

Like many Hibbys, I thought the absence of a commemorative

video of the game was because release of the recording had been blocked by a miserable Jambo git at BBC Scotland. Then, thanks to my journo-colleague Jim, Sky News's man-on-the-spot in Scotland and a big Hibby, a recording appeared. I bought it but quickly realised it was superfluous to my needs: the VCR in my head had preserved every goal without embellishment, apart from an extra tumble I'd given Hearts' Jim Jefferies as Erich Schaedler battered through him to set up the seventh and best goal from Alan Gordon.

Conspiracy theories abound in derbylore:

There was the time that Hearts, fearing another annihilation from their regular first-footers, are supposed to have got the fire brigade to drench the Tynecastle pitch so it froze, causing the game to be postponed.

*The bitterness never leaves you.* In 1990, after Hearts tried to kill off Hibs, some Hibbys boycotted Tynecastle. Fourteen years later, they've never been back. Some Jambos even switched sides in sympathy, and Alec, who's currently tiling my bathroom, is typical of them: 'I went and watched Hibs for four years because I was so scunnered by Wallace Mercer for trying to put them out of existence.'

*Passions run high.* To look after the wheelchair-bound at matches, you might think that only tolerant, placid individuals need apply. Last season at Easter Road, following a red-card decision against Hibs, a carer jumped the fence of the disabled area to run onto the pitch and attack the ref.

*Those in public office are not above the relentless squabble.* In Edinburgh's City Chambers in 1995, a Hearts faction of Labour councillors, including the Lord Provost, tried to push through a cryptically-worded motion concerning the colour of the official livery for the capital. Hibs-supporting Labourites scratched their heads. 'Pantone 201? What colour is that?' they asked. 'It's . . . pantone 201,' came the reply. This was an attempt at painting the town maroon by stealth.

*The young study history and learn.* In 2003, the 30th anniversary of *that* match, the Hibs captain Ian Murray, not even born when it happened, took the field at Tynecastle with '7–0' etched into his hair with green dye.

*And the beaten never recover.* For Gordon, another journo-mate, January 1, 1973, was his blackest day as a Jambo. Thirteen years later, Hearts only had to draw their last game of the season away to Dundee to win the league, but blew it. Surely next to that, 0–7 was a little local difficulty? Surely as a hack he has a sense of perspective? He's almost trembling at the memory. 'That was the worst. The only way I'll ever get over it is seeing Hearts beat Hibs 7–0.'

### 24 October. Hearts 2, Hibs 1

Herriot, Brownlie, Schaedler, Stanton, Black, Blackley, Edwards, O'Rourke, Gordon, Cropley, Duncan. These are Turnbull's Tornadoes, the greatest Hibs team of my fantime – the 7–0 team. In the film version of Irvine Welsh's *Granton Star Cause*, a radge gadgie played by local comic Alex 'Happy' Howden is being given one by his wife who's equipped with a fearsome strap-on. As 'Happy' grips onto the imitation marble fireplace in their manky flat, he recites Eddie Turnbull's brilliantly-realised vision of total fitba, presumably to heighten the sexual ecstasy.

Or maybe he's just trying to think about nice things, wonderful things, to make the pain go away. This is why I'm chanting the swashbuckling line-up, so that I don't have to contemplate how the buggering hell I'm going to get through the first proper derby of the season being stuck in the Jambos end.

'Herriot, Brownlie, Schaedler . . .' And of course, I have to say it to myself. I can't let *them* hear me.

Beanie pulled down tight over my face, even though it's a mild autumn afternoon, leaves orange and yellow and tumbling softly in the whispery breeze, I have a new route to Tynecastle and my first match-day companion. My brother Sean is offering me moral support for what promises to be a testing day and it's his idea that we walk most of the way along the Water of Leith, Edinburgh's excuse for a river, so that we avoid contact with the Hearts – and Hibs – hordes until the last possible moment.

It's a pleasant stroll along part of the city's extensive network of walkways and cycle paths, many of which were reclaimed from the long-disused suburban railway line. In times past, we reckoned, some fans probably journeyed to Tynecastle and Easter Road by this service, some of them after a morning shift at the factory, many in a collar and tie and everyone in a hat.

We have to agree beforehand how we're going to behave during the game, which is ridiculous considering the gloriously unpredictable nature of football, and how the sport subsists on spontaneous reaction from the crowd. We cannot urge on Hibs, obviously, and if Hearts score, we will have to stand up amid the thunderous acclaim going on all around us and . . . clap? Cheer? Taunt the Hibbys?

This kind of depends on the fans we find ourselves alongside today: they could be real head-cases and we'll have no option but to join in, demonstrate our Jamboness with extreme prejudice.

Now I'm thinking: why didn't I get a season ticket? At least that way, by this stage, I would be on muttering terms with my near-neighbours in the Wheatfield, and if I'd already revealed to them a habit of acknowledging good play by the opposition – a cunning plan with today in mind – they would not be surprised. In fact they would probably be expecting it, no matter that today's opponents are Hibs, 'the wee team'.

For this is our intended tactic, the method by which we subliminally support Hibs, and the only way I am going to get through today. I cannot be vocal for Hearts. Obviously. And I cannot be silent either. Brilliant! I feel like Dickie Attenborough in *The Great Escape*, shortly after the big break-out, holding onto a tremendous secret. No, no, not Dickie, because, after drumming into the other POWs how they could not drop their guard, not even for a second, he mucked up and was an easy catch for the Gestapo.

We get in early enough to see the warm-ups. All over one half of the pitch, the Hearts players engage in games of three-a-side keep-ball using only one touch. The patterns are like Spyrograph, the ball retention impressive. The ground is filling up and over at the Hibs end, the fans are goading their hosts about their current financial plight and the enforced move to Murrayfield.

> No Hearts in Gorgie
> Oh there'll be no Hearts in Gorgie

And . . .

> It's coming down
> It's coming down
> Tynie's coming down

Sean nudges my leg as all this is going on and I feign a scowl in the hope it's noticed by the Jambos close to me, but inside I'm laughing my head off. This is easy. And then the game starts. The bloody game. Right from kick-off, Hearts replicate their one-touch training routines and this gives them an immediate edge. Hibs, in their kinky boots, can't get going. Some of their players look overawed; others try too hard. Dean Shiels scampers down the right wing but is easy meat for Alan Maybury. Then Derek Riordan, born a Hibby and too desperate to score, snatches horribly at a half-chance.

Hibs haven't put together a single move worth my exaggerated, grudging credit, so I try another tactic: slagging off bad play by Hearts. But there isn't any of that either. The Jambos get right behind the team in the ascendancy and it's dispiritingly impressive to see players and supporters in perfect harmony, inspiring each other. It's a closed feedback loop and I'm trapped in the middle. Then Hearts score, Patrick Kisnorbo gets it and . . . what the hell do I do now? From the bottom of my trainers, I try to summon up an ecstatic expression. Imagine a gravedigger in an Ingmar Bergman film, sucking a lemon in a thunderstorm – that's how happy I look.

The whole stand is on its feet, hugging, cheering and – what a horrible sight – twirling scarves. Sean and I give grudging applause and he pretends to be a ventriloquist's dummy, like Lord Charles, grinning dementedly through gritted teeth: 'Gluddy glastard!'

I feel like a fraud. I feel I've let myself down, my father down, the entire Hibee Nation down. Life in the Jambo Village just isn't going to work. I mean, how can I pretend, how am I ever going to learn to love, the sight of a sclaffed goal for Hearts against my team of nearly 40 years, scored by a balloon more suited to Aussie Rules than the beautiful *geme*?

Then the Jambos in front of us start up a chant: 'Oh the Hibees are gay . . .' I've switched off watching the game and I'm waiting for the second line to kick in; it never comes. 'Oh the Hibees are gay/Oh the Hibees are gay . . .' Is this song heard in other Derbies? Do Sheffield United taunt the Wednesday like this, or vice versa? Presumably it doesn't apply to every team, but how are Hibs gay? The white boots, the haircuts? Lots of teams are much of a muchness, but being labelled queer is a pretty exotic piece of abuse and, to me, is yet more evidence of Hibs' individuality. And to Jambos I say this: don't knock it 'til you've tried it.

The outers occasionally turn round and urge the rest of the stand to 'sing, ya bastards!' and I'm thinking, *come on*, as the noted philosopher Daniel Bedingfield put it, *you've gotta to get through this*. 'Herriot, Brownlie, Schaedler . . .' But even I get bored with this mantra after a while so I start assembling random lists . . .

- *The Great Escape* – Who Got Away, Who Didn't.
- Forgotten Children's TV Classics (*Rag, Tag And Bobtail, Hector Heathcoate, The Magic Boomerang* . . .).
- All The Girls I've Loved Before.
- Great Lost Sweets (Hmm, bit obvious that one).
- Best-Ever Derbies (More like it . . .).

Then, bang on cue, to the tune of the Pet Shop Boys' *Go West*, the Hearts fans sing '4–2, and you blew it', goading Hibbys about the 2003 derby when they surrendered a two-goal lead with strikes in the 98th and 152nd minutes of injury time. Hibs wet their knickers that day and while I wouldn't say this lot are doing the same, they are allowing themselves to be bullied out of what I presume to be their usual gameplan by a Hearts team who expect to get a result; Hibs are merely hoping for one.

I feel like I'm in *The Singing Detective*, played backwards. Unlike Dennis Potter's hero Marlow, who compiles a litany of boring things ('A speech by Ted Heath, a particularly long sentence from Bernard Levin, a Welsh male-voice choir . . .') to numb the pleasure of being greased off by a pretty nurse, I'm thinking of stuff I love so I don't have to acknowledge the awful truth that is Hearts' pumped-up domination of this game. All the Hibs young-sters look terribly puny, as if they need to sign up for a Charles Atlas correspondence course in body-building and it really is men against boys. Steven Pressley versus Steven Fletcher is a contest that's a long way from even-Stevens. This has not been a controlled perfor-mance from the Hibs kids. They've been Brat Pack flops in a movie with one of those generic, lazy, unexpressive two-word titles like *Maximum Force* and *Sudden Impact* except theirs would be called *Premature Ejaculation*.

And yet I can't criticise them. Forced to get by on meagre Hibs titbits this season, I devour the scraps of this performance. I admire the subtle midfield promptings of Boozy, and so do some discerning Jambos behind us, until eventually he gets overwhelmed. But in the second half, as I'm reduced to counting up the number of power-points in my flat, to stop me thinking of the heaving inevitability of a Hearts win, Joe Hamill – Hamster – gets a second for Hearts and, feeling utterly depressed, Sean and I head for the exits before the end, thus missing Riordan's consolation goal which *Scotsport SPL* will confirm the next night as being yet another zinger.

But that was awful. Not the game, the whole sitting-on-hands, biting-of-tongues, suppressing-of-reason for being, denial-of-Hibbyness *hell*. If your team's result dictates your mood for the rest of the weekend, then derby outcomes can determine your state of mind right the way through until the return match. Even now, even after divorce and death in the family, it can bend and shape the character you thought was fully-formed long ago. As a kid after a derby defeat you can't think of anything but revenge. The re-match can't come soon enough. So what, then, a derby win you cheered but did not want . . . ?

Some people prefer their heroes to be brilliant but flawed. After *For Your Pleasure*, Roxy Music sold more records, but thrilled less. I still read every new Martin Amis from cover to cover on the day of publication, but even the great man admits that every author ends up repeating himself. Oh, that Hibs repeated themselves! Since 7–0, they've given us, precisely, the Skol Cup. Hey Faither! Dot-dash, dot-dot-dot! What did you used to say to me? 'Oh ye of little faith', was it? You should have been at bloody Swinecastle today!

On the walk home, Sean and I wonder what the old man would have made of the match. 'As a Jambo, you mean?' He's always taunting me like this. Because of our grandad's Gorgie connections, he likes to believe that both our father and our father's father were Jambos, and that after I declared myself a Hibby, Dad was forced to live a lie, which he took to the grave. We'll probably never know the secret, having lost touch with his side of the family long ago. Was his younger brother, a doctor last heard of as living somewhere in deepest Africa, even still alive?

If Faither's football back-story was cloudy he was always clear-sighted about visual art and knew what he liked, particularly among the Scottish stuff. He was a fan of the New Glasgow Boys of the 1980s, the movement which produced Peter Howson's grunting, bull-necked foundry-workers and stevedores and Adrian Wiszniewski's wan, floppy-fringed mummy's boys. Today, it's impossible to avoid the conclusion that Hearts were a Howson painting, Hibs a Wiszniewski. Today, perspiration triumphed over inspiration, style over sinew, brawn over brain, athletics over aesthetics, attrition over attraction and haymakers over playmakers. OK, so we claim the moral highground, but we've left the three points at the bottom of the hill. And yes, 'we', for me, still means Hibs.

Back at my flat, Sean and I watch a delayed transmission of Man U vs The Arse but the so-called 'Game of the Century' – the one that would finish in Pizzagate, the Old Trafford food-fight during which Arsene Wenger challenged a soup-spattered Sir Alex Ferguson to a square-go – passes in a nanosecond. I take none of it in. Mentally exhausted from having to internalise so much emotion, I go to bed at 8.30pm but can't sleep because of the knots in my stomach.

And the pain in my heart.

### 25 October

With apologies to Stanley Kubrick and that scene in *The Shining* when Shelley Duvall stumbles across Jack Nicholson's literary labours, just before he turns into the mad axeman . . .

I hate Hearts. I hate Hearts. I hate Hearts. I hate Hearts. I hate Hearts. I hate Hearts. I hate Hearts. I hate Hearts. I hate Hearts. I hate Hearts. I hate Hearts. I hate Hearts. I hate Hearts . . .

### 27 October

Craig Levein is raging. Tony Mowbray, in his post-derby analysis, has a dig at Hearts for putting the emphasis on muscle; he has a beef about beef. He's right, of course – Hibs have a tradition of being a flair team, Hearts do not, and this result was a triumph for physicality but Levein can't see it, accusing Mowbray of offloading 'a lorryload of sour grapes' in Princes Street. 'I'm fed up hearing about teams who want to play lovely, flowing football,' he says.

### 30 October. Hearts 3, Dundee 0

He's gone. Craig Levein has taken his baseball cap and his brutish football philosophy to Leicester City. Can I be the first to say 'Good riddance'?

I won't miss him, but I share something with the managerless

Jambos today: a feeling of dislocation. I cannot persuade Sean to come back to Tynecastle with me, and although I meet my Dundee-supporting friend Alan for a top pre-match scran at La Bruschetta, the classy Haymarket trat, we go our separate ways at the turnstiles. Alan has his mates, Neil and David, to keep him company and they're not even Dark Blues; they're just a couple of metrosexuals. But I am back to being on my lonesome in the Gorgie Gulag.

However briefly, Sean and Alan provided the moral support necessary for me to provide Jambo support, because I don't think I can do it on my own. Why should I have to? Why should any fan? The SPL is so scary these days it should carry one of those 'Don't watch alone' warnings that used to be flashed up before horror flicks. When it's not your team, this applies with knobs on. (Knobs turning slowly, creakily, in big, heavy doors, throwing long, jaggy, *Nosferatu*-like shadows . . .).

When you're young, and you live inside your own head, and you're *absolutely obsessed*, you don't notice the lack of companionship at football matches – same with pop concerts – because you don't need it. And you don't miss the conversation because, really, you don't have any opinions worth airing. It's just you and your big, bumper book of scorers and set-lists, colour-coded, real or metaphorical, in my case real.

But then you undergo changes. You sprout body hair. You spend longer in the bathroom. You become clumsy. Your voice deepens. You use it to express yourself, like this: 'Uh, you know what? Hibs are crap.' I was posted missing from Easter Road for long periods during the 1980s and the 1990s, only returning for Euro games and cup finals. Yes, I was that glory-hunter.

Aren't most fans like this? Surely we all have time away from football now and again. Surely, if you're a Scottish football supporter, this is an absolute imperative.

When you're sprouting opinions almost as fast as body hair, finding your voice, trying on radicalism for size, you might decide that football is no longer cool. Or maybe, in a league table of pastimes if not passions, football suddenly finds its lofty position under threat from a newly-promoted rival: women.

The first spell when I went AWOL from the Hibee Nation was the least cool for football, ever. One stadium disaster – Hysel, Bradford, Hillsborough – followed another. Football is notoriously insular and cynically 'I'm all right, Brian', but I know people who turned their back on the game after that terrible triumvirate, and never gave it a moment's thought or care, ever again.

Around the same time, the late 1980s, I met a girl and married her. Now it would be easy to claim that football's ability to kill completely disillusioned me, at the same time as I got entrammelled in marital life, and that these things explain and justify my non-attendance, but it wouldn't be true. I just got bored with Hibs.

They'd flirted with the idea of winning the old First Division and the Scottish Cup in the 1970s, but the next decade brought no success and Hearts were Edinburgh's best-in-show. It was a gimmicky time in the sport, an era of shiny strips that tampered with tradition, and the skimpiest of shorts. Footballers were ugly, all lank hair and moustaches. Grounds were tired, puffed out. And I felt *old*. Thirty isn't ancient, but suddenly I was older than the vast majority of players, and with that came the awful realisation that I would never get a game for Hibs.

Also, a new soccer tribe came to town. And the Casuals didn't wear club colours. They confounded staff at Edinburgh's most label-conscious clobber-store, Cruise, by forking out the average monthly wage on a Stone Island jacket, then going fighting in it. And they confounded the polis by bypassing the grounds and fighting on trains (passenger-service, not football-special) and in pubs, or simply phoning ahead for a pagger whenever the mood took them.

Previously, the hooligans' league didn't look much different from the football league: the biggest clubs, Celtic and Rangers, were the most violent. But the Casuals kicked out the old order, and the Old Firm, and in that sense I should have vaguely admired them; all the more so because Hibs were right up there with

Aberdeen and Motherwell as being the baddest in Scotland. And Hearts were nowhere. To the tune of 'Magic' by Edinburgh chart-toppers Pilot, the chant was:

> Hey hey hey, it's magic, you know
> Hearts and Casuals don't go

But I couldn't admire the Casuals because they weren't *my* youth cult. Not that I was a bona fide boot-boy, but the bovver brigade with their *Clockwork Orange* stylings provided the colour and incident during my teens, so of course I was loyal to them.

Each youth cult thinks itself superior to those that came before or follow it; same with music tribes. New Romantics picked up the baton from Glam, and the baton was an eyeliner. But Glam rooled, OK. Glam produced Bowie, Roxy and Slade, and I'd put up Chicory Tip against the entire New Romantic scene for a square-go on a crumbling, weed-strewn terrace, and the only issue in doubt is which bunch of 1980s ponces would wet their brocade breeches first: Spandau Ballet, Flock Of Seagulls . . . or Blue Rondo A La Turk.

Lynn, who was younger, dragged me to see a lot of these bands, including ABC, Duran Duran and Haircut 100, but it wasn't New Romanticism which split us up. Nor, really, was it her refusal to allow me to display, anywhere prominent in the marital home, the classic *Edinburgh Evening News* giveaway poster of the classic Turnbull's Tornadoes team.

But divorce hastened a retreat back to the familiar, the reassuring, the safe – Hibs. Ironically, Hibs themselves at that time were not safe; Hearts were trying to take them over. So they needed me, and the rest of the Hibee Nation, as much as I needed them.

The fans helped save the club. The club, by way of thanks, won the 1991 Skol Cup. After the fad for all those prissy cocktail bars and wine bars of the 1980s – when, after wearing a suit to work, you were supposed to change into another one for a night out . . . ridiculous – this was a welcome, beer-flavoured success for a team who returned to baggy shorts, kicking out the era of football in tiny trunks.

But it didn't last and soon I was straying again. Faither stopped going and the family bond was broken. Hibs became dourly defensive under Alex Miller's management and the flair bond was broken, too. Over the next few seasons, I'd sometimes hear a little voice in my head. It would be peddling macaroon bars and memories and asking why I didn't go to football anymore. But I had my reasons, and the more football got trendy, the more I dug in my heels.

*Loaded*, Laddism and Liam Gallagher's loutish support for Manchester City upped football's cool quotient around the time of Euro 96, but it is surely typical of the thrawn Scot that he hunches up his collar and shuns such hype. And anyway, very little of the stardust fell from the sky, or Sky TV, onto Easter Road.

After Dad died, my brother would occasionally accompany me to matches. Even more perversely, he preferred Hibs when they'd been relegated and were playing, and being beaten by, the likes of Stranraer. But if I was going to return to football for good, I needed a friend who would stay loyal and true.

I even thought about advertising for one:

*Middle-class fan approaching middle-age supporting mid-table team seeks similar for companionship, beer, rock-gig reminiscing and (if we must) football. Must have GSOH (good sense of Hibs) and be HIB tested. No smokers, opera-lovers (liar), long-walkers, time-wasters, playing-for-timers, and definitely no girlfriends.*

I despaired of finding anyone, then, in the summer of 2000, in the canteen at *The Scotsman*, I got talking to a colleague who until that moment had hid his face behind huge curtains of hair. I assumed he was a stray member of the Edgar Broughton Band; then he revealed himself to be Rab from Broughton High School, sporting a prog-fan's haircut 27 years too late.

We didn't really know each other at school, but quickly became match-day mates. He was even more lapsed as a Hibby than me, but the Franck Sauzee-Russell Latapy team of international patter-merchants lured us back to Easter Road as we tried to remember what we'd been doing since the last time my playground kickabout collided with his, back in 1973.

Soon we hooked up with David, who in a previous life we'd known professionally as a rising star in the New Labour firmament, and whose passion for Hibs was almost equalled by that for trains. By then he was the man Tony Blair phoned an hour before his turn on TV's *Frost On Sunday* to ask: 'David, what shall I say about the railways?'

Through David we met Ivan, a Humanist minister, and the four of us would convene in swish restaurants for pre-match lunch. Ivan was always rushing back from a non-religious hatch, match or despatch, but don't get the wrong impression about him. Despite – and I quote from the Humanists' website – being opposed to 'fruitless arguments between religions', he's not adverse to arguing with Rangers fans using language that's extremely fruity. And despite believing that 'humanity is capable of solving its own problems' he's always ready to advise 'that baldy eejit' John Rowbotham exactly how he should be refereeing a game. Oh, and like Rowbotham, Ivan has no real need for a hairbrush.

We went to home games the four of us, then we hit the road, although because David believes the internal combustion engine to be one of the sins of the age and doesn't do cars, we travelled to away games by train.

We hunted the corn-fed chicken through the streets of Kilmarnock. Using the extra-virgin olive oil and the balsamic vinegar as the wing-backs, we delineated the course of the match and likely outcome on the bistro tablecloth. We'd win – we were good then – and sing *The Joyful Kilmarnock Blues*, The Proclaimers' number about away victories in Ayrshire. Then, on the packed railway platform, David would order us to 'Stand here' and sure enough, we would be nearest the carriage doors when the train stopped, so we'd get seats for the journey home. Did we intellectualise football? Of course; that's what Hibs fans do.

But sometimes, during the Williamson era at Easter Road, it was touch and go over the pre-match tuck whether we went to the match or ordered more wine and pondered a phenomenon which really fascinated us: ladies who lunch. David had no need for the condiments to illustrate tactical subtleties because Mr Bobby was demonstrating every week that he had no need for tactics. But try as he might, Mr Bobby couldn't break up our group.

That happened by natural causes when David moved to London and Rab to Shetland . . . and now I'm trying to shift my allegiances to Tynecastle. If our little group ever re-assembles, I might not be allowed back.

Football by yourself is a tough, tough gig. I mean, if absolutely necessary, I could probably go to Easter Road on my own, because the club is my friend, the place is my personal heritage site, having been designated (by me) as one of Grade 'A' listed special emotional interest. I could go there on my own because the ghost of my father is always at my side, telling me about football and art, and the art that's in football.

But, adrift from Easter Road, my team, my mates and my memories, football is no fun. Not when you like to shout, as I do, because shouting as a lone fan draws attention to yourself; people think you've got a weekend pass from a local institution and that it's their bad luck you've decided not to talk to the trees and pitched up at the football instead.

Hello, oak. Hello, poplar. Hello, larch. But hello, Dundee, today's Tynecastle opposition, and a club for whom all Hibbys have a soft spot. In 1986, Hearts were certs to win the league. On the last day of the season, they were seven minutes away from doing it. Dundee stopped them.

The Jambos, I have to admit, were relentless that season: a tough, dynamic unit with John Robertson – the new Tynecastle manager-in-waiting – thumping in the goals with a schoolboy's glee. Understandably, as the finish-line neared they got nervous, allowing Celtic to climb onto their shoulders, but they still headed up to Dens Park knowing that a draw would clinch the title.

Dad and I trooped along to Easter Road for a meaningless Hibs-Dundee Utd match and we feared the worst. We didn't have a radio and so had to rely on updates from Dens to be passed down the line. No news – no goals – was bad news. The clock was ticking. Then Dundee Utd's David Narey took a throw-in and Easter Road went berserk. My first thought was: 'That was a good throw-in but was it really that exceptional?' Then we realised Dundee had scored. Moments later, more wild whooping. At the end of a mad afternoon, Celtic had tanked St Mirren 5–0 to nick the title.

That's local rivalry, the *Schadenfreude* of football. And I can't deny I chuckled when Tayside's top Bobby Ball impersonator, Albert Kidd, emerged as the unlikely hero. Years later, I'd spot a Hibs fan walking in front of me with 'Remember' printed on his replica strip. Remember *what?* Then his mate would catch him up on his right-hand side, always his right. His shirt read 'Albert Kidd'. And years after that, the great man emigrated to Australia, but his deeds have never been forgotten. A guest-of-honour at hastily-convened supporters' functions during his trips back to the old country, he'll never have to buy a drink in Leith for as long as he lives.

Now I'm thinking of my friend Ivan again. His son Kieran was too young to appreciate the tragedy and, oh, the comedy of events at Dens 18 years ago, but that didn't stop his father, the Humanist, trying to explain, teach, pass on wisdom. 'Look at these men!' he said as the telly cameras panned across the devastated away end. 'Grown men, crying! What a wonderful sight!'

How I laughed, at the time. But sitting among the Hearts hordes now, breaking pie-crust with them, I look at their funny, wee pinched Jambo nappers and concede that, yes, it must have been a terrible day, so near but yet so far. It is a holding-bay of emotions that Hibs have never, *ever* visited in my fantime. Ivan is probably cheering on Hibs at Kilmarnock today, keeping the side up despite Rab, David and I deserting him, and our team. Well, I hope he's not watching alone . . .

Young and ambitious, Craig Levein was always going to quit Hearts at some point. Meanwhile, he's marked the card of the board as they search for his successor. 'Give the job to John Robertson,' he says. Surely, as a prolific striker in days gone by, Robbo has got more football in him. He must have. And surely there are some Jambos crying out for their team to play with a bit more flair. Levein hated the word. *'I'm fed up hearing about teams who want to play lovely, flowing football.'* As far as I'm concerned, this is a fitting epitaph for the man, in much the same way that 'If you want entertainment, go to the cinema' was for Mr Bobby.

The posh papers report Levein as saying he made up his mind a year ago that he would try management in England. The small, funny papers report that his marriage had broken up and hint at the involvement of another woman, a member of the Tynecastle staff. His behaviour had become strange, says one tabloid. There was the time he punched a dressing-room wall at Motherwell, and of course his big moody with Tony Mowbray. But in one area he remained thoroughly consistent: punishment-beating football.

I slope off home, quickening my pace as I pass the Balmoral pub where a scuffle spills onto the pavement. It involves a youth with tattooed tears who, I'd like to think, is now crying the crocodile variety for his former manager. I'm really going to have to meet some of this fan's type, you know – I can't just sit there, hating every minute. I've got to find out what Jambos think about football, how they want it played, whether they want it played at all. The song running through my head is *Lonely Boy* by Andrew Gold and I can't believe I've dredged that up from the soft-rock past I thought I'd managed to obliterate, in the quest for ever more cool music.

In my personal reality-show hell, I am participating in a version of *Faking It* or *Wife Swap* and failing miserably. What I need is more of a makeover element, in the style of *Queer Eye For A Straight Guy*.

Or, *Jambo Eye For A Hibby Guy*.

# NOVEMBER

### 4 November. Hearts 0, Schalke 1

So where is this Hearts-style match-day mate going to come from? Football-wise, apart from Rab, David and Ivan, my friends fall into two categories: they're Hibs nuts or they're the kind of football 'casual' who gathers in the pub for the big stuff on the telly, like we all do, but doesn't watch games in the raw.

If pushed these non-practising supporters will declare allegiance for the likes of St Johnstone, Montrose and, for goodness sakes, Wrexham. In the time I've known them I've worn them down and turned them into Hibs sympathisers and therefore Hearts unsympathisers. Some have kids and charge-cards for out-of-town one-stop-shops; they're not going to give up their valuable *leezure*-time for the Jambos.

What I need is a Jambo from my past. There were plenty of them at secondary school but I'm not so sure I want to go back that far. The most fanatical Jambo I knew, from the 1970s or since, was Kenny, a straw-haired boy with a hen-toed walk. He liked to amuse the rest of the school by reciting his name backwards and with a cry of 'A-hee-hee!', in celebration – comical, not boastful – of the healthy size of his tadger. But there was an air of impenetrable sadness about Kenny. His great loves were golf and Deep Purple, with whom he was so intimate that he could refer to them merely as 'Purple'. One of the great behind-the-science-lab smokers of my school, Kenny died of cancer in his thirties.

From the 1980s, when I played five-a-sides at a community centre in Pilton, one of the sink estates which helped Edinburgh earn the title 'Aids capital of Europe', there was another blondbarneted lad who turned up every week without fail, tried hard, but was supremely rubbish. This was Billy and he was the second-most fanatical Jambo with whom I've ever engaged in mildly internecine, my-team's-better-than-yours hostilities.

Back then Billy worked for one of Edinburgh's major insurance houses and I was pretty sure he'd still be there. 'Hello, personal pensions, can I help you?'

'Hi Billy, it's Aidan.'

'What do you want, you Hibby git?'

Cheers, I say, I hope this call isn't being monitored for 'training and quality' purposes. I explain that I don't want him to sell me a pension – a cautious, Hearts-style concept if ever there was one – what I need is a Jambo Lifeplan.

Billy has been supporting Hearts since he was seven years old. His father was a Hearts fan in a family of Ulster Protestants. Dad had seen the best of the Jambos in the 1950s but had fallen out of the habit so a neighbour took his laddie until Billy was old enough to go by himself. In his debut season, Hearts were pipped to the old First Division Championship by Kilmarnock on the last day of the season, on goal difference, but he was too young to understand the significance of this, and to be devastated by it. He would come of age in this respect 21 years later, when the exact same fate befell Hearts at Dundee.

I am hoping some of his Jamboness will rub off on me. Now this is obviously a dangerous game. Too much, and I may touch the void, caress the polyester match-wear, and never return. But I think I can trust myself not to do that.

It's quite exciting, challenging yourself like this, wondering how far you can push things. This must be what it's like to go to a swingers' party, I'm telling myself, but as I'm thinking about a delirious, writhing mass of bodies beautiful, I'm picking my way through a crowd of Hearts fans in Mather's Bar, just about the most defiantly unsexy pub in Edinburgh.

Billy is deep in conversation with his friends and it's difficult to tell where his group ends and the rest of the rabble begins. Does he know everyone here? It seems that way. From the start I can tell he's suspicious of me. He probably thinks my agenda is all about piss-taking and, right at this moment, I'd be hard-pushed to convince him otherwise.

October was a bad, bad month. Livingston was the worst game of football I'd seen for years and on those trips to Parkhead and Feyenoord I felt alone and, at times, scared. Then there was the derby, where I applauded Jambo goals and, consequently, a little part of me died. I have a long way to go if I am to understand Hearts' reason for being, never mind start to experience even just a flicker of feeling for them.

Billy has retained most of his hair – and third-form wit – but you would euphemistically say that these days he enjoys a pie or three. He introduces me to his oldest friend Colin; they met on the first day of primary school. On my first day at primary a boy called Robert announced without shame to the entire intake that he couldn't tie his laces. He even made up a little song of celebration and I was tremendously impressed by his impudence.

Over four decades Billy and Colin never lost touch and now they share an office. It's stories like this that convince you of the chronic smallness of Edinburgh. Despite its pretensions to be a city, and its ambitions to be recognised as the international capital of literature and suchlike, it is more accurately categorised as a large town whose life-long inhabitants can, at any given moment, turn a corner and walk straight into an invite to a class reunion. My father wrote the foreword to a travel guide for Edinburgh in which he described it as a city of two certainties: the east wind, and the fact an extra-marital affair cannot be kept secret there for very long; sooner or later it is bound to be blown off course.

As Billy and Colin eye me warily, I try to make small talk about big matters involving stunted men, such as the appointment of Robbo as manager. Under Craig Levein, according to Billy, Hearts were successful and boring. Does he mean 'successful *but* boring'? Or, for a Jambo, is success everything? Colin says that instead of Robbo he might have preferred Terry Butcher, the manager of

Motherwell, who's proved as adept as Levein at building up a team from ground-zero but, crazy guy that he is, likes to see the ball passed around more.

Euro nights are still special. If this was a midweek match in the SPL or the CIS Cup, the Jambos in Mather's would not be dusting down this old chant:

> *Na na na na*
> *Na na na na*
> *Whey hey hey*
> *Georgie Fleming*

Or this one:

> *We don't need your Colin Stein*
> *Drew Busby or Alan Gilzean*
> *We've got somebody twice as good*
> *His name is Wilson Wood*

Or indeed this one (though it does require an attractive WPC to be trackside):

> *Get it up you while you're young*
> *Get it uh-up you-hoo*
> *While you're young*

The old songs are the best, but we've got to get to the game. We jump on an airport bus and are offloaded at Murrayfield which, this time viewed in darkness and all lit up, looks big and space-shippy and mightily impressive. Our seats are in the top tier and, gazing down on the serried ranks, it seems that every single inhabitant of the Jambo Village is here tonight. But there's a sizeable Schalke support, too, a bouncing blue-and-white mass filling one end of the ground who wave banners bearing the legend 'Iron Blue 83' and sing one song that lasts a full 15 minutes. I have grudging respect for German football. I mean, I prefer the silky, free-flowing stuff from South America and I absolutely adore classic Brazil, but there's something deeply impressive about German never-say-die-ness, German *Vorsprung durch Technik* and, yes, German arrogance. MC Tynie may well be a Hun-lover as well, for he extends fraternal greetings to the opposition in their native language just before kick-off.

Then . . . ''MON THE HEARTS!'

Where on earth did that come from? From right next to me, that's where. I don't know it yet, but this big, growly roar of encouragement is Billy's traditional greeting to his team. It's so loud his body is shaking. It's so loud *my* body is shaking. Colin smiles. He's heard Billy do this many times. It tells him everything is all right with the world. It tells him the match can begin.

Where do Schalke play their football? When they win, do their fans dance in the streets of an eponymous town? Football has taught me a lot – all right, it's taught me the South American capitals – but I'm dismayed at my ignorance here. I tell the guys I remember diddley about O-grade Geography. Then, across the mouth of an exit, I spot a lad with whom I flunked the exam: Norman, a fine footballer in his youth and a leading teenage authority on Krautrock. His mum used to meet my mum at parents' nights and together over tea and empire biscuits they'd discuss the menopause and their useless sons. I squeeze through the crowd to speak to him, Norman laughs at everything I say, even when I'm not being funny, just like he used to do in Geography. I half-wondered if he'd come to the game out of respect for the tremendous teutonic triumvirate of Can, Faust and Amon Duul II. 'Nah,' he says, 'I don't like that stuff anymore.' He's a Hibby but was keen to be part of a big Edinburgh football occasion so has tagged along with some Jambo mates. We exchange phone numbers and promise to catch up properly.

Robbo is the new Hearts manager. He's in the dugout tonight but these are still Levein's Jambos. You can see his influence in the stands: a lot of the fans have adopted his baseball cap-and-rectangular glasses look. And you can certainly see it out on the pitch, in a performance that could never be described as gung-ho.

But the king is dead, and while the bloke in front of us might be sporting a Levein memorial cap and Levein memorial specs – plus regulation Dalry Public Baths yellow swim-band – he clearly believes his team should be casting off their traditional caution. 'Fuck's sake, Hearts, he's gone!' is the desperate cry. 'We don't have to play ten men behind the ball at home anymore!'

The gung-*no* approach gets Hearts nowhere. They're far too clunky and it takes them an age to construct a move, whereas Schalke break at will, at speed, and ruthlessly in the German style, score the only goal they will need. I'm not entirely sure whether Schalke are, as we used to say about top Euro teams, a 'crack outfit', but they're as good as they need to be to dispose of Hearts, for whom Levein's old lieutenant, Patrick Kisnorbo, stupidly gets himself sent off.

This has been Hearts' poorest performance of the season and, rather than gloat about this, I sympathise with my new Jambo mates. Not wanting to embarrass or inhibit Billy and Colin, I submit to the night, allow myself to get caught up in the big-match atmosphere, and join in the exortations. And for once, I don't feel like a complete phoney.


**5 November**

I'm thinking of Norman and how we used to play Subbuteo together: epic, four-team, inter-house tournaments that also featured Kenny (Rest In Purple Peace) and Jim, another fanatical Jambo in his youth and, last heard of, a policeman. Five minutes later, I'm on the phone to the Lothian and Borders Fuzz, the firearms department, and Jim and I are soon reminiscing . . .

'Gerry Cruikshank – she was sexy,' he says, reeling off the school pin-ups. 'Valerie Farmer – she was dirty. And Isobel Brewster was that dirty wee thing from Abbeyhill. Girls and football, Aidan, that's all we cared about at school. You could tell that by our exam results.'

Half an hour after that, he's dropped into my office – dark curls greying, eyes like Alan Hansen, brilliant blue – to explain how he's of mixed origins. 'My dad was a Jambo and my mum was a Hibby. I could recite the Famous Five at two years old but then I decided to support the Jambos.'

Jim's devotion to his team has never waned, even though he can't get his 23-year-old son excited about Hearts and he's run out of match-day mates. He retires from the force next year after three decades of solid service.

'It's amazing how many folk we knew from school are either dead or in the cops,' he says. How many coppers are Jambos? He doesn't know a single Hearts supporter on the force. 'Bang goes one theory, then. And I'm not a Unionist or a wash-hand basin – I'm not a mason.'

But Jim admits to loving Tynecastle traditions and one of them is the honouring of the club's war dead. In 1914, 16 Hearts players swapped their football boots for army ones and became the only British team to sign up en masse for the First World War. Four of them were among the 20,000 Brits killed on the first day of the Somme; in total seven did not return from the battlefields of France.

Jim is a member of the Great War Memorial Committee who, in recent years, has been raising the money to have a commemorative cairn built in the war cemetery at Contalmaison and he's going out there for Remembrance Sunday. 'Here,' he says, handing me a booklet, 'give me a couple of quid and you can read more about it.'

Jim's got to go; I tell him I bumped into Norman the other night and suggest we should all meet up. 'Glad you don't do the funny handshake,' I say.

'Do you know,' he says, showing me his wrist, 'I broke a bone here trying to save a shot in that bloody Subbuteo tournament. My worst-ever sporting injury. That was pre-spring-powered goalies, of course.'

## 6 November

In central midfield Hibs have Guillaume Beuzelin, an artist who won't be hurried, while Hearts have Patrick Kisnorbo, who just rushes around banging into things. Here is the crucial difference between Edinburgh's football teams.

The other day in *The Independent*, the veteran sports columnist Ken Jones was reflecting with his usual lyrical weariness about the modern game and how so many of today's players are athletes, first, footballers a not-even-close second. He might have had Kookaburra in mind. Recent performances have been wretched. The only way this useless Aussie – laughingly labelled a 'playmaker' by *The Herald* – was going to successfully complete even a three-yard pass was if he borrowed a trick from that old kids' telly show from his homeland, *The Magic Boomerang*, and threw the famous curly stick, freezing the opposition in its tracks.

All right, that's my view, but what do Jambos think of him? Today, I go onto the Jambo website, Kickback, for the first time and as luck would have it Kookaburra is the subject of debate. 'Tons of energy,' says Chris, 'and he wins the ball well. Unfortunately he nearly always gives it away.' Rod is less kind, telling him direct: 'You never have been and never will be a footballer.' Ditto, Tazio: 'Complete and utter mince.' So maybe Jambos *do* know a bit about football after all.

After the glitterati of the Champions' League on TV every midweek, I'm afraid that on Saturdays it's back to the shitterati of the SPL. And Kookaburra stands feet and ankles below the rest of Scotland's *gallumphicos*.

**7 November**

Craig Levein is hoping to make a name for himself as a coach in England, but he's got a bit of work to do. Some people down south have never heard of him.

Front page headline in today's *Sun*: 'You're Levein Me For *Who*?' It appears that the husband of Levein's lover Kerry Staniforth – communications manager for Hearts' sponsors All:Sports – was told she was having an affair with 'a famous football manager'. But spurned Russell had never heard of Levein. When he was shown a picture he laughed.

'It's horrendous being cheated on,' he tells the paper, 'but having your wife run off with a bloke who looks like a cross between Harry Potter and a nerd from PC World makes it even harder to bear.'

## 10 November. Dunfermline 1, Hearts 2

Dunfermline, on the coldest night of the season to date. A mascot – how much do I hate thee, Sammy the Tammy? – cavorts on the pitch. The Athletic's theme tune, *Into The Valley* by local heroes The Skids, is belted out at 11 on the dial, turning the tartan-punk classic to sonic slush. A steak bridie – a delicacy of the ancient capital of Scotland – lodges in my stomach like a depth-charge. But, hey, don't worry, it's the CIS Cup!

In all my years as a Hibs fan I've only ever seen them win a trophy twice, and both times it was the least shiny of the chamber-pots offered up by the domestic game in the Ratneresque closing-down sale that is oor fitba. Back in 1972, the CIS was merely the League Cup. In 1991, it was the Skol Cup. And even though its status diminishes with every round that's played, I stay perversely loyal to it. Hibs have won it, so it's great.

But they went out of the competition 24 hours ago, so it's Hearts as usual and tonight Billy has brought along a skinhead mate.

Ricky works at the same insurance house as Billy, and I'm thinking, does he deal with personal damages? Or rather, does he *deal out* personal damages? You should never judge a man by his haircut, or lack of one, but Ricky's in the passenger seat, I'm in the back, and I can't see his face as I explain the concept of my book – but I'm sure his expression must be one of deep distrust. 'I used to go weekabout to Easter Road and Swine- . . . Tynecastle,' I say, pathetically, and somewhat desperately.

It's a short journey over the Forth to Fife but before we leave Edinburgh, Billy has to stop off at home. 'Just got to turn on the lights and close the curtains,' he says. I thought only old people did that, but it would seem to confirm my theory that Jambos are a cautious lot. Can such a safeguard sum up a club's entire philosophy? I think so. Not that I feel like pointing this out to Billy, far less Ricky.

We arrive in Dunf and Ricky reveals himself. Big, burly, *scary*. I ask him if he was sorry to see Levein go. 'Dunno, maybe he was only as good as his team.' (Or as bad?). 'I mean, I loved him as a player, really aggressive, and as a manager he did well with what he had. But maybe he couldn't take this lot any further. Maybe Robbo, being a striker, will be different.' Different? Does he mean more attacking? Does he care? Or does substance – the chunkiness of the challenges – win over style for the Jambos?

'To be honest, all I care about is us being a successful team – I'm not really bothered about playing fancy football,' admits Ricky. 'As long as we're winnin' the physicals, rollin' teams over at home, doin' you boys three times a season because you never make the Top Six for the fourth game – and finishin' third and qualifying for Europe. That'll do me.'

And that could do me. I could go home now, having had my suspicions about Hearts confirmed. But we're at East End Park and the Sammy-choreographed preliminaries are over and, right from kick-off, Steven Pressley shows that Hearts mean business in the numpty cup with a steam-hammer tackle. 'Get in there, Elvis!' roars Ricky.

'I'm aw' aboot centre-halves,' he tells me, after another cruncher from Andy Webster. I don't think I've ever been aw' aboot centre-halves in my life, but each to his own. Ricky has a centre-half's build, and he confirms that this was his position when he played the game, before injuries caught up with him. Injuries received, or dished out? 'Once I got banned for 16 games.' What for? 'Off-the-ball incident.'

He tells me about some of his friends, such as the pal – he could have been a player – who was kicked out of his team for battering a referee and challenging the whole of the opposition to a fight. 'Total headace but a good lad, and he *loves* his football.' Then there's the chum who was going to thump ex-Hibby Grant Brebner – who could have been a player, too – for chatting up his bird in the

Edinburgh nightspot, the Opal Lounge. Both mates were going to come to Dunf, he says, but got 'held up'. What, at the Forth Bridge, because they've got Fife exclusion orders on their heads?

Hearts are making heavy weather of the tie. Billy is quiet but he becomes slightly more animated when a Hearts fan walks past us carrying a couple of bouncing-bomb bridies. Billy and Ricky are pointing at his quilted coat; they haven't seen that style before, with club sponsors' All:Sports logo stamped across the wearer's ample arse, and it's obvious they're impressed.

More revelations from Ricky: he's 'big into the Mafia'. He collects hooligan memoirs and is something of an expert on the local scene: he knows of Hearts lads who switched to Chelsea, Millwall and even Hibs because these clubs offered more 'action'. Swapping teams *is* possible, then. He sneers at the ultras who used to inhabit Section N at Tynecastle for their rotten renditions of the Hun anthem, *The Sash*. 'If you're goin' to sing it, sing it properly,' he says. And he admits: 'I'm a wee bitty racist.'

These all seem like good reasons why I should dislike Ricky, why my prejudices against Hearts were entirely justified, but he says other things which intrigue me and make me think there might be more to him than this grunty exterior suggests.

He's got a sense of humour. The unprepossessing Neil MacFarlane, he reckons, looks and plays like a schoolboy. There's a comedian's keen understanding of timing before he adds: 'Maybe Primary 6 or somethin'.' And I think I prefer Ricky's nickname for Hearts' petrified striker – 'Dennis Shyness'.

He's a student of the game. I thought my knowledge of football beyond these grim shores was pretty sound, but I might have to conclude I've met my match. We're talking about the Euro opposition facing Scottish teams this season when Auxerre crop up, and Ricky says: 'Aye, and don't forget they lost their four best players before the season started.' It's difficult not to have respect for a subscriber to the old-skool football mag, *World Soccer*.

Or for an Edinburgh football fan who loathes Capital-based Old Firm supporters: 'Just the shite that comes oot of those guys' mooths!' Or for an Edinburgh football fan, all right a Jambo, who rates beating Rangers in the 1998 Scottish Cup Final the best day of his life. Respect, yes, but also envy. Hibs haven't won that trophy since nineteen-hundred-and-bloody-two.

Dennis Shyness, for it is him, scores a last-minute winner and on the walk back to the car the lads are discussing Hearts' semi-final prospects. This is what I wanted, a feeling of kinship, so I join in. Then Ricky tells me he loves German football. I love Brazilian football but also have a soft spot – perverse, I know – for the German variety. Maybe he and I can get on after all . . .

### 12 November
Backpage headline in the *Edinburgh Evening News*: 'Robbo Wants Sexy Football'. The new boss says he'll be relying less on the height of Mark de Vries and Kevin McKenna. 'I like to see the ball passed,' he says. I should be pleased, but am I? Hibs are the sexy team, I don't know if I want Hearts nicking their clothes, or non-clothes . . .

### 13 November. Kilmarnock 1, Hearts 1
Ricky can't make it, he's going to a booze tournament with darts sideshow, so it's just Billy and me for the trip to Ayrshire and after the curtain-closing episode en route to Dunfermline, I'm thinking, Kilmarnock is a much longer round-trip: will he need a house-sitter today? Ayrshire is Beyond Glasgow, which means I never went there as a lad, and made my first trip to Rugby Park only three years ago. Billy, of course, has been there so many times that he knows the best route and the best garage on the journey for car mags.

Billy is a petrol-head. I've just remembered this. When we first knew each other, at the five-a-sides, he always missed games because of the Round-Britain Rally, which is a kind of muddy-hillside endurance tournament with car sideshow. I don't really like other sports apart from football; I'm a monomaniac and proud of it.

During one close season a few years ago, *The Scotsman* sent me to watch so-called minority sports, in a doomed effort to get me to broaden my horizons. By the summer's end, I'd managed to upset fell-runners, croquet players, women cricketers, dry-slope skiers and the karate brigade, who all sent letters of complaint to my editor about the sneering tone of my reports. Greyhound owners were so angry at me for reporting confessions of 'nobbling' that they threatened a demo at the newspaper offices, complete with pie-stuffed mutts. And, when I speculated that a small-bore shooting contest might set up as its targets Ronnie Corbett and other tedious short-arses, trigger-happy types from all over the world – all over Bumfuck, Idaho, at any rate – dubbed me a 'limpwristed guno-phobe' and threatened to use me for practice. My bad attitude was all down to summertime grumpiness at the absence of football.

So, onwards and westwards for my latest experience of a minority sport: Hearts. What do you think, I say to Billy, will a couple of hours do it for Kilmarnock? He sniffs. 'I'll be disappointed if we don't do it in one-forty.' Billy chooses the 'back way', across Eaglesham Moor, but there will hopefully be enough time for us to chat, to catch up on the lost years, and for me to gain his trust.

There are, I reckon, seven ages of football fandom in the progression from boys' gate to pensioner concessions. The high-water mark, which comes immediately after half-mast-breeked half-interest, is teenage obsession. After that, girls can get in the way, then you might get married, and women will form an impregnable defensive wall against football-watching.

Some wit once described *The Simpsons* as appealing to all ages: as a kid you start out watching it because of the pretty colours. And while you might graduate to laughing knowingly at the satire, even to intellectualising the cartoon, you go back to liking it for the pretty colours when you're old and dribbling into your soup. Football functions in a vaguely similar manner in that it's not the play you like when you're young and have a poor attention span; it's the size of the crowd, the adult behaviour, their swearing – anything but the play. And when you're older, you're equally disinterested in what's happening on the pitch. You go to be with your mates or to bond with your dad because you might have a keen sense of your mortality and that of others. You also have a keen sense of your team's all-round crapness.

In all his time as a Jambo – and what are we up to now, the fifth age of fandom? – Billy has never allowed other distractions into his life. The only thing that occasionally gets in the way of his Hearts obsession is his Scotland obsession, and swinging his kilt with the Tartan Army. He's never been married.

An addiction to football can restrict a man's personal development, and leave him socially challenged. You'll always find us in the kitchen at parties, the remedial class in the school of life, and the gutter-side of the velvet rope barring entry to the Disco of Human Relations. But are we unhappy? No, not at all.

I recently totted up all the 90 minutes, plus extra time, plus added-on minutes to enable Rangers to sneak a gobby winner – off a square Ibrox post or the bonnet of a disabled vehicle parked trackside – that I'd spent at Easter Road and was disappointed to discover that it only amounted to about one month. Billy, unlike me, wasn't posted missing from Tynecastle for large chunks of the 1980s and 1990s; he didn't trudge off at half-time for a pie one cold, wet afternoon at Airdrie and never come back.

Being a petrol-head, he remembers that I used to drive my mum's 2CV to five-a-sides. 'Poofy lemon, wasn't it?' he says. He lost both his parents recently and somewhere over the moor the chat turns to death, or rather pensions, because we're Scottish and can't get too penalty box-intimate with our feelings, at least not yet. Pensions is how he earns his petrol-money, and his pie-money. I don't have a pension, or at least one that's doing anything for me, and at odd times of concern about this I've consoled myself with the thought that this was a very Hibby state of affairs. Live for the moment, be wild and free.

I know other Hibbys who don't have pensions and this may be a fanciful notion, but I've viewed this as just one more expression of club philosophy. Worry overmuch about the future and you can't play dazzling attacking football in the present, or in the case of the fans, enjoy it. The current team of Hibs sprats are too young to be bothered about pensions, and are starting to perform with great verve every week, the little bastards. Hearts, on the other hand, have a much more prudent outlook. Their football is calculated, cagey, as if they're worried about what's round the corner, or at least this was the case under Craig Levein and, personally, I can't see it changing under Robbo. Here again, we're talking about club philosophy. Which maybe explains why Billy opted to sell pensions for a living.

We stop at his favourite garage where he scans *Car*, *Autocar*, *Auto Express*, *Intersection* – really picking up speed on the shelves now – *Top Gear* and *Fast Car* before finally settling on the latest ish of *Max Power*. Billy may work in pensions but today on the A77 he turned up the power to max and we've arrived in Kilmarnock way too early. Correction: we've arrived not a minute too late to grab the prime parking spot in a residential street full of curtain-twitchers that's closest to the route we will use for our sharp exit – 'it's a single-track, non-classified road that runs past an abattoir,' confirms Billy, hoping I'll note this key info in the book. He's also bought himself some sweets – a packet of Rolos, two Turkish Delights, some Marshmallows – and in his methodical pick 'n' mixing, without offering me any, it's clear that with my presence I'm intruding on a very private match-day ritual.

If Perth is unfailingly described as 'douce', and Callander and Crieff and similar-sized Scottish towns as 'prim', then Kilmarnock is 'perjink'. We're in a sturdy stone suburban area that I assume is a long way from the stadium; it looks too prosperous. Suddenly, Rugby Park materialises, almost apologetically. In a newish hotel next to the ground, Billy once again appears to know the entire Jambo contingent. Most address him as 'Sid'. I meet Carol, from the club shop, and her friends who work at Tynecastle, one of whom says they knew all about Levein's affair but were sworn to secrecy. Still on matters sexual, I ask them how they view Robbo's plan to inject the players' half-time oranges with Viagra. No-one seems terribly excited about this mission statement about sexy football. One guy wearing the full range of Jambo accessories, including watch, sovvy ring and necklace, is more concerned that Robbo doesn't 'spoil the legend' and ruin the memory of his own heroics as a player. See: they're cautious.

Billy and I get to the old wooden main stand in time for the 1970s throwback of a majorettes display. Killie, featuring the wonderfully-named Danny Invincibile, take the field to Thin Lizzy's *The Boys Are Back In Town* and Steven Pressley, suspended today, comes up and sits alongside us and starts to munch his way through a jumbo packet of Wine Gums. What is it with Jambos and confectionery? This makes Billy peckish and he strikes out on the half-time pie run, 45 minutes early. Killie caterers Brownings regularly finish top of football's pie league and you can tell they're masters in their field from their slogan. 'Say Aye To A Killie Pie' is adman classic and was quite clearly minted on Madison Avenue, Manhattan, home of the huckster.

Killie score first and are good value for the lead at half-time, when Rugby Park legend Davie Sneddon takes a bow in the centre-circle. 'Who *are* ya?' shout the Hearts fans in derision. Only the guy who scored the Killie goal that cost you lot the League Championship in 1965, that's who.

So what of the supposedly sexed-up Hearts? So far, so flaccid.

A man along the row from us shouts 'Fuckin' boo!' after a typical piece of ineptitude from Robbie Neilson – Lumberjack. Three minutes later, he shouts it again, and again. Fantastic: a majorettes display *and* a Tourette's display, all in the same sultry autumn afternoon.

Robbo, in his role as chief fluffer, is having trouble stimulating his side. Then, in desperation in the second half, he suggests a three-some. Mark de Vries and Ramon Pereira join Dennis Wyness up front and the trio combine for the latter's equaliser. But sexy? In *those* maroon socks? I'm not convinced . . .

Billy and I begin to trade what little info we know about the whereabouts of our old five-a-side mates. Kenny – lost touch. Alan

– lost touch. Robin – divorced. David – divorced. (I went to his wedding after being at the final Scotland-England Home International, when Graeme Souness rooled, OK, over both Bryan Robson and Ray Wilkins in midfield, the last time a Scot played with such strutting imperiousness). Pete – lost touch. Donny – lost touch. The two Colins, no hang on, the *three* Colins – lost touch. Derek – lost touch, but almost certainly still married to Val, Jambo legend Willie Bauld's niece. Then Billy admits arguments over extra-marital affairs resulted in him falling out with some of our old crew; he strongly disapproves of playing away.

The list goes on, and when I said before that Edinburgh is a small place, that you're always bumping into people you know, maybe it's not.

But, Billy – not lost, reunited. He may not have shared his sweets with me but he gets me home from Killie in world-record time. Maybe he's not so cautious after all, a view re-enforced by the truth behind that nickname.

'They call me Sid because I'm unpredictable. You know, like Sid Vicious . . .'


### 14 November

Robbo needs a nickname, so he can properly join the Jambo gang. I'm yet to be convinced of his credentials as a soccer satyr, but the moniker is going to have to be something to do with sex. It could be Alfred after Alfred Kinsey, or Alex after Alex Comfort, author of *The Joy Of Sex* which of course featured a bearded Steven Pressley lookalike as the bedroom-demonstrator. Throbbo? Dr Sex? Got it: think, small, chunky relationships experts . . . Dr Ruth.


### 15 November

As a joke, Billy emails me some bumf about pensions. 'I know you won't get one,' he says. I laugh when reading about the low-risk investment of a Cautious Managed Fund and write back: 'How very Hearts'.

## 23 November

The best Hibs legend – and there are a few – is that we taught Brazil how to play football. That Famous Five-referencing encyclopedia I mentioned before is viewed by Hibbys as conclusive proof that, not only did the great Easter Road forward line of the 1950s influence the development of the game in South America, but they were actually the blueprint for Brazil's 1970 World Cup-winning team.

I'm a boy from Brazil, or at least I wanted to be, 34 years ago, when Carlos Alberto's joyous blooter for the fourth and final goal against Italy crowned the most beautiful expression of football there has been in my fantime.

They played with unrivalled élan, never more so in the delirious build-up to the captain's clincher when, the split-second before he hit it, the ball bobbled on the concrete-hard pitch, just as it did before Jarzinho's cross onto Pele's head against England. That header didn't go in, Gordon Banks pulling off the greatest save of all time, but it was part of the greatest hat-trick not scored in a tournament, Pele's audacious halfway-line attempt against Czechoslovakia and outrageous dummy against Uruguay being the others. Oh, and another thing: Mexico '70 *looked* different, it was the first major sports event on new-fangled colour TV, so that first glimpse of the canary yellow was a unique experience.

Immediately after the tournament I got out the atlas, studied Brazil's position on the globe, and planned my move there. Only out of politeness, for my successful integration into samba culture was surely a formality, I advertised for a Brazilian penpal (female). And from *Charles Buchan's Football Monthly*, I ordered a child's size Brazil top bearing the legend 'CBF' and wore it all summer long. All the next summer too, and when it got too small for me, my mum cut it into dusters.

At every World Cup since, or at least every one where Brazil have been true to the spirit of '70, I've cheered them on. In this I've been relentless. Not radical, perhaps, but it's only recently that Brazil tops have become omnipresent. Thirty-four years ago, they were more scarce, especially on the Angus coast. And that summer in particular, the canary yellow attracted butterflies everywhere I played, everywhere I recreated the final: little brother as the bad boys, the *pension*-peddlars of Italy and me as beautiful, beautiful Brazil.

Flash forward to another beach, not Montrose, not the Copacabana, but Portobello where local kids in bibs await the arrival of their soccer-skills teacher, possessor of the best beard in football, captain and orchestrator of the greatest Brazil team since '70 . . . Socrates.

He's actually here but the kids can't get to meet him because the tartan tabloid hack-pack are trying to ask the same question 1001 ways: why is his countryman Juninho proving such a flop at Celtic? The scene is mildly tragic – the football education of the nation's youth being scuppered by a bunch of professional groupies for the Old Firm – and seems to sum up the current peeky state of the game in Scotland.

But after the hacks have gone, and after the kids have learned how to make the ball sing, I get the chance to ask my question: did Socrates know that my team, Hibs, had played a crucial part in the development of Brazilian soccer?

'Your team?' he says. 'Your team?' He ponders this. '*Cool* . . .'

What a man. A smoker, a drinker, a doctor, a political activist, a cultural commentator, a playwright, a stupendous footballer, a giant with tiny feet and a narrow stride . . . and now he's a Hibby.

Socrates, just for being Socrates, deserves the highest honour Scotland can bestow on a footballer – an honorary knighthood, a macaroon bar and a DVD of *Scotsport SPL Uncut: The Even Pisher Stuff*.

Jambos mock Hibbys for being Brazilophiles. In the most recent issue of the fanzine *No Idle Talk*, they scoffingly speculate on the existence of Hibs websites called www.lochendbrazil.net, www.greencowdenbeath.net and www.wetaughtbrazil.net. Hearts have got their own version of Socrates, Neil MacFarlane, but they can keep him.

## 25 November. FC Basel 1, Hearts 2

I can't get time off work to go to Switzerland. Billy's at a family wedding – in Brazil – so not only is he missing his first Hearts Euro tie since 1976, he cannot be my guide for a tour of the Jambo Village's hairiest outposts, where a boozer might be bending its aerial into the shape of a Toblerone to pick up this Uefa Cup game for free.

I'm contemplating a visit to Robertson's but when I phone to check if the match is being screened in the dread-pub, a man with a lisp says he's very sorry, but they're showing a Rock Hudson film season.

I listen on the radio and despite my mind wandering as I try to remember the very first sports event to grip me on the wireless – a Walter McGowan fight, maybe? – this tie throws up a thrillingly improbable finish thanks to a last-minute winner for Hearts from Robbie Neilson.

In Portugal, according to the fansite Kickback, the Euro-centric Jambos taunted Hibbys with the chant: 'What's the weather like in Leith?' In Holland it was: 'What's the hookers like in Leith?' In the Swiss capital they couldn't decide between fondue and skiing, so sang both versions. Yeah, yeah, very funny . . .

But the singing had to stop. In the jubilant Jambo dressing-room after the final whistle, the players were celebrating with the team Dansette turning up to 4 on the dial, maybe even 5, only for the Vladimir Romanov-appointed director of football, Anatoly By-shovets, to switch it off. He then delivered some stern words about the need for the team to stay completely focused on the next match. I'm intrigued. Which Steps track is the players' favourite?

**26 November**

Billy is back from Brazil, home of celestial soccer.

'So is the Maracana Stadium just heaven on earth?'

'Dunno, I didn't go.'

Typical Jambo . . .

**27 November. Leicester City (managed by Craig Levein) 2, Plymouth Argyle (Mr Bobby is their – master tactician) 1**

There's always someone worse off than yourself. I may be a reluctant Jambo, but at least I don't have to sit through what surely must have been the most un-Brazilian game of football in the history of the sport.

**28 November. Rangers 3, Hearts 2**

There may be 1690 reasons why Rangers are so great, and I assume this is why that statistic is so often quoted down the Copland Road. I reckon I can probably think of 16, which is plenty.

1. 'Hullo, hullo, how do you do . . .' Such a warm welcome! And it sums up the whole Ibrox experience, doesn't it?

2. Ice cream-sundae ties. Standard issue, my old school chum, club chairman David Murray wears them, so does manager Alex McLeish and the entire team when they (briefly) compete in Europe, and they too exemplify the sunny disposition of the club.

3. Respect for family and kinship, e.g. the preoccupation with heirlooms, e.g. the sash apparently worn by everyone's father.

4. The overwhelming sense of Scottishness, from the moment you hurry past the unofficial orange away-strip vendors and enter the stadium. It completely grips you. Usually round the throat.

5. Tan loafers. Not to be confused with Emerson, Marco Negri and other tired and emotional Gers of swarthy complexion, these were the official team shoes before being adopted by spivs and chancers everywhere.

6. The no-beard rule. Does it still apply? No matter. Of all the bans that Rangers could enforce, of all the clamp-downs aimed at making Ibrox a nicer, kinder, more human place, wasn't it brave of them to come down hard on facial hair?

7. Loyalburgers. Another myth? Who cares, we just want them to exist, to be the half-time snack-of-choice. ('Ur yez whantin' Nae Surrender Sauce wi' that, bud?').

8. The pre-match medley (The Dam Busters, The Great Escape, etc). So apt for a game of football played in Scotland in the year 2005, don't you think? (see 4).

9. The oompah-pah band who keep that essential World War Two spirit going in the Broomloan Stand. Truly honking (see 4).

10. Being able to call Bob Malcolm a team-mate (and getting a card from him every Christmas, signed in his own special way: 'F.T.P.' – Fuck the Pope).

11. Being able to call Michael (*Aspects Of Love*) Ball a team-mate as well. And Alex (*Aspects Of Bampotishness*) Rae, too.

12. Great Marketing Ideas In Action: The Burberry Baseball Cap. No longer a frumpy tartan for tourists, the beige check's stunning reinvention is best viewed at Ibrox. In marketing-speak, this is what's called a 'reverse Ratner'.

13. Penalties. Most of us think of buses as being like girls, and vice versa. At Rangers, they have a different method of measuring frequency, and of reassuring the populace: 'There'll be another one along any minute.' Spot-kicks for them, naturally.

14. The Ibrox treatment-room. A world-class centre for the care of groin strains, especially in the weeks leading up to international matches . . . ('Hullo, Wattie [Walter Smith, Scotland coach]? No, he won't make the Italy game. Slipped on the marble staircase again. But don't worry, as of next Monday all our tan loafers are going to be fitted with skid-protection devices . . .').

15. Those brilliant fans. They get right behind their team and never let up, from the first whistle until 20 minutes before the end.

16. Ease of access. Because Ibrox empties 20 minutes before the

end, you won't get stuck in traffic on the journey back to your Rangers-style residence in Bothwell or Bridge of Allan.

A visit to Castle Greyskull is a must on any football odyssey and no less so on this football idiocy. 'I love comin' here for the culture,' smirks Ricky as we pile off the train at Glasgow's Queen Street Station, with Billy leading the way to the Horseshoe Bar. Billy is an aficionado of the best-value lunch in the world, £3.95 for three courses. He's hoping to find the signature sweet on the menu: tinned rice and tangerines (also tinned), but stocks up with a bag of Sports Mixtures en route, in case it's not.

We talk about the first time we saw Rangers, in the raw, and, as usual, compared to these guys, I find I was a late developer (if indeed gazing in awe from the terrace wall at John Greig's ginormous *gluteus maximus* as he wound up for a throw-in could be deemed necessary to one's development).

My first match at Ibrox was, I think, Rangers' first home game after the 1971 disaster in which 66 people were crushed to death. As Dad and I hurried past stairway 13 and its hideous tangle of metal stanchions, vendors shouted 'Erra *Rangers Protestant News!*' and a Bluenose tried to yank my green-and-white scarf from round my neck until the old man chased him off. Little did the Hun know the scarf had begun life as a Celtic muffler. Hibs didn't win that day, or any time since when I've been present.

I grew up loving to hate everything about Rangers; well, everything apart from Lex McLean, the Gers-supporting variety comic with the tremendous conk who could terminate the Ibrox career of his goal-shy namesake George McLean, such was the sheer, elemental power of the music-hall running-gag. I hated the squareness of the Ibrox posts and the squareness of the sideboards sported by the likes of Alex MacDonald and Derek Parlane. Briefly in the 1970s, Hibs threatened the Old Firm duopoly, the old enemies' act. After one Hibee defeat of Rangers, the Ibrox chairman, Willie Waddell warned his opposite number at Easter Road, Tom Hart, to be sure to pack the steel shin-guards next time. But the Hibs challenge faded, and John

Greig's massive bahookie shut out the sun down Easter Road way.

The fans who follow, follow Rangers have master-race conceit. 'We arra peepul!' is one of their oldest chants. It gets an early airing on this dank afternoon but the Jambos, bouyed by their Euro win in Switzerland, are keen to make their presence felt.

'Ya bams, ye cannae even read the *People!*' shouts one. The next minute he's starting the song about the Gorgie Billy Boys being cruciate ligament-high in Fenian oxygenating fluid like the Ibrox hordes, much to the consternation of those in the home stands. Ibrox is one of Scotland's big grounds, a cathedral – ha! – of football, but the Jambos are exquisitely indifferent to it.

The game starts – a thunderous "MON THE HEARTS!' from Billy – and the Jambos score early, a penalty converted by Paul Hartley. Woohoo! I cheer because, well, it's a goal against Rangers, and they're fundamentally good things. Hearts are really going for it – this is not Craig Levein football, this is not Cautious Managed football. Now the travelling contingent are singing about their Basel heroes and I can only admire their resident songsmith for burning the midnight oil on these lyrics:

> *There's only one Dennis Wyness,*
> *He used to be shite, now he's all right . . .*
> *Walkin' in a Wyness wonderland*

And . . .

> *Oh Robbie Neilson*
> *Scored a fucking great goal*
> *With a minute to go*
> *In old Basel*

Hearts are comfortable and three passes in succession, none of them more than two yards in distance, get the Jambos excited. 'Passin' game, Hearts, passin' game!' enthuses one. To which his friend adds: 'This is just like watching the Hibs!' The Rangers fans are deadly quiet and the Jambos are taunting them by putting fingers to lips, but it's the Hearts defence who go to sleep and the Gers draw level before half-time.

During the break, in a fascinating new development, Billy hands round the Sports Mixtures and we resume the debate about our mean and snarly hosts. Hearts fans are viewed by some as Rangers Lite, but the lads get irked by this. Ricky admits that, aged 14, he bought a tape of Orange songs. He says he probably hates Celtic more than Rangers, but it's a closer contest than you might think. Billy confesses he, too, used to be a 'daft wee boy', flying a Union Jack at Tynecastle during the 1970s. Around the same time, across the city, I was probably trying to learn the words to IRA songs.

These days, though, Billy is a patriotic Scot and a fully paid-up member of the Tartan Army Travel Club. He's cheered on his country at World Cups and European Championships, right round the globe, and good for him. Not everyone thinks this is good, though. He gets hassle from Hearts Casuals for wearing the kilt. Ricky shakes his head. 'Look, I'm no big Scotland fan but that's bang out of order.'

It is. Billy is unswervingly loyal to Hearts, but following Scotland as well does compromise his commitment to his club. That he is questioned and challenged for being in the Tartan Army rather undermines the image of Scottish football fans as passionate, colourful, humorous and sporting, never mind that right now, the national team need all the support they can get.

The horrible brass band are giving it laldy and it's hard to believe that all these Gers fans in the Broomloan are loving the fanfare. Surely some are Scotland fans, too? I scan the faces, and there are plenty who are not singing along, and a few of them look a bit embarrassed.

The second half, and even when Rangers start flexing their muscles, Hearts hang in there, then fight back. Joe Hamill dinks a delicate cross into the box – this will almost be Hamster's last meaningful contribution to the entire season – and Mark de Vries stoops to score. He beats Marvin Andrews to get on the end of the cross which prompts a Jambo behind to shout: 'Get it up ye, ya black fuck!' Elmer Fudd is black, too, but I decide against pointing this out. Then, just as it looks like the Jambos will hold out for a deserved draw, Rangers grab a winner.

This is a bog-standard Ibrox defeat – I've had many as a Hibby – and perceived injustices such as ref Dougie McDonald's failure to show a red card at the penalty to Jean-Alain Boumsong almost make it seem like a win.

As we're walking out of the ground, swinging behind the Copland Road Stand, Ricky points to a burger van bearing the sign 'Excellent Food'. 'Aye right,' he says. 'Told you this place was good for *yer actual kultyur.*'

We find a pub to let the throng die down. The District Bar close to the stadium is wall-to-wall with Hun knick-knacks. Lots of pictures of the Nine-In-A-Row team in action, in trophy celebration or doing some big-game fishing: Coisty, Durranty, Goughie, Atilla, Bomber, Gazza, The Two Andy Gorams. Then another snap of Durranty on his own, in specs and a ludicrous bouffant, looking like a barber's shop model.

We queue for ages for beer – 'Hud oan, Bert,' says the barman to the old soak with a tab, 'a've goat some payin' customers' – and chat some more about Rangers, by implication, Hearts . . . and Scotland.

Billy loves following Scotland all over the place and doesn't understand Ricky's lack of interest in the national team. I think I can: Ricky is almost 20 years younger than us and so didn't see the likes of Billy Bremner, Joe Jordan and Kenny Dalglish in their prime and has only known dull or crap national teams. Mind you, I also think Ricky is thrawn, maybe a bit perverse, partial to the odd wind-up, and very much his own man. 'Ingratiate' is probably not a word in his personal lexicon, and the same goes for 'affectation'.

We're talking about how today's game will look on *Scotsport SPL* – nothing like the original, we reckon, once it's been edited with a breadknife and some Blu-Tac – and Ricky says he hopes there are no female sports journalists on the show this week.

'Birds and fitba, they just dinnae go,' he says. 'They should stick to knitting and sewing.' Billy asks what Ricky's girlfriend thinks of this viewpoint. 'Oh, she knows I'm sexist, racist and bigoted. Sometimes I play that old Orange tape, just to wind her up.'

The Union Jacks I saw among the Jambos at Parkhead the previous month were not in evidence at Ibrox. A single Saltire flew in the away end today, and the three of us agree it would be good to see more of them on days like these, in defiance of Rangers' triumphalism.

This boozer is full of fans in orange tops, the shirts that were supposed to be banned by Rangers as part of the drive against sectarianism. But they're on sale outside the ground: the Rangers black market is an orange market. And here comes another. Its wearer hollers: 'Anyone seen Rod the Prod?' and we're disappointed when the response of 'Aye, which wan?' doesn't materialise.

And here comes another. This lad is flogging home-made posters. 'It's the Govan Young Boys Protestant Flute Band, ur yez whantin' wan, guys?' Ricky smiles at him. 'Love the orange wash you've put on it, mate – very classy.'

So another week, another Jamboesque experience – and elsewhere, another win for style-conscious Hibs featuring yet another wonder goal from – yes, for it is him – Derek Riordaninho. I'm seeing as much of Deek in the pasty flesh as are the clodhopping defenders detailed to mark him: absolutely diddley.

On the train home, Ricky and I discover a shared enthusiasm for the unhinged comedy genius of Will Ferrell. Well, you've got to laugh when you visit Ibrox. Unless you're a Rangers fan; what a glum bunch they are. Not that I feel sorry for them. They don't give a damn about us, they're ignorant about all the other teams swilling about in the SPL, and I'd love to be in the District Bar on quiz night, just to hear Rod the Prod stumble over an easy-peasy question, like why Hibs *are* Brazil.

By the way, there were no tinned tangerines on the menu today. Just way too much orange.

# DECEMBER

**4 December. Hearts 3, Dunfermline 0**

Hibs are playing glistening football now; almost every week, Tony Mowbray's young hearts run free. They're making friends, influencing patronising west-coast hacks, attracting back the lieges of Leith who had given up on them, and winning top marks for artistic expression. A scintillating 4–1 triumph at Dundee last month being typical. Still, the revival should come to a juddering halt today at Parkhead. Selfishly, perversely, I'm almost glad. If I can't see Hibs, why should they be thrilling anyone else?

Meanwhile, across at Tynecastle, I'm starting to feel more involved. The recent away trips, especially Ibrox, have been good fun and the guys seem to have accepted me into their company. I'm certainly less apprehensive of Ricky. He's the type who gives up a smile slowly, makes you work for it, but when it arrives, a small electrical current surges through the room. He doesn't suffer fools and Hibs gladly and fair enough; I respect that. He also seems to have a good eye for colour and detail and the quirks of fandom, and this could prove useful. I've already started to appropriate some of his vignettes of the Hearts playing personnel, such as: 'Neil MacFarlane – just two shots on goal in his entire career.'

In the build-up to this game, Vladimir Romanov has been claiming Hearts can improve on being the third force. In fact, Vlad The Impaler says he's going to spear the Old Firm duopoly. Before too long, he reckons, the Jambos will boast a bigger fanbase than Celtic and Rangers. The Big Two will be kebabed, left in a gutter like one of Ibrox idol Barry Ferguson's late-night takeaways.

A bold statement of intent, but you have to wonder where these new Jambos are going to come from. OK, *apart* from me.

If they've any sense, Hearts will use me in promos, like old army recruiting ads, or commercials where the sceptical are eventually won round to a radical new way of thinking, then provide endorsements for catchphrases, such as 'I never knew this could be so much fun' or 'I'm convinced this is a major addition to road safety' or 'That girl's wearing Harmony hairspray'.

This isn't the best time to be trying to dragoon new fans through the turnstiles. It's December, Christmas shopping is hitting crowds everywhere, and these days fans never require much in the way of an excuse to give football a bodyswerve. But Hearts start the match playing some nice stuff. In a radical departure from the norm, the ball stays pretty much on the ground. Admittedly Dunfermline are tripe, but Robbo's message about sexy football appears to be getting through to the players.

Dr Ruth has been praising Hibs on their great season thus far, which is a far cry from the sneering, superior tone adopted by Craig Levein during his last days at Tynecastle. Levein stuck rigidly to the Hearts template he created and could not be seduced by other football philosophies. Dr Ruth, as well as being a Jam Tart, is also proving himself a bit of a tart.

Good for him for being so swingingly liberal. Everything gets boring after a while, even sex, and under the unyielding Levein Hearts had become as predictable as the Victorian gent who always keeps his spats on, then post-coitally reaches for his pipe. The entertainment level, at least to these eyes, peering through my metaphorical what-the-butler-saw contraption, was pretty dire. Dr Ruth, tumescent with possibility, and at least a willingness to try to show supporters a good time, is experimenting with new positions.

Size isn't everything, so the big strikers aren't getting it all their own way anymore. Dr Ruth is also into fantasy role-playing, for he's clearly said to Dennis Wyness, the club's troll mascot, usually perched on the dashboard of the away-games bus: 'Why don't you try centre-forward?' This is Shyness's actual function, but Dr Ruth must reckon he has to make him believe that strange fruit is on offer, in order to tease goals out of him. Time will tell if his coaxings are going to succeed, but the sight of Michael Stewart, also unused by Levein, lovingly caressing the ball in white boots, could not be more dramatic if he was wearing a gimp-mask.

Me, I'm wondering if I might turn into Al Pacino. Pacino in *Cruising*, that is. That was the crime movie where, as a determinedly straight cop investigating a brutal gay killing, he went deep cover, dallied overlong at a Hi-NRG disco and started to doubt his own sexuality.

In probing the Jambo netherworld, might a similar thing happen to me? What if I emerge, blinking at the sun at the end of the season, sporting maroon leather shorts and sailor's cap and a tight sleeveless T-shirt emblazoned with an image of Steven Pressley and Paul Hartley standing facing each other, so close they could kiss, naked from the waist down and comparing stud-spanners, in classic Tom of Finland style?

I am becoming strangely accustomed to these alien surroundings. Hearts, under Dr Ruth, him on top, don't make my eyes run as much as they did when Levein was cracking the whip. MC Tynie doesn't nark me so much either, and you might have noticed that I've stopped calling the place Swinecastle. I slow down when passing Gorgie City Farm, to make sure I hear the cock's crow. Before disappearing into the Wheatfield Stand, I glance back at Gorgie Parish Church and offer silent prayer: 'Be with me, Lord.' I wait for the chummy reassurance of Pressley greeting Andy Webster with a pre-kick-off high-five. And, back on my own again, I study the upcoming fixtures in the programme and wonder if my new best Jambo mates will be going to the next away game and whether there will be room in the car for me. Well, I suppose even death-row cells must, after a while, have a familiarity about them that is oddly comforting.

Hearts are certainly cruising today – this is a decent performance. I'm thinking of Billy, who always checked home security under Levein, and wondering if with Dr Ruth running the show he'll head out to games leaving his back door open, which used to be a motif of the good old days and a sign of trust, but could in Gorgie be viewed as an invitation to experiment, such as with three-in-attack sex romps. Then I hear from the fans behind me who are tuned in to the Hibs game on *Sportsound* that John Hartson has scored a late winner for Celtic. 'Yes!' they shout. 'Yes!' I say, to myself, sort of. Well, that's the result I wanted, isn't it?

Two days later I'm reading Mike Aitken's match report in *The Scotsman*: 'What was most impressive was Hibs' desire to play the beautiful game . . . maximum score for artistic merit . . . lovely to watch . . . an astonishingly assured performance from a group of young players – just one outfield was older than 24 – developing into the best footballing side in the SPL.'

It seems that Hibs completely outplayed the champs, they murdered them 1–2. Admittedly that is a very Hibee scoreline, a glorious Glasgow defeat, but Hearts have just lost their sex appeal.


### 11 December. Inverness CT 1, Hearts 1

Is this game even on? It's ten past three and we're walking to Pittodrie, Billy and I, and we can't hear a peep. In fact, there's more noise coming from the cemetery next to the stadium.

(Question: why are so many Scottish football grounds – Aberdeen, Hearts, Hibs, Dunfermline, Rangers, etc – built just goal-kicks from graveyards? Answer: so the clubs don't have far to travel when, to paraphrase the poet Tom Leonard, the ball lands on the slates for the very last time).

There was a brief moment on the car journey to Inverness's temporary home, 100 miles from the Highlands capital, when I wondered if the match would be fogged off. A thick haar hung over the Mearns like a giant, scabby dog-blanket. I thought back to a misty afternoon at Parkhead years ago when, after what seemed like 46 consecutive 5–0 thrashings, Hibs were winning 2–0 with mere minutes left, only for the ref to abandon the match because of poor visibility.

The cars decked in red and white travelling in the opposite direction, out of the fog, had the right idea. They were bound for Easter Road and the game of the day, Hibs vs Aberdeen. (*Sigh* . . .). Then I thought: nah, this stuff will lift. Fog isn't fog anymore, I reassured Billy. Bad weather isn't bad weather anymore. Winter isn't winter anymore.

The Mearns used to be my summer playground. My family had a holiday home in the Angus fishing village of Johnshaven and we spent all the school-holidays there. On the one side, the North Sea, fearsome even when calm, while on the other, the red-soil farmland so beloved of the painter Joan Eardley. The car journey by Saab Estate, blinking headlights at other Saabs because Dad said they were so rare, soundtrack to the hippy musical *Hair!* on the in-car eight-track cartridge, took two whole hours . . . aeons as a kid, and Johnshaven, to this boy, was a long way from Edinburgh so I could properly unwind from the stresses and strains of supporting Hibs . . . and follow Johnshaven Dauntless. The Dauntless – great name for a football team, as is Queen of the South and, er, Heart of Midlothian – played on a daisy-strewn public park with goal-nets stitched from old lobster creels. They were an amateur side, of course, a wildly disparate band of fish-gutters, fish-curers and fish-smokers, and everyone seemed to be called Taylor, most notably Magnus Taylor, a big, bearded, barging centre-forward who flattened defences in the local summer league. I used to pester Faither to drive me, blinkingly, to their games in Auchenblae, Fettercairn and Stone-haven. Summers were special then, as of course were winters.

Remember, pre-Adidas Sambas, when players sported basic, flat-soled pumps, when goalies wore baggy tracky bottoms, and when the bounce they got off the cold, hard surface was akin to that of the playground favourite, the Superball? Back then, snow wasn't cleared from the terraces and there must have been afternoons when I was unable to feel my toes through my desert boots, and I wished I was at home in front of the fire watching *Grandstand* as Chester Barnes and Desmond Douglas engaged in some gladiatorial ping-pong.

But there was a real I-may-be-some-time valour about football in wintertime. Once, Faither and I battled through a snowstorm to get to Dundee, only to discover on the trudge up Hilltown that Dens Park had been frozen off. We were disappointed, but there was also acceptance of the fact that bad weather happened, that you did your best to overcome it, and if the conditions beat you, that the old man would still turn his bohemian-style bunnet to the snell wind and say: 'Son, let's find out if Dundee's got a snooker-hall.'

Football fans these days wouldn't tolerate such uncertainty – rightly so. Players won't risk injury on icy pitches – rightly so. Undersoil heating means matches go ahead anyway, but I can't help feeling that football, like so much of life now, is prey to nanny-state strictures, and that we've all turned into a bunch of big jessies and nancy-boys, scared of a wee bit cold.

Billy achieved another personal best behind the wheel today so we're kicking around Aberdeen for something to do because even the pubs haven't opened yet. There's an interesting colour contrast in the main drag, Union Street, that I don't remember from my youth: the grey of the granite usually makes the city look drably Eastern European in wintertime, but today it's got a glow to it on account of the large number of fake tans. You didn't see complexions like this in the North-East when summers were summers, and Aberdeen, drenched in oil money, is now starting to resemble Glasgow for swankers.

What are we going to do now? Billy has an idea. We return to the car and head out to one of his favourite local attractions, the city's Porsche garage. These are his dream-machines. He runs me through their specifications. I ask if he wants to go inside for a closer look but, no, he's happy with his family packet of Revels, gawping in silent wonder, as if the cars were snoozing cougars in a zoo.

It's a moment of reverential awe, and as we approach Pittodrie and that riotous graveyard, I get to glimpse another one. 'Haw, Sick Boy!' A Jambo sticks his head round the door of the Saltoun Arms as we pass the pub and shouts this greeting at Billy, who acknowledges it with a little wave. Last time we hit the road with the Jambos, he was Normski – is he going to have a different nickname for every away game?

'Well,' says Billy, 'I got that one in 1986, on a bus to the old Czechoslovakia, we were playing Dukla Prague, and I was absolutely guttered. These border guards stopped us and other buses were being held for six hours, but I threw up and they ran off.'

It's slowly dawning on me that I am in the presence of a Jambo legend, albeit an extremely modest one. Billy does not wear his Hearts on his sleeve; there are no souvenir badges of places visited on Jambo duty on his scarf, and getting him to tell me about the trips is like persuading him to share his Revels.

Here's the list: the aforementioned Dukla, Paris St Germain, Bayern Munich, Velez Mostar of Croatia, Estonia's Tallinn, St Pat's of Dublin and Dnipro, when he was one of only 26 fans allowed into the Ukraine, Dnipropetrovsk being a closed city because it was the centre of the arms, nuclear and space industries of the old Soviet Union. And you just know that on each of the other 25 at that game, he'll have made the same quiet, soulful, impression, broken only by the occasional ridiculously crap joke.

Me: 'Billy, have you ever gone an entire season without missing a single game home or away?'

Him: 'I think I must have gone ten seasons with a perfect attendance record.' And he says this without the merest hint of boastfulness. Supporting Hearts, all the way, is what he does.

This game is on right enough but only 2,011 hardy souls have turned up for the curiosity-value of squatter-soccer. Inverness are set to move back to their own home in the new year so their remaining fixtures at Pittodrie have taken on an I-was-there cachet for football anoraks.

But the idea that some fans might be here just to add a game to their collections seems completely derogatory when applied to Billy. Try Ross County on a midweek night when you've got work the next day. Try Watford for a testimonial at the fag-end of a rotten season. Billy's been there, done that.

This game is boggin'. Hearts get a draw with yet another penalty;

they've scored only 19 goals so far and ten have come from the spot. Whoopidoo. On the journey back, I drive. It's dark when we pass the turn-off for Johnshaven, but my mind is soon drifting back to those long days of summer, when the Dauntless substituted for Hibs. I'm about to ask Billy if he ever had a summer team, a second team, an any-team-apart-from-the-boys-in-maroon, but he's sleeping.

I turn on the radio. Hibs have beaten Aberdeen 2–1 and the *Sportsound* pundits are raving about them. 'Hey, Sick Boy/Normski/ whatever your name is, the Hibees played like Brazil today!'

But he's fast alseep, dreaming of a customised Porsche with sweets dispenser.


### 16 December. Hearts 0, Ferencvaros 1

Hearts are the last team in Europe. The previous night at Ibrox, Rangers crumbled under intense pressure from an Auxerre team roared on by 16 of their fans, and were dumped out of the Uefa Cup on their sizeable backsides. Training trends come and go but Govan arses are always big. Thus Hearts are the last men standing.

I check the website on this historic day but the Kickbackers are distracted; the pressure must be getting to them. There's a debate about favourite Who songs ('The Kids Are Alright', surely) before the chat returns, judderingly, to football with this urgent enquiry: 'Just how fat did Phil Stamp look at training the other day?'

But then it's back to those infernal lists, such as best/worst pub. These guys must rate Robertson's the best, yes? Well, no. 'I wouldn't go back even if Pamela Anderson was working behind the bar,' is a typical comment. 'I've never seen so many unsavoury characters in one place in my life. The quickest pint I've ever had.'

Mather's is one of the best, though. An unfussy, wooden-floored oasis in a desert of bright, female-friendly lighting, magnolia and chrome. When I get there, Billy is talking to his friend Robert and they're sharing an Estonia moment together. Both know the country well. Billy has visited many times, on Hearts and Scotland duty, but for a while he also had an Estonian girlfriend. Before his first trip, he was warned not to go, or he'd be shot.

Robert worked at a bar in the capital, Tallinn, called Ruby Tuesday and ended up marrying an Estonian girl. They've settled in Fife and he's in the spray-tan business.

After only a couple of minutes in their company I'm mightly impressed by these guys' knowledge of Old Russia, New Russia, the Russian Mafia, the Russian Oligarchy, and I'm thinking, yes, it's right and proper, with fans who are such men of the world, that Hearts are still in Europe.

Tallinn is the new Prague, says Billy, the city being caught at a good moment in its westernisation where the hip, discerning chap will book up for a stag weekend . . . but *before* the lapdancing chain Spearmint Rhino expands there.

And, of course, they both knew Estonia when it was even more interesting, when you could hire an old mansion with jacuzzis, champagne-on-tap and '12 crackin' wummin' . . . all for the price of a goat, or maybe even a stoat. Immediate post-Commie, you could get anything you wanted there. AK-47s? No problem, sir. How many?

Robert's biased, obviously, but he reckons the Estonian women are the most beautiful in the world. Before Billy's fling in Tallinn, he went out with a Czech girl. He talks authoritatively of Estonia's place in the new world order, and how in so many ways it's more advanced than Scotland . . . and I'm thinking of his experiences of the East, and my experiences of Easter Road, and his relationships with women of different nationalities, and my four Leith Walk girlfriends, and I'm telling myself: I'm not worthy.

If Hearts are to progress in the Uefa Cup, they need to win tonight and must hope that Basel fail to beat Feyenoord. Ferencvaros are Hungarian, even a homebird like me knows that. I'm not old enough to remember when Hungary was truly a giant among football nations, but the likes of Ferencvaros and Ujpest Doza were still top sides by the time I started to become fascinated by Euro competition, the exotic names, the elaborate tumbling routines.

Another big crowd, more than 26,000, has converged on Murray-field. We take our seats, Billy, his friend Colin and I, in front of some bad yins in the toppermost row who stay standing through-out, behind a bedsheet banner proclaiming: 'Ulster Hearts'.

As at Pittodrie, we've missed the kick-off so Hearts are denied Billy's rasping roar of encouragement. I'm surprised the ref let the game start without it, frankly. But Hearts get in the groove early – the enigmatic Michael Stewart at last producing some form worthy of his Man U credentials – only to fall behind after half an hour.

Hearts fight back and as fans hanging over the electronic score-board thump it with their fists, as a giant bottle of Irn-Bru is passed along our row and quickly consumed by order of the stewards – with a slug revealing mostly vodka – I'm thinking: at last, this place resembles a football stadium. But Hearts can't turn the match around. They slump out of Europe, the big adventure over.

On the way out of the ground, I meet John, these days completely bald, but once bubble-permed, and I'm further re-minded of how far some have ventured for football thrills, and how determinedly EH7 I am. John was in Argentina for the 1978 World Cup. He knows of at least two fellow travellers on that ill-fated sojourn who stayed, met South American girls, and married them. The diamonds on those sweethearts' fingers certainly shone brighter than the ones on the Scottish team's shirtsleeves and, famously, John didn't miss the chance to remind the players of how rubbish they'd been.

In a classic piece of grainy footage – '78 was by far the darkest World Cup there's been – the team have just held the mighty Iran to a 1–1 draw when they're ambushed by a group of extremely hairy fans. John is prominent with his perm in a clip that's always shown to remind us that this was a thoroughly desolate experience, and the players can count themselves bloody lucky the chant was no more vicious than: 'We want our money back.'

But, never mind the football, the Tartan Army have stories they're still telling from Argentina and the Jambo Village will be exaggerating the misadventures from the UEFA Cup 2004–05 for years to come.


**17 December**
Dr Ruth is snapped on just about every back page *kicking* the Ferencvaros coach. No, not the team-bus, their manager, Csaba Laszlo. Dr Ruth tries to deny the wee, sly dunt after the final whistle, but the evidence is in the screen-grabs for all to see.

He's a bit of a radge – gratifyingly so.


**18 December**
There are lots of football comedy shows around these days, but because so much Scottish football is comedy – or tragedy, one or the other, I always forget which – we can justifiably claim to be top of the league in this field. Radio Scotland's *Off The Ball* bills itself as 'the most petty and ill-informed sports programme on air' but is also hilarious and essential listening if you want to get through Saturdays with your sanity more or less intact.

I've been invited on to today's show to talk about my Jambo life but don't want to blow my cover, not with another derby coming up in two weeks' time, so presenter Stuart Cosgrove suggests a nickname. Minutes before we go on air from the Glasgow studio, we're still trying to think of one. 'I know,' he says finally, 'who was the surgeon who carried out the world's first heart transplant . . . South African guy . . . got it, you'll be Christian Barnard.'

Cosgrove is a renaissance man among football pundits, which is damning him with faint praise because only Pat Nevin's post-punk obsessions (notably for Half Man Half Biscuit) comes close to matching his list of hip credits as Channel 4 executive, cultural commentator and author of the definitive *Hampden Babylon*, in the style of Kenneth Anger's *Hollywood Babylon*, a searing exposé of a football nation's bloated underbelly of booze, birds, big ties and boating trips. Cosgrove supports St Johnstone. His sidekick is Tam

Cowan, Ernie Wise to Cosgrove's Eric Morecambe, the eternally-striving small man, Motherwell bauchle, *ra* punter incarnate, who pronounces my pseudonym 'Bar-*nard*' (this is the Lanarkshire way, with the emphasis on the second syllable). The show passes in a flash. Cosgrove and Cowan's soccer Casual-sweetie wifie routine is well practised, but I can't use that as an excuse for my poor showing. Nervous, I revert to juvenile jibes and jokes about Jambo dress-sense. I feel like Lisa Rodgers, dullest of the talking heids on those Channel 4 '*100 Greatest . . .*' list programmes.

Cosgrove asks me if I'm warming to the Jambos; I say I'm becoming 'curiously endeared'. Cowan reckons that's my cover virtually blown; only two newspapers in Scotland would use such a poncey phrase. Still, at least I learn which player possesses the biggest cock in the SPL. It's Jim McIntyre of Dundee United and the boys tell me there's pictorial proof: he was snapped at a team Christmas party, dooking his walloper into a pint tumbler. 'Like a giraffe taking a drink from a pond,' confirms Cosgrove. The lads wish me well for the rest of the season. 'I suppose the hardest part must be trying to shake aff the HIV,' says Cowan. Thankfully, he didn't say that on air and I leave the studio pretty confident that my presence will have barely registered in the Jambo Village, especially as Hearts don't have a match today.

### 18 December. Livingston P, Hearts P

What was I saying last weekend about bad weather never affecting football anymore? On a bitingly cold but bright day, we set off for Livingston. From the outskirts of the new town (no different from the inskirts) right the way to the throbbing pulsebeat, we negotiate all 742 roundabouts successfully. To the inexperienced motorist they're like a hovering cluster-cloud of asteroids, motionless but still capable of bouncing you seriously off course.

We've got Billy as our guide, however – 'The Human Map,' quips Ricky – and we're soon parking up in a shopping centre . . . only to discover that the game has already been called off due to frost. This is especially annoying, because on current league standings this looks like being Hearts only trip to Livi this season, and unless I can make the rearranged match on doubtless some midweek night in deepest, darkest January, my cunning plan to see them at every ground will be scuppered. But as I potentially lose a fixture, I gain a new Hearts chum. David is a solicitor who, according to Billy, is Ricky's only rival in the Jambo stats stakes. He's a wee wiry guy in specs with a shaky leg and on the way back to Edinburgh, the pair are soon competing for the scariest, hairiest story about Billy's driving and even I can join in when the reminisces reach Kilmarnock. But these two are soon out on their own again, it's Mr Memory from *The Thirty-Nine Steps* versus someone really smartypants from telly quizzery . . . I know, Robin Ray on *Face The Music*.

Starter for ten: the worst-ever Hearts strike force, the *Truly Terrible Trio*, if you like? 'Has to be Musemic, Eskillson and Baird,' suggests David. 'Musemic was a Yugoslav and his sole claim to fame was scoring the only goal in a derby. Eskillson – no relation to the word "skill" – once complained that the noise of the crowd made him miss a sitter at Easter Road. Baird was an English journeyman battering-ram, a poor man's Sandy Clark if you like. I didn't like.'

Ricky smiles. 'Fair play, David,' he says. But I know, we all know, that the big man will be back.


**19 December**
Uh-oh. I've been rumbled. Post-*Off The Ball*, the Kickbackers are giving me a kicking. 'This guy is laughing at us,' says Maroon-Platoon, 'and if I see him I'll be telling him exactly what I think of him.' Steph 98 says: 'A boot in the Denis Laws should put an end to his wee storey [sic] book.' For the benefit of like-minded Jambos, my photo is posted; already it's been downloaded 662 times. Colonel H offers hope I can avoid the inevitable. 'I heard the show, can't remember the guy's name, but it wasn't Aidan Smith,' he says.

But Lenny confirms that 'Christian Barnard' was a pseudonym

and no relation to Christian, the panto veteran and second-most-famous Motherwell showbizzer after Tam Cowan. 'Condescending bastard. Never liked Smith or the crap he writes,' adds Lenny. 'The guy was a disgrace,' says Fine Scottish Wine. Finally, Gizmo: 'This twat . . . ironically, while he's watching the Jambos, his beloved Hubz are having their best season in many moons and he's missing it. Get it right up ye, ya biased wee Hibs cunt!'

**26 December. Hearts 0, Celtic 2**
No leftover turkey for me today, I'm too chicken. Too scared to go to Tynecastle after publication of that 'Wanted' poster on the internet. I sneak down to Bert's Bar, at the foot of my street, to watch this game on Sultana TV. Hearts fans are in an anti-Aiden mood – they boo Aiden McGeady for choosing to play for the Republic of Ireland rather than Scotland. Meanwhile, as Hibs give Dundee United a goal of a start and bang in another four – that's 35 to date and I've missed the lot, including all those Riordaninho stoaters – I ponder my derby disguise.

# JANUARY

## 2 January. Hibs 1, Hearts 1

Edinburgh at Hogmanay – it's the only place to be. Well, isn't it? Nobody knows how to celebrate New Year quite like the Scots. This is what we've been telling the rest of the world for donkey's.

But until a few years ago, when Edinburgh decided to invite the rest of the world to a ginormous piss-up, everyone had to take our word for it. For Hogmanay before then was a domestic festival, celebrated in your own house, your neighbour's house, or a complete stranger's house, to which you had gained admission only after production of these credentials: a couple of cans of Tartan Special, a fetching smile and the assurance that 'Wullie said it'd be OK.'

Now the party is a massive communal affair, out-of-doors, against the backdrop of the Castle Rock, with pop bands, processions, highbrow events, a big wheel and a mountain of tat. It lasts for five whole days. 'Edinburgh's Hogmanay', as the super-swally is called, succeeds on many levels, not least in changing Embra and Hogmanay out of all recognition.

A large chunk of Sydney, most of Surrey and a quarter of a million revellers from all the 'airts take the place over. The bulk of them are young, dressed in parkas and silly ear-flap headgear, and as they hug each other in the rain on the street-corners of this (to them) foreign city, displaying a lack of reserve that (to us) is completely alien, they look like they're auditioning for one of those wistful, twentysomething Richard Linklater films such as *Before Sunrise*.

There is more posh totty on the streets of my home town than you can wave a hand-held rocket-launcher at. With all this multi-farious entertainment, and plenty of English pounds in their pockets, these Abigails and Sashas will never want for anything. What a contrast to 30 years ago when Edinburgh, in common with the rest of Scotland, completely shut down over Hogmanay. On January 1, and the day after that, you couldn't even buy a loaf of bread or a pint of milk. This was Before Sunblest.

So imagine my delight, therefore, when the great waft of strange accents, the sheer un-Edinburghness of 2005 to date, is blown apart by this: 'Ya fuckin' skinny wee gay mongol junkie Drylaw shite!'

Deek Riordaninho has just scored for Hibs in the New Year derby – once the only live event in Edinburgh during the hangover holiday, and now just about the only one that's quintessentially Edinburgh – and I have to say that's brilliant.

Not the goal. I'm talking about the reaction of the Jambo behind me. By anyone's standards, that's an impressive buckshot of abuse – instant, comprehensive, sound local knowledge, you could call it gutter poetry. And it's almost as impressive as the dead-eye aim with which two barely-nibbled pies are hurled at Riordaninho as he taunts the Hearts end with a right-up-you celebration.

I want to note this lyrical description for posterity but must not draw any more attention to myself than *Off The Ball* has done already, so I text it to myself. Then I hunch up the collar of my snowboard jacket, the one with the whistle on the zip in case of emergencies, and tell myself, try to convince myself, that there's nothing like the Ne'er Day derby.

*Jingle bells, jingle bells*
*Jingle all the way*
*Oh what fun it is to fuck*
*The Hibs/the Hearts* (delete as appropriate) *on New Year's Day*

Thanks to Noel Coward for that festive jollity, and it's true: in the Edinburgh football calendar, the Ne'er Day game is *the* fixture. Before this book came along, I'd organised to go on a holiday using that snowboard jacket for its proper purpose. This was back in the Bobby Williamson era and, remembering the Ne'er Day game under his command when Hibs blew a 4–2 lead in injury time, I thought I could cheerfully miss this one.

But then Mr Bobby quit, Tony Mowbray – Lord Shaftesbury – arrived, and by 2004's end, Hibs had become the deeper-thinking pundits' idea of the most attractive team in the SPL. I can't miss this derby, I just can't. Result: I cancel the trip to the French Alps, kissing goodbye to £600.

This is my first trip of the season to Easter Road. In 37 years of watching football, such forgetfulness is unique. Even when Hibs were truly crap in the 1980s, I never completely boycotted them. And I never missed the Derbies because in those matches anything could happen.

Anything . . . such as, a Jambo spots me from the 'Have you seen this Hibby?' poster displayed on the website and I get a £600 doing. I am nervous about this game, the worst I've been. I've mastered the trick of being invisible at Hearts matches, of staring glumly into space for 90 minutes, but that might not be enough today.

Billy is as edgy as me as he hands me my ticket. We walk down Easter Road, a street I could do blindfolded, and it's just as well Billy's here because I'm heading to the home gates as usual until he grabs my arm and leads me along the away fans' route, across Bothwell Street Bridge.

Before segregation, I was often on this bridge. Rather, I was swept along it by the clomping crowd, all of them sporting Freeman, Hardy & Willis' finest stackheels, when this was one nation under a stompy glam-rock beat. My feet never touched the ground. On this bright but bitingly cold afternoon, a group of Jambos have plonked a large carry-out on the tarmac and, like toll-enforcers, are demanding we sing 'the Gorgie Derry Boys song as we cross. I raise a wimpish arm in salute and quicken my pace. On the bridge's metalwork, Vicki Pollard's soul-sister in the Leith branch of *Little Britain* has felt-penned the legend 'Derek Riordan is sexi'. I scoff theatrically at this declaration of devotion and think: you balloon, that fooled no-one.

Another first: I have never before watched a game from the Whyte & Mackay Stand. In fact, I didn't even know that was its name. I remember when all this was terracing, when this section was known as the Dunbar End, and I'm pretty sure I was last on these slopes in 1979 when a beer-gutted George Best, who, for all that oor fitba demanded of him, could play in his sleep and in his stupors, was tripling Hibs' home gates with the occasional, brilliant shimmy done from memory. He couldn't save Hibs from relegation, though.

Today, I've got a cracking seat: front row, upper tier, no-one ahead of me, so minimum possible Jambo integration situation. Billy is on one side of me and Carol, from the Hearts Shop, who I first met at Kilmarnock, is on the other. Ricky isn't with us; he tends to avoid the home of 'the vermin' if at all possible and he can watch this game on the box.

The pre-match chat is all about the players who might be leaving (Mark de Vries, Alan Maybury, Paul Hartley) and those who might be arriving (a batch of 20 young Lithuanians, boxed up like veal calves, who then presumably skitter down the lorry-ramp into Edinburgh, wonder how such parsimonious surroundings can be playing host to so much hedonism and ask each other: 'Ver *are* ve?').

In the Whyte & Mackay, I can sense some unease about the match, which is different from my unease about the occasion. Hibs, the form team in Scotland, and of course the flair team, are favourites. But this doesn't prevent the Jambos from drowning out *Sunshine On Leith*. At all previous Derbies, from all other sections of Easter Road, their jeering never registered and I always believed the rendition of The Proclaimers' lament carried right across the Forth; in fact, from deep in the bowels of the Whyte & Mackay, the booing of the song is all you hear.

The atmosphere is fantastic. Abusive chants are acknowledged by one lot with something approaching reverential silence; then there's a response with knobs on.

*Tony Mowbray's got a fuckin' monkey's heid!*
*Tony Mowbray eats bananas with his feet!*

Hal David, Burt Bacharach's great lyricist, would surely be proud of a winsome couplet like that. The Jambos then indulge in some traditional junkie-jibing by turning their twirly scarves into tightened tourniquets. The Hibbys in the East Stand respond with their version of *Hearts, Hearts, Glorious Hearts* – identical to the original apart from every mention of 'Hearts' being replaced by 'shite'. And I cannot help thinking that in another part of the city I no longer recognise, some people will be sitting down to a classical musical recital. Each to his own, I suppose, but I know I'm in the right place, or at least the wrong section of the right place.

Hearts struggle to get into the game, and de Vries and Hartley – transfer targets for Leicester and Celtic respectively – are toiling in their efforts to impress the Jambo contingent with their commitment to 'the jersey'. The derby commands total respect from both sets of supporters and woe betide any player who isn't prepared to die for the cause in a 30–70 challenge in favour of an opponent.

The East Stand, in reality the old main terracing sawn in half, roofed and 'seated' using basic plastic trays, is where the bad yins among the Hibs support hang out; the greying, gnarled Casuals, the Tricolour revivalists, the terracing traditionalists, and all of them stay on their feet from first whistle to last. But, from where I'm perched today, the East has lost its growly defiance. It looks different, the whole place looks different. This has been my ground for three decades but I barely recognise it. What is happening to me?

I barely recognise Hibs either. Never mind the roughly similar rugs, I am a stranger to their style of play, which is very fast and fluid and to-feet and I should love it, but all football fans want to engage with a team, their team, and give them the benefit of their stunning football insight, but as far as Hibs are concerned this season I cannot acknowledge them.

Because all fans think – *know* – they are more tactically astute than all managers, I want to shout out something fantastically perceptive, but I have no frame of reference for Hibs so have nothing to contribute to their cause.

Ah, but Hearts are a different matter. I know this lot. I know their style of play, I know their key players, I know how they can win this game. Like it or not, in this half-season they have become my team, and this afternoon, in the derby, they're means by which I can pro-actively engage with the game.

Before the Drylaw goal-addict scores, Hearts had some success down the left flank through Joe Hamill. So now I'm saying to anyone who will listen, but not in my radio voice: why has Hamster come off the wing and moved into the middle?

Then later, in the second half, Phil Stamp is substituted despite being the key man during a crazy 15-minute spell when Hearts have got Hibs rocking and reeling. Pas des Bas trudges off, seriously dischuffed. 'What's that about?' I say to no-one in particular.

It's difficult not to be impressed by the sweaty vigour of Hearts' comeback, or the rumbustiousness of the Jambo support. From this vantage point, the Hibby parts of the ground have been neutered, emasculated, almost silenced. A flare, or some sort of guffy bomb, goes off in the Whyte & Mackay, and, quick as a flash, Billy quips: 'That's the only flair at Easter Road today.'

I'd never heard of the word 'brutalise' until the first controversies over small children gaining access to violent videos. The shocking acts in these films lost their terrible power by dint of repeated exposure, and the kids lost any appreciation they had of right and wrong. Is this game my *Child's Play 3*? Have the senses I thought were so refined been dulled by so much Jambo bludgeoning?

The equaliser is scored by Hartley. A few minutes earlier Pauline had muffed an easier chance and, bearing in mind his Hibby past, and the doubt hanging over his Jambo future, some in the Hearts support had started to turn on him. But he goes mental at the goal, the Jambos go mental back, and everything's all right with the world again.

Hibs come back in the last 15 minutes and now it's Hearts' turn to hang on. Steven Pressley has pretty near perfected his art of winning free-kicks this afternoon, falling on the ball when a Hibs toerag tries to nick it from behind his big hurdies, and when Lisa-Marie tumbles for the umpteenth time, I'm whispering in the hope he can hear me: 'Take your time, big man, stay down.'

I jumped to my feet to applaud the Hearts equaliser, and if they'd gone on and scored a winner I would probably have reacted in the same way. For the second derby in a row, Hibs have played a lot of football, but was there too much of it? From me, this is a heresy, a disavowal of my creed. But Hibs, I cannot help thinking, have been slightly disrespectful towards the derby, of the way it has to be played if you're going to achieve the desired three points. Ricky, whose gnarly wit has been missed today, told me back in November that he liked to see Hearts 'winnin' the physicals' and today this seems less of a personal preference, more an SPL prerequisite than I was prepared to acknowledge before.

A draw seems a fair-ish result though I don't suppose I would have been saying this six months ago, if I was in my usual spot in the West Stand, gazing over at the Jambo hordes and scoffing: 'What a rubbish away support!' You had to be there. In the Hearts end, that is. The view of the ground, the match, life itself, is completely different. Today I walked over Bothwell Street Bridge for the first time in yonks and I may have crossed another bridge as well.

Of course, I cannot forget that, finally this season, I have seen a Riordaninho goal, and maybe it'll be his last if he sneaks out of the transfer window like a Drylaw housebreaker making good his escape with a VCR. But I feel no shame or embarrassment being among the Jambos, roaring appreciation for a great fightback, and I really don't think that had anything to do with my relief at avoiding being doubted, outed and given a stiff kicking.

In the Windsor Buffet, in the world-class centre of excellence for getting blootered that is Embra, my city, Billy and I drink long into the night.

## 3 January

Edinburgh is the city of *Dr Jekyll and Mr Hyde* and the dangerous allure of dual identity endures here. For something has changed in me: Dr Hibby is in severe danger of turning into Mr Jambo. In a reversal of the usual trend, it's a case of too little green potion rather than too much. What was it I said on *Off The Ball*? Am I becoming *curiously endeared* to Hearts?

Because I couldn't be seen to be fraternising with them at the derby, I phone some Hibs friends to wish them a Happy New Year and tell them, truly, about my feelings during the game. There's a long pause. 'You need a doctor,' is just about the only printable reply.

And I do. His name is Dr Mike Smith and he's my dad's brother. Last heard of, he was in Zambia. Previously, during the apartheid years, he had slaves. This was what the old man told me at any rate. He visited us only a couple of times when Dad was alive and I remember him as a nice man. *For a Jambo*. But was Faither one, too? My brother Sean's taunting to this effect is starting to niggle me. Uncle Mike is my only link to Dad now but all I have as a means of getting in touch is a number for a PO Box – 6109. Do people still use them? I decide to write a letter . . .


## 4 January

Funny time of year, this. Funny time of season. The first half is over, and you're sitting in the metaphorical dressing-room, peeling an orange, peeling back the layers on what's just happened, and facing up to the fact you need goals, the kind that are also aims. You've got to look forward, but the only certainty is more uncertainty. No wonder we all bloody drink so much.

For Jambos, the New Year hangover is lasting longer than usual. At first, the emergence of Vladimir Romanov, pockets apparently groaning with lats, the Latvian currency, was reason for optimism, if not an excuse to throw a wild party. Now, in the cold light of the morning after, once the Craig Levein memorial specs have helped Jambos re-focus, some healthy Scottish cynicism and gloom has descended on Gorgie and Dr Ruth is being swept up in it, too.

On Kickback, Only A Game!! points out that the coach is 'moaning his face off' about refs, rival managers, the financial uncertainty, everything. He's raging against the machine. 'We're not looking too professional at the moment – we shouldn't be washing our dirty strips in public,' adds Rod. And PivotMember80to86 says: 'I hope I'm wrong but I don't think he'll last to the end of the season.'

Now I'm thinking, he already has at least eight nicknames . . . that's three more than my friend Billy, who in his own quiet way is as much of a Hearts legend . . . does the manager merit another one, namely Calimero? This was the cartoon chicken who used to trudge around with half an eggshell still on his head and wimper: 'It's an injustice, it's an injustice . . .'

As for Romanov, some Jambos have clearly been expecting a quick fix, fancy-dan foreign signings and a romp up the league, re-asserting city superiority over good-news hoggers, Hibs. But Kick-backer Paul Valente cautions: 'Romanov is the only game in town and we have to be patient or our Lithuanian friend could pull out of the takeover.' Rottenref agrees: 'If we miss this boat I can assure you there will be no lifeboat.'


## 8 January. Partick Thistle 0, Hearts 0

The only public place in Scotland where you can hear, on a regular basis, the prog-rock classic 'Sylvia' by Focus is Firhill. This 1973 instrumental hit from the Dutch combo – a duel between Jan Akkerman's guitar and Thijs Van Leer's organ, which the latter wins by breaking out into some bonkers yodelling towards the end – is dusted down for a crackly spin before every Partick Thistle home game, a typical piece of eccentricity from the Jags, which illustrates their individuality, much like this chant:

*Hullo, hullo, how do you do*
*We hate the boys in royal blue*
*We hate the boys in emerald green*
*So fuck the pope*
*And fuck the queen*

It used to be 'Firhill for Thrills'. This was the legend on a sign on the high wall below the old terracing, and the League Cup – won in 1971 after a viddy-printer-melting 4–1 triumph over Celtic – glinted under the trophy-room strip-lighting as thrilling confirmation that wee teams could have their day in the sun, even daft wee teams like the Sizzle.

But Partick have slipped down a league and are in danger of slipping further. How many of the luvvies have stuck with them, I wonder, and especially on this dull-bone-ache-cold afternoon?

Because of their proximity to BBC Scotland's HQ, Thistle used to attract a lot of West-Endy trendies who delighted in telling any fool who would listen, in a camp Glesca accent: 'No, I simply cannae be doing with the Old Firm and their bitchiness and spite. I cheer for the Harold Wraggs.'

But Thistle to them, I bet, were just like a rubber satchel or a pair of clear-framed specs – in other words, a fashion statement, a faddish concern. As the team disappeared from the top-flight, these prats will have moved on to book clubs or pilates or some such frappucino frippery, leaving only diehards like my friend Richard's dad, who's recovering from illness but will be here today in spirit.

I wish I was only here in spirit. The wind is biting, the rain is horizontal. The faraway terracing is shut-off and ghoulish. But the commissionaire is still brass-button smart at the front door, the club shop is still advertising cup-triumph videos from '71 . . . and, bang on cue, here comes 'Sylvia'. This may no longer be Firhill for Thrills but it's still Firhill for Thijs.

It's the Scottish Cup 3rd round, a day of hopes and dreams and crazy schemes for many clubs, but the other certainty apart from 'Sylvia' is that in this competition Hibs will fail. Maybe not today –

they're at home to Dundee – but sometime before May when the old trophy is garlanded with ribbons on the Hampden steps. It's written in the wind.

Hibs have not won the cup since 1902. Think about this for a moment: *1902.* Buffalo Bill was still alive, the Boer War was still raging, the first manned flight by Wilbur and Orville Wright was a year off and Albert Einstein's Theory of Relativity was three away from publication. One hundred and three years of pain in the Scottish Cup can make a Hibby feel a bit like John Hurt in *The Elephant Man* as he rages against a cruel world laughing at his hideous misfortune. 'I . . . am . . . a human being!' cries the appropriately-named Hurt. Well, I . . . am . . . (still, just, more or less) . . . a Hibs fan.

The cup roll-of-honour for this century and a bit has a gruesomely deformed look: triumphs for East Fife, Falkirk, Morton and even the long-defunct Third Lanark, but none at all for Hibs. It's a pathetic record: defeats snatched from the jaws of victory, glorious failures. There has also been woeful underachievement, cringesome embarrassment, and crushing ignominy at the hands of teams from towns that don't even have a Tesco – plus the odd tanking from Celtic. And that's simply the story of my three-and-a-half decades as a sufferer.

I should have known from the start – having arrived on the planet just in time for the 1958 final – that my life would not work out as planned. Much-fancied then, Hibs lost to Clyde, who've become even more peripheral to Glasgow's football culture than Partick Thistle since moving to the new town of Cumbernauld.

I plot the map of Scotland by Hibs' cup graveyards. The East Coast Main Line is a 'black tourism' heritage trail of hopeful travelling turning to horror, and I have seen us crash out of the competition at almost every stop (in Dundee, three times). You dream of great goals, gleaming silverware and victory parades in wheezy, open-topped buses. Then you wake up and smell the Bovril.

In 1978, the ritual task of obliterating our patently ludicrous cup fantasies fell to Arbroath. The ticket for the tie – no, 'Grand

Football Match' – at gale-lashed Gayfield cost 30p, and for some perverse reason I've kept the stub along with the programme. Hibs managed to hold the mighty Red Lichties to a draw before succumbing to the inevitable at Easter Road.

From boy to man, of course, I watched Hibs with Faither, who frequently had to reassure his eldest son that, yes, life could be cruel and football vicious, but the Hibees would win the infernal thing one day. Because children think of their fathers as big, strong, capable of retrieving balls from trees without using a ladder and most importantly all-knowing, I believed him.

It's said that you don't truly understand cup failure until you've been beaten at Kilbowie Park. Who said that? Me and my dad, after witnessing Hibs' 1988 wimp-out at the hotch-potch of huts which used to serve as Clydebank's home, where even winning a game was a thoroughly depressing experience.

Ah, but that's Hibs. Forget about them, they're never going to win the cup. Hearts, meanwhile, did it in 1998, and the triumph is still fresh in the minds of Billy, Ricky, David and a couple more fellow-travellers, Grant and Dougie, when we meet for a pint before the tie in the Iron Horse in Glasgow's city centre.

'It was four in the morning when I got home from celebrating,' says Ricky. 'My mum had made a replica of the cup out of Bacofoil for me and stuck it on my bedroom wall. I pulled the downie off my bed and slept in my Hearts flag that night, then I took the week off work and went on the sauce.'

A cup win gives you credibility, this much is clear. You can dine out on it for ages, longer than in the past because triumphs outwith the Old Firm are more rare now. I'm definitely the odd one out and feel like I'm missing a leg or half my head.

We take our places in the old Firhill stand. It's got a wooden floor caked in pigeon shite and leg-space is at a premium (the structure clearly dates from a time when the average male height in Scotland was 5ft 2ins, with rickets and a humpy back . . . fact: I never knew what a poultice was until Paw Broon required one in the *Sunday Post*, the same day I discovered what lumbago was).

I look around me and, despite Hearts' recent poor form, there's confidence in the air, some of it bordering on arrogance. This is the cup, Hearts have won it recently, so chests are puffed right out. Billy and Ricky are even sporting new footwear for the occasion – futuristic Prada trainers designed for the moving walkways of the space-age that, like food in pill form, never arrived. 'Harvey Nicks,' confirms Ricky.

They're smug gits, for sure, although I could talk to them all day about their cup memories, and as the rain batters down it seems like an excellent idea to reconvene in the boozer, but it's game-on this afternoon after a ref's inspection.

OK, it was always going to be tough for the match to better another rendition of 'Sylvia', but this one doesn't even try. It's hideous. Hearts are playing like poultices. They're playing *sideways*. Robbo has been urging his team to express themselves as foot-ballers, as *individuals*, but as long as Patrick Kisnorbo is thudding around in the middle of the park – and especially when he's joined there by Neil MacFarlane; Kookaburra and Socrates, what a pair of numpties – then these remain Craig Levein's Hearts.

Dr Ruth's predecessor liked to crack the whip. He was into domination. By the time he quit Tynie, his players would probably have licked toilet bowls for him. They were slaves in a weird, perverted version of football, programmed to give their master dull satisfaction. Under him, the sum of Hearts was greater than the parts and that sum was a group-sex version of football, a Gorgie orgy.

Levein's slaves were like robots but Dr Ruth is trying to squeeze a different chip into the slots in the back of their heads, and as a result, they're going a bit haywire. Now I love robots, grew up with them, beginning with Robert the Robot in *Fireball XL5*, but much as I appreciated Robert's unflustered efficiency on the XL5 flight-deck, I'd never have handed him a central midfield berth. Kookaburra's brain has shorted and smoke is spewing from his ears: 'P-l-a-y f-o-o-t-b-a-l-l? D-o-e-s n-o-t c-o-m-p-u-t-e! Phzzzzz!'

Students have their own discounted turnstile at Firhill, in an attempt to lure those in the uni flats close to the south stand out of their scratchers in time for kick-off. The sensible ones today will have yanked the duvet further over their heads, safe in the knowledge that they wouldn't be disturbed by noise from the crowd. One Jambo in front of us gets up out of his seat to complain about the total and absolute lack of thrills. Ah, I remember him from Kilmarnock. 'Fuckin' boo! Fuckin' boo!' But he's a lone voice; a game *The Observer* will rate as 'abysmal' leaves the rest of us too stupefied to make a protest. Hibs win their 3rd round tie 2–0 and are acclaimed by *Scotland On Sunday* as 'mesmerising'. For them, another great cup adventure is under way. Without me.

This has easily been the worst game of the season. If Thistle were just a wee bit less honking themselves, they would have dumped Hearts out of the competition. In a further demonstration of the Sizzle's singularity of purpose, they field a giant striker from France called Armand *One*, but such incidental pleasures are thin on the ground and long before the end we're screaming to get out of Firhill. One Jambo has endured the raw day in just a T-shirt – one with a special message: 'Century's up with no Scottish Cup – never be a Hibee' – and I hope for his sake it's been worth the risk of pneumonia.

We return to the city centre and find a pub where we can kill time before the next train. It's a converted bank on George Square full of shoppers laden with outrageous Glesca fashions and we're talking about football in other countries, the expectations of it, and wondering whether there's a phrase in Brazil for 'He put in a good shift', and deciding there can't be . . . when the mood of the place darkens. I've never seen a pub taken over by a gang of Casuals before and this lot swarm around like locusts . . . locusts in overpriced, over-labelled sportswear, Stone Island and the like. They're a Hearts mob, about 20 in number, some are on mobile phones, all of them throwing darting looks in different directions. I know I'm not the bravest but they've got me terrified without even doing anything. Ricky recognises a couple of them and is quick to take stock of the situation. Remembering Billy's hassles with the Casual fraternity because he follows Scotland – and never mind my presence – Ricky bundles us out the door. I feel pretty sure he could have sorted out all 20 by himself; nevertheless I'm relieved.

Part of me wants to go back and challenge the Burberry-ed buffoons for giving Billy a hard time for being in the Tartan Army. The Casuals presumably think this is counter to Hearts as they understand the club; they're morons. But I have to say it's a very small part of me that wants to do this. It's the part that at one time yearned for a little Action Man scar, to signify that I hadn't lived such a sheltered life. Ricky must see straight through my hud-me-back (*please*-hud-me-back) bravado. But he's decent enough not to mention it.

On the train back to Edinburgh, Ricky tells me about a work colleague who's been quizzing him over the book. 'He said to me: "I hope you're going to batter him." ' I told him: "Aidan's an alright guy, beat it." ' I don't say anything for a bit. Are Ricky and Billy compromising themselves for me? I have no idea how these guys behave normally at matches, but is my presence inhibiting them? By not slagging off Hibs, like everyone else around them, are they risking getting themselves into trouble? But just when I think they might, perfectly understandably, draw away from me, the opposite happens.

We pile off the train, the brush with the Casuals a distant memory and now something to chuckle about, and head for the Haymarket Bar where we stay until closing-time. I wish I could remember what we talked about, but we got really pissed.

It's a safe bet that girls and music were involved. In fact, something's coming back to me about unlikely lust objects and I think I surprised the guys with my choice of Ellen McArthur, pixie-featured princess of the oceans, and I guess the nomination must have something to do with a respect for the seas bordering on pathological terror.

On the subject of conventional beauties, Ricky and I would have to fight over the honour of our shared No 1 . . . if only we could remember her name. The black supermodel who's not Naomi Campbell.

*Fight Ricky*. I don't think I'd like that very much. I've never been in a fight before; he has. He moves his nose from side to side as if it was made of Play-Doh. 'Been broke a few times,' he says. There also appears to be something wrong with his right hand – the pinkie shoots off at a funny angle, so he can't form a proper fist – although it's probably safe to assume this hasn't always been a problem.

Some more Ricky facts: his paper of choice is the *Daily Star*. He drinks only Becks. The black supermodel apart, he prefers blondes. He's one of Giorgio Armani's best customers. Food-wise, he doesn't like 'any of that fancy shite' and puts chilli on everything else. He thinks the current trend for the male satchel is '. . . as gay as . . .' He has definite views, some of them as we know are fairly extreme, but they're his own views; no-one tells him what to think or say or do. He used to be wild, having been arrested a total of seven times. Once he was questioned about a murder. But he hasn't hit anyone for four years.

But if there's one thing this hard man really hates, it's phoney, pseudo, ring-the-doorbell-and-run-away hardness. For instance, before games at Tynecastle, Billy drinks in a pub called the Fountain, which he nicknames 'Vietnam' and Ricky sneers at this because the bar is 'no' hard at all'. He snorts at fans who do the carpet-fitter's walk – arms by sides and curved, as if carrying rolls of General George – because they're 'no' hard at all'. Then there's me. He doesn't have to say it. *No' hard at all.*

Billy is such a meek and mild guy, insisting he must get home soon because he's got a big washing to do tomorrow, but there was a time when he hung about with some right bad yins. This was the 1970s of street-gangs. At the Ferencvaros game with him, minutes after we'd been talking about the gangs, Billy spotted the (presumably) former leader of the Young Mental Drylaw, proving once again that Edinburgh is a wee place, and that 30 years can be the blink of an eye.

'Fitba chants were crap in your day, yeah?' says Ricky (he's 18 years younger than Billy and I). We harrumph at this impudence before Billy informs Ricky that he's probably sung a few of 'our' chants without realising it. 'Where do you think the "Oh, Mikey, Mikey . . ." one about Mike Galloway came from? It used to be sung about Alan Anderson.'

'And Ernie Winchester,' I add, 'and the pop classic that inspired it was "Son Of My Father" by Chicory Tip.'

'Who the fuck were *they*?' says Ricky.

'Glam-rock frauds, so you would have hated them.'

And that was how it happened. That was how the first entirely electronic hit, written by the great Giorgio Moroder, performed by a bunch of brickies in drag, and which was first bastardised into a terrace-song about a redoubtable Hearts centre-half, then a barn-door-bypassing Hearts centre-forward, then a ging-er Hearts utility man – we didn't need *them* in the 1970s – glued the friendship between the three of us, long after the worst match any of us could remember had been forgotten.

Somehow, though, I don't think Ricky would approve of the term 'male bonding'.


**11 January**
Hearts aren't going anywhere. The universally-loathed plan to sell Tynecastle and move to Murrayfield is scrapped. 'I am delighted that the Hearts shareholders have voted so decisively to support the plan to keep the club at Tynecastle,' says Vladimir Romanov. 'It is after all where we *vide*.'

OK, he might have said 'bide', as in the old club song. Either way, Jambos who wore Russian-style hats to mark the announcement – 'a day of drama,' according to *The Scotsman*, 'that matched anything the old ground had seen in its 119-year history' – probably rated the declaration on a par with John F. Kennedy's: 'Ich bin ein Hibby.'


**15 January. Hearts 3, Dundee United 2**
Suffering from a potentially fatal sniffle, I fail a late fitness test. But I tune into *Sportsound* from my sickbed and . . . bloody typical. Then

I get this text from Ricky: 'One of more boring five-goal thrillers. PS, remembered the supermodel's name . . . Tyra Banks.'

**19 January. Hearts 2, Partick Thistle 1**

Ah, the romance of the Cup. A home replay, at night under lights, a flurry of snow as we hurry towards the ground, and the opportunity for football to fleece its most loyal fans, asking the season-ticket holders to rebuy their seats.

Ricky and Billy have seasons, although not in the same parts of the ground, and I had hoped we might watch a home game together for the first time, but Billy is sick so Ricky takes me to the old main stand. While this is my first match in it this season, and the first for a few years, I'm no stranger to the corrugated-roofed construction. It was from here that I watched my first Tynecastle games with Faither, including Hibs' 7–0 annihilation of Hearts on New Year's Day, 1973, when – this was pre-segregation – every Hibby goal was greeted by a growl of 'Fuckin' IRA bastards' by the cigar-chomping man sitting next to me in a best coat of the most luxuriant camel-hair.

With Tynie saved – I'm loving the place tonight, and happy to use its nickname – it is right and proper that we are in this stand tonight because although it will almost certainly be knocked down and re-built as part of the decision to stay put, it is the one with all the history, and the ghosts.

It's a Leitch; that is, it was designed by the great stadium architect Archibald Leitch. It bears less of his imprint than others, such as Goodison, Craven Cottage and Ibrox. At the time of construction – 1914 – Leitch was being commissioned by three other clubs and, as the pre-eminent stadium-spotter Simon Inglis says in his biography *Engineering Archie*, he may have taken his eye off the ball at Tynie, not least because of the outbreak of war. A plaque listing the directors at the time of its completion does not include his name.

But here it sits, just, and still exemplifying Jambo personality. As Inglis writes: 'Every club derives much of its identity from the character of its ground, Hearts more than most. Tynecastle's neighbourhood setting, its maroon detailing, the intimacy of its approaches – the club offices are, for instance, located in a Victorian police station – even the sickly odours from the nearby distillery, make it unique.'

Since Inglis completed his book, the Fountain Brewery has closed. The pong it produced ensured that no other ground in Scotland *smelled* like Tynie. Now the old place has to survive just on looks and location; this it does effortlessly.

We climb the stairs, pass the sign warning: 'Causing a nuisance will result in ejection from the ground(s)', and almost inevitably, when we find our seats, one of the goalmouths is obscured by a pillar. This seems apt as well. The seats are cramped, but snug. This is the original, ancient, never-say-die-or-hud-oan-not-yet home of HMFC, and it feels good to be here.

Some things will never change, and Steven Pressley is still falling down all over the shop, and at the slightest provocation, too. Norman Wisdom made an entire career out of tripping over his own feet and he seems to have been a role-model for the Hearts captain, the Sacred Cow of Gorgie.

Ricky is a big Elvis fan, and I thought I might be offending him by mentioning the great man's free-kick-winning masterclasses, but he's picked up on my oblique references to them and concedes the captain does go down easily, although he insists that his hero has 'earned the right'. So we've developed this little smirking routine when the big tumshie hits the turf. The acknowledgement 'Elvis is down again' is in danger of becoming as over-used as 'Elvis has left the building'.

Ricky used to have a season ticket for the Wheatfield Stand, but the cost was getting too steep for his friend Peter so they moved across the park with Peter's son Lewis. The Wheatfield replaced the old shed where Ricky started watching his football. He'd stand up the back and by the final whistle, after all the surges, the 'Get intae thum! We're over here!' calls-and-responses, find himself right down the front. Fantastic fun.

He gives me the lowdown on a player I've not yet seen in action, Steven Simmons. He's not enamoured. 'Simmons thinks he's hard, he'll stick his foot in, but then he'll run away,' he says. 'I *hate* players who do that. You've got tae stand and take it.'

We talk about the job-lot of East Europeans – Lithuanians from Kaunas and Belarussians from Minsk MTZ-RIPO, teams sponsored by Romanov – who are currently trying to impress Calimero and win contracts. Ricky thinks it would be bad if players from abroad without a proper feeling for Hearts became the dominant force in the dressing-room.

Hearts' experience with foreign players is similar to other Scottish clubs. They've had good ones and bad ones. For every Stephane Adam there's been a Gordan Petric. The two most recent cash injections into Tynie – the involvement of the Scottish Media Group and Hearts' share of the Sky TV money when the network thought oor fitba was worth screening – helped build stands the club were prepared to rip down, but little else of permanence.

Tonight Dennis Wyness avoids asserting himself in any way. He's not causing a nuisance, as the Thistle defence will confirm, and so tech-nically cannot be ejected from the ground(s). But his diffidence is in marked contrast to the stadium, which is forcefully re-establishing its place in Edinburgh life and culture through this tense cup-tie.

Thistle take a shock early lead, Hearts bundle in an equaliser and extra-time seems to be looming when with two minutes left Shyness suddenly finds himself on the end of a cross he never expected would reach him. He's only five yards out, the Partick defender who gifted him the chance is sprawled on the ground . . . Shyness takes an age to get the ball down, to tame the wild, bucking leather sphere . . . *come on, Dennis!* . . . goal.

The cup dream lives on. I tell Ricky that it's a foregone conclusion we'll meet Hibs in the quarter-finals and what a stormer that's going to be. He smiles. 'That's the third game running you've called us "we".'

## 22 January. Dundee 1, Hearts 1

Before this game I'm in the health club, in the jacuzzi. This is what men do now, Faither – oh how the life of the football fan has changed since we went to games together. But football is still the universal language. Two complete strangers – Scots as well – can share a whirlpool together and, within minutes, will be blethering away like they've been leaning against the same terrace stanchion for years.

Gordon supports Hearts. 'Me too,' I say. (Thinks: can I pull off an entire conversation as a jacuzzi-ed Jambo?). 'So what's your take on the Lithuanians?'

'Three months ago I thought that if Romanov came, and Levein left, but we stayed at Tynie, that would be the price we would have to pay for keeping our home,' says Gordon. 'Now, I'm not so sure. Robbo's not as tactically astute as Levein, and I'm thinking about what we've lost. Robbo's too hot-headed, he's always picking fights with refs. I've got some sympathy for him; it can't be easy having a bunch of Lithuanians foisted on you. But Levein was cleverer; he was *premeditated*. So anyway, you're going to Dundee, are you? Give them a cheer for me.'

I truly lead a double life now. Sushi for lunch with my meeja mates through the week; pies with the Jambos on Saturdays. I look at my reflection in the changing-room mirror; I'm putting on weight. *Super Pies-me.*

Dundee, for the football fan, is the spiritual home of the pie, or as the locals prefer it, *peh*. Dens Park, for the Hibby, is special, too: this was where Hearts lost the league in incredible circumstances in 1986.

My pal Jim from school, the Subbuteo rival who's now a rozzer, was so convinced Hearts were going to win that day that he bought a load of champagne for what should have been the triumphant return to Edinburgh. 'It's still in the garage – I see the boxes every day,' he says. 'I can't touch it and think maybe I should just chuck it out. That was my worst-ever year. First I got a vasectomy, then my dad died and then *that*. Losing the league in the final seven minutes; the ultimate kick in the balls.'

I want to ask Billy and Ricky about their memories of that fateful day. But they almost certainly still carry the emotional scars, so I will have to choose my moment carefully, especially with Billy. He tells us that he didn't make the Thistle game because his doctor had just strapped him up with a 24-hour self-monitoring device to check on his high blood pressure. He was worried the ploddings of Socrates and Co would send him shooting off the dial.

He's fit to drive today, however, and on the road and the miles to Dundee, we talk about music. 'Who are you intae?' says Ricky.

'Well, Roxy Music's *For Your Pleasure* is my favourite album of all time because it was the first, proper, serious one I bought, but these days I like hip hop.'

'None of that shite will last – nothin' current will,' he says. He likes The Drifters and Frankie Valli and the Four Seasons. He loves the Beach Boys. And he absolutely adores Elvis, the King. Favourite Elvis song? 'Maybe *Always On My Mind*. To be honest, I prefer his love songs, but dinnae tell my girlfriend that.'

His taste crashes into the 1970s only for soft rock – which I don't think was so termed back then – and the likes of Rick Springfield, the Eagles, Chicago. 'Were Blue Oyster Cult 1970s? *(Don't Fear) The Reaper* is *quality*.'

First I'm thinking, Ricky beats Billy and I on sports questions, but 1970s music is something he's going to have to consult us about. Next I'm thinking: is *(Don't Fear) The Reaper* the choon that's piped over the PA of Ricky and Billy's insurance house, in an effort to up pensions productivity? ('Come on, Mrs McSnafferty, you've no need to wet your pantaloons over hooded strangers turning up at your front door without ID and wielding scythes if you sign up for one of *our* policies . . .').

Then Ricky, the skinhead with the bashed nose and the bust hand and the life ban from the nightclub across from the office where he now puts in an honest day's graft . . . who says there's no feeling like the 'pure, mad, mental' adrenalin rush you get from being in a fight . . . reveals he's a massive Abba fan. 'Have you seen *Mamma Mia*? *Quality*. I've been three times.'

We reach the Tay, silvery in the winter sunshine, in good time and climb up through Dundee to grab Billy's carefully-researched prime getaway parking place . . . then the Cautious Managed Jambo Soft-Rock Boys pile into the Clep, an old-fashioned boozer which honours the city's famous footballing sons in faded monochrome, including Alan Gilzean, Ian Ure, Ron Yates but outrageously not Charlie Cooke. It's busy with Hearts fans and a couple of them look at me twice. But I'm thinking: I'm going to the game on a baltic afternoon, not like the guy in my health club, so you can't jacuzzi me of anything. I'm with two good Hearts fans and they don't seem to mind me being here.

We've got our running gags now. Even our non-running ones. Since Billy casually mentioned he was a not bad sprinter in his youth, this typically small boast has, er, grown legs. If he breaks into the merest suggestion of a slow jog to catch us up after yet another visit to a sweetshop, Ricky will go: 'Look at that pace!' Billy is Billy Whizz.

Then there's Steven Pressley, who is of course a falling-down gag: he could be Elvis, the King of *Roll*. And Ricky is especially fond of the joke that is the Old Firm-dominated tabloids' over-hyping young Celtic and Rangers players. Other clubs have no choice now but to rear young, local talent, but whenever a promising teenager emerges at Parkhead and Ibrox, which isn't as often as you might think, he's viewed as a daring alternative solution; as someone who holds the key to the meaning of football. The list of those who've followed Simon Donnelly to football's equivalent of the end-of-the-pier is a long one.

'Aye, but you wait and see,' says Ricky, 'Aiden McGeady will still win Young Player of the Year over Derek Rear-end.'

Lee Miller has a Deek Riordaninho haircut. He's Hearts' new on-loan striker from Bristol City. And Jamie McAllister – Dine-Out – has just gone blond. Maybe Hibs are influencing Hearts on the park in the same way that Jambos seem to be influencing Hibbys in the stands, well this one at any rate.

What is happening to me? I used to be a rap-loving Hibby who lived for today and didn't worry about tomorrow. Now I'm hanging out with pension-workers who support the hated Jambos and, music-wise, like it mellow, with lots of gloopy guitar from leathery-skinned LA sessionmen.

But here's the thing: I have supposedly groovier friends than Billy and Ricky but they're no longer interested in football and music and all they talk about are pensions, savings policies and what they're going to do when they retire. Billy and Ricky might sell pensions for a living but their conversation is dominated by the great twin passions.

On the walk to Dens, Billy is intrigued by music all right; for the past couple of hours he's been trying to remember the name of a song, his favourite song. 'I dunno what it's called. I think it's . . . uh.' New or old? 'Oh, it's old, definitely old.' Sung by a male or female? 'Male . . . I *think*.'

Ricky: 'You *think*? Can you no tell the difference between a bloke an' a lassie?'

Hang on, I say, it wasn't that easy, 30 years ago. I thought the Alessi duo of *Oh Lori* fame were two girls until – confession-time – I bought their debut album. 'Check out the cover,' I tell Ricky, 'then tell me it's not where Paul Hartley got the inspiration for his feathercut.'

It's £20 to get in to Dens, which is pretty steep for away games outwith the Old Firm. I'm spending a lot of money on football right now. As a member of the socio-economic grouping, 'Fifty-Quid Blokes', I have little left over for music. (Tragically, there are no real bargains in life anymore, not since cheapo LPs like Amon Duul II's *Live In London*, £1.49 at 1970s prices; Pink Floyd's *Relics*, 99p and Faust's *The Faust Tapes*, an incredible, unrepeatable 49p).

I'm spending a lot on *pehs*, though. The Dens ones are two quid each and, given the city's reputation in this arena, they turn out to be anti-climactic. Ricky has the same attitude to pies as he does music – old-skool is best – and says that when Chris Robinson's catering empire moved into Tynie, the quality dropped. 'The ones before were greeny-yellow, lots of grease on top, like pies *should* be.'

You need something else to talk about when the football is rank, some other big interest sitting on the subs' bench for those moments when an attempted cross from Dine-Out or Robbie Neilson – Lumberjack – fails to clear the first man. I could prattle about stadium architecture – Dens is another Archibald Leitch design – but I don't think the lads share my fascination for its angled main stand and shallow-raked enclosure. 'Thought you'd like it,' is Ricky's only comment.

If we didn't have a counter-attraction for those dire times, then surely Billy would be nervously glancing at his blood pressure reading and Ricky would be scrutinising the small print of his pension. And this game *is* a shocker. The *Edinburgh Evening News* will report: 'The Jambos yet again failed to create any meaningful openings.' They leave it late – a recurring theme – but this time can only salvage a draw, and I glance across at Billy, to make sure he's OK.

The lingo of any team's travelling support is always a bit more ribald than you hear at their own grounds. At Dens, the 'Oh the Hibees are gay' chant is trotted out many times, but on this afternoon it's accompanied by a shout of 'Elton John, Elton John', the tantrums 'n' tiaras pop legend having just announced he's bound for Easter Road for a summer concert.

'That was Sinky,' says Billy, identifying the author of the new version. 'An absolute legend,' confirms Ricky. 'He arrives at games late because he's been in boozer, falls asleep at the pie stand, leaves before end to get back to the pub, and usually gets chucked off the bus home.' Then I see him: he's a short-arse in a completely unprepossessing woolly hat.

In the black-and-white world of the Jambos, it seems that you're pink merely if you dye your hair. Lee Miller, for instance, looks like a 'fuckin' stupid Hibby poofter' according to Geoff, who works in the same office as Billy and Ricky and has just joined us in the away end. Miller will be nicknamed Lee Hibby, then.

We pick up the general theme. Ricky is a big fan of organised crime, old-time gang lords, their hitmen, and the fiendish contraptions they used to electrocute rivals through their testicles. He says he used to like the Krays until he found out about 'the gay vibe'. Then we're talking about movies while Dine-Out fuds around with the ball in the corner and Ricky says that the previous night he saw *Alexander*, the swords 'n' sandals epic. 'No' bad,' is his considered verdict, 'and no' too much homosexuality in it.'

Billy mentions a bar in Thailand where you can receive a blowjob without knowing the sex of the fellatrix and the big man turns white. 'No way! *No way!*' roars Ricky. 'If you found out it was a bloke you'd have to kill him. And then you'd have to kill yourself.'

Possibly this little group of ours is on safer ground when discussing football, and only football.

On the journey home, Graeme Souness is 'At-the-end-of-the-daying' and 'To-be-fairing' on Five Live and Ricky says how much he admired the Newcastle United manager when he was captain of Scotland.

'A tragedy he didn't play in the 1978 World Cup until it was too late,' I say. And I tell Ricky, who was too young for that tournament, how the BBC signed off its coverage with 'Don't Cry For Me Argentina' and a camera-pan along the Scottish squad which stopped at Souness when Julie Covington reached the line: 'The answer was there all the time . . .'

Only Souness could get away with a Randy-From-Village-People mouser, I say. But it was still brave of him to flaunt it, given the clunky nature of the average footballer's 'gaydar'. Almost certainly the most personally groomed Scot of his generation, thanks to his spell in Italy, Souness's room-mate on away trips, Kenny Dalglish, was convinced he was homosexual purely on the evidence offered up by his hairdryer: it had three heat-settings.

'The first World Cup I watched was 1982 in Spain,' says Ricky, 'when Souness scored that last-minute equaliser against Russia.'

'Then stripped to the waist for the post-match interview?'

'Aye,' says Ricky, with what can only be described as a manly purr. 'You're talkin' about the first footballer to properly understand the concept of the six-pack.'

### 25 January. Livingston 1, Hearts 2

Terry Waite was blindfolded and chained to a radiator in Beirut for five years. David Blane starved in a glass box suspended over the Tower of London for 44 days. Me, I'm making my second trip to Livingston in a month, as a surrogate scarf-twirler.

This will sort out the Jambomen from the Jamboboys: the game that never was, finally played in the town that isn't one, in January, on a Tuesday night, when all the back pages are being hogged by Hibs and in particular their Drylaw goal fiend Deek Riordaninho.

The *Sun* today has no less than four stories on the boy – calling him 'Del' when of course it's 'Deek' – and the clamour to have him picked for Scotland, so he can swap the Leith San Siro for some park in Milan with a similar-sounding name, is growing by the day.

I feel sorry for Jambos, trudging through to West Lothian to watch their struggling team in such toytown surroundings as Almondvale, while their capital rivals bask in the glory of third place and all this sexy-football drooling. I certainly have sympathy for Billy and Ricky, who if they were making this journey without me, would surely be slagging off Hibs, good-style.

So, feeling bad about inhibiting them, I do the job myself. 'Don't you think the coverage Riordan's been getting is a bit excessive?' No response. 'Yeah,' I say, 'and if he goes all the way to the top he'll have to get some serious dental work otherwise he's not going to achieve the ultimate approbation for any player these days – a sportswear modelling contract in the Far East.'

'Aye,' says Ricky finally, 'remember that twat at Real Madrid who said they weren't going to buy Ronaldinho because he was too ugly?'

OK, so the buck-toothed Brazilian does look like one of the Sea-Devils from *Doctor Who*, but Barcelona are romping La Liga so

Real's rejection of him is right up there with Decca Records reckoning The Beatles couldn't sing for toffee.

Toffee? Deek must like it. Riordaninho might be in the running for a full Scotland debut against Italy, but we spend a few minutes on a mercifully mild night speculating on the kind of hard centres that did for his gnashers.

Ricky tells me he has always been a stats freak, for all kinds of sport, not just Jambo-style football. 'Aged nine, my mum and dad would line up a team of 12 uncles and older cousins against me for *A Question Of Sport* and I'd destroy the lot of them.' Ricky likes all sports. Well, apart from rugby. He has a favourite American football team, a favourite in everything. In skiing competitions he supports Austria. He thought about a career in sports-writing, before the lure of pensions became irresistible.

Billy is quiet. The journey is short but tricky, even for The Human Map, and he's got to concentrate to get us through all 742 round-abouts. He's either wondering how he'd fare in *A Question Of Sweets*, a choc-nostalgia quiz face-off against Deek Riordaninho . . . or he's *still* trying to remember the name of his favourite song, a searing personal inquiry he began back in Dundee.

Talk of tuck makes Billy hungry and he decides to beat the queue for the half-time pie run by a full 45 minutes while Ricky and I search for our seats. We're done for £20 admission again, that's £55 I've forked out on games in just six days.

Almondvale is totty, a uniform 20-odd rows of yellow seats right the way round, and, hoping for a choice observation, I ask Ricky, a first-timer here, what he thinks of the place. 'It looks like it was built by Meccano Boy, with maybe the loan of just a small amount of kit from the lad next door,' he says. *Quality*.

It could be my rampant paranoia, but I reckon I'm getting more dead-eye stares with each passing match. And I'm right. 'That was Chris – mind the guy at my work I was telling you about,' says Ricky, as we plonk ourselves directly above a corner-flag. Chris is the unofficial local recruitment officer for the Masons, the one who wanted Ricky to hit me, on behalf of him. He smirks as he passes, sits down behind us, and I can feel his eyes on the back of my head.

Billy returns with two pies for himself, plus a packet of Starbust. Deek won't remember but Billy and I knew these as Opal Fruits. And Snickers as Marathon. And when Snickers was Marathon, it was so named because it was reckoned to be an aid to running one. This was when Mars was still the choc by which you could work, rest and play. Aztec Bars gave us a little bit of insight into the history of the Incas. And Zoom ice-lollys, produced during the Space Race, got us thinking about the infinite possibilities of the Solar System.

The finite possibilities for Hearts tonight as the rain starts to fall are three points from Richard Gough's basement boys. Livi, the Lions, are propping up the table, and after a 4–1 spanking at home to Inverness on Saturday, even their annoying drummers are muted. The Hearts fans, meanwhile, are in a foul mood and round on their players for each mistake. There are plenty. They're even booing the Keepy-Uppy King providing the half-time entertainment.

'Aye,' sneers Ricky, 'balancing the ball on the back of your neck when you're doin' press-ups is all very well, but can you actually *play* the game?'

The King finishes his routine with a donkey-kick over his head, volleys in the direction of the empty net from just ten yards out . . . and misses.

It sums up the match so far, and the Jambos resume showing no improvement. Jamie McAllister and Simmons – he needs a nickname – are both having stinkers. 'Get tae fuck yooz two!' roars Ricky.

Funny place, Livingston. This is a new town, but, according to an advertising hoarding, discos are discotheques here. And football doesn't fit in. The sights and sounds of a real football community are missing. There are no shops close to the ground, so you don't hear the shutters crashing as traders head for the hills on match-days. No boozers either – so no bored small boys kicking empty juice cans in the doorways waiting for their dads – and we had to be directed to the nearest faraway pub with this bizarre instruction: 'Turn right at the water-feature.'

Ricky tells me a bit more about Chris. 'He says the other day: "Come and join us, Ricky, the Muslims are scared of us!" I told him: "No thanks, I'd rather sign up with Combat 18. You're just a gang and all your mates are polismen."'

Then Livi score. In what seems like a last, desperate gamble, Dr Ruth chucks on two skinny kids. They make Deek look like Schwarzenegger. They're pale and frightened. But they scamper about and lift the crowd, who assume them to be the first of the intake of Lithuanians.

Some Jambos leave but Paul Hartley hits a cracking free-kick which some would lazily call Beckhamesque, but not me: the Painted Fool does not have the monopoly on them. And a minute later Lee Miller directs that Hibby haircut at the ball to head an unlikely winner. It's another last-gasp salvage job from Hearts and I'm about to ask Billy how he's coping with his blood pressure, but he's biting the heads off Jelly Babies.

A temporary reprieve for the beleaguered, Jambos, and that's the cue for a singsong. 'Tony Mowbray's got a fuckin' monkey's heid.' 'If you hate the fuckin' Hibees . . .' 'Stand up if you hate Hibees . . .' They're all sung with spitting venom by Chris, directed straight at me.

And there's no hiding place here. I'm not standing, or singing, and neither are Billy or Ricky on either side of me. We're the only three staying put and remaining silent. But, with the most loyal Hearts fan on my left, and one of the most indomitable on my right, I feel more or less safe.

Sometimes I've wondered what meeting other Jambos would be like. Sometimes I've actively thought of finding some. But every time, I've reckoned I would be letting down Billy and Ricky, cheating on them.

Looking back, I probably started out using them. I probably exploited them. I am sure I thought I would get a maximum five anecdotes each, then move onto another bunch of poor suckers, rob them of a reminisce, pick at the sore of a prejudice, then onto the next lot.

But slowly and surely these two are becoming my friends. The chat between us always starts off gruff, gradually increasing in frequency to dour, but I'd hate it if we gabbed away like reality-show berks.

I am feeling part of the Jambo Village now. Proper Hearts fans I know have out-of-joint noses because I'm going to games and they're not. A few months ago, I would be at pains to stress that I went to Livingston because I had to. Now I go to Hearts games like this one because I want to. There's a masochistic, made-it-through-the-rain streak in all Scottish fans and I'm glad I was there tonight.

And Livi-ed to tell the tale.

# FEBRUARY

**1 February. Hearts 2, Motherwell 3**

'*Gardyloo!*' Such a quaint Edinburgh custom, the depositing of shite from tenemental windows onto the streets below, pausing only to holler this warning to the teeming populace. And, because Hibs fans have such a keen sense of history – we know everything about all other noteworthy events in 1902, the year of our last Scottish Cup – I guess that's why Hibbys living in Albion Road have chosen to re-enact the tradition tonight. I mean, it couldn't possibly have anything to do with all these Jambos streaming into the Famous Five Stand, could it?

Easter Road is the neutral venue for this semi-final in the CIS Cup and Hibs aren't going to win this one either, having been knocked out a couple of rounds ago. So Hearts have the run of the place. The West Stand, the East Stand, where the mentalest Hibbys hang out, and the Famous Five Stand . . . and to add insult to invasion, Jambos call this one the George, Anne, Dick, Julian and Timmy the Dog Stand, after Enid Blyton's quintessential quintet. It's too much for locals to take. Hence most of the houses being dark. Hence the Albion Bar being firmly shut for the night. Hence the big splash of . . . well, what was it?

I lived in a double-upper flat in one of the grandest thoroughfares of Edinburgh's New Town during my young football life, but I would have gladly swapped Great King Street for Albion Road and its proximity to Hibs. My brother and I shared a bedroom and yet it was still big enough to have a set of park swings bolted to the floor. Still big enough, despite the swings, for epic games of one-a-side football, Sean shooting against the wardrobe, me against the ornate Georgian dado. Three times the dado was reduced to dust and had to be re-plastered.

On the bedroom wall was a poster, given away with the *Sunday Times*, illustrating the tricks of the legends. The only one I can remember was the Franz Beckenbauer Relaxed Ankle, a technique for hitting a pass with the right amount of speed so that it eluded opposition players, but then slowed down sufficiently for a team-mate to collect. I remember this one simply because of Faither's typically percipient debunking: 'But every ball travels like that, fast then slow – it's called velocity!'

There was still enough space in the most decadent kids' bedroom in the whole of Edinburgh for Sean and I to stage action-theatre, usually on a war theme ripped off from our comic collection, usually *Commando* or *Victor* – a strip called Dusk-To-Dawn Vigil was a particular favourite – and Sean's Trackmaster go-kart was pressed into service as an armoured carrier.

Downstairs, there was a vast hall, excellent for games of long-bangers. And there was a room where the au pairs lived. Some kids are raised by wolves; I on the other hand was brought up by Carole from France, Herta from Austria, Agnes from Holland and the luminous Vittoria from Italy, who once managed to lose me in Goldberg's, the first department store in Edinburgh to boast an escalator, when I would have happily settled for losing my virginity.

But I would have even more cheerfully swapped all of this, the succession of ever-more exotic home-helps, the tutoring in the mythical powers of the Relaxed Ankle, everything, for a house with a view of Easter Road. What a Dusk-To-Dawn Vigil that would have been! And imagine Saturdays, not leaving your favourite chair all through the first half of *Grandstand*: *Football Focus*, Harry Carpenter's boxing round-up (eternally featuring horizontal heavy-weights Billy Walker, Brian London and Jack Bodell, 'the chicken farmer from Swadlincote,' as he was always described) . . . a bit of rugby league with Eddie Waring from somewhere muddy like 'unslet or 'Ulkingston Rovers . . . then at bang on 3 o'clock turning to the window to watch the game!

Apart from this stunning vista, I wanted to live in Albion Road because I guessed everyone else there was working-class and I wasn't. I remember a class debate in the school quad, and how my friends looked up their noses at me when I tried to suggest I was like them. 'Mum, are we working-class?' I asked in a state of mild panic as she tucked me in that night. 'No, we're middle-class,' came the reply. Nevertheless I posed at being working-class, or working-class as I viewed it, which was sexy and hard.

I wasn't very good at this. I thought shite was spelled '-ght'. My few graffiti escapades were carried out with an aerosol of artist-quality glittery gold paint nicked from my father's study, where he pretended to be Jackson Pollock. Mum wouldn't buy me a Crombie, so I had to make do with a ludicrously long, belted, Gestapo-ish greatcoat from C&A. I wanted to wear rubbish clothes and eat rubbish food and watch rubbish ITV; none of these things were permitted. *The Frost Report* was a satirical, (very) BBC show of the 1960s, in which there was a running gag where upper-class John Cleese looked down on middle-class Ronnie Barker who looked down on Ronnie Corbett at the bottom of the heap. I was Barker but I wanted to be Corbett, who I would learn later, was a Hearts fan. Ironic, really, since I'm now trying to emulate him in a different way.

I was truly rubbish at being a bovver-boy. From the affluent streets near my house I would flick half-formed gang-signs at rival youths on corporation buses, then when they got off to give chase, I'd run away. Pissed on one pint of lager and lime I rolled up at our youth-club disco and let it be known, through some girls, that I was extremely dischuffed by the presence of a hard-nut from the Young Mental Drylaw. But when a challenge to a square-go was messaged back, I slipped out the back entrance.

My friend Bob took the knife in the stomach that was meant for me, and all the swooning from the sexiest fourth-year girls that went with it.

I was all talk and Levi Sta-Prest trousers (at least Mum allowed me to have them). Really, I was Steven Simmons whooshed back to the 1970s and Ricky would have been ashamed of me.

Tonight I'm with Ricky, Billy, Colin, Peter and Don – a big crew – but they're self-conscious about their surroundings. They're not from these parts, and their anxiety is apparent the moment we meet up in the Windsor Buffet. A pint of lager is not always *just* a pint of lager. Not when it's pulled in a Hibs pub.

This one is sufficiently far from the stadium so as not to be draped in green-and-white memorabilia, like the Cabbage & Ribs – Hibs' cockney nickname, though why we need one is beyond me – but the guys are shuffling nervously in their Jambowear. Normally, I'm the interloper, the anxious one. I should be glad that tonight it's more of a level playing-field, or rather one that's sloping on both sides. Still, I wish they would relax.

Ah, but semi-finals are tense occasions. They're never great football matches, no-one remembers the losers, blah, blah. 'So how do you think we'll do?' I say. 'See?' says Billy, cracking the tension. 'He's saying "we" again!'

I ask them what they think about the resignation of Chris Robinson. This is news to them. 'I read it on Kickback,' I say. Don't they spend all day on the fansite, like me?

We head to the ground, me leading the way, them almost getting lost behind me, and I'm thinking: I know their patch, and not just from my time there this season – why don't they know mine?

The stadium is full, with the biggest Motherwell support I've seen in my life and Hearts fans squirming around everywhere else. 'Ah fuckin' hate this place – it's shite!' says one restless Gorgie native. A plastic pop-up seat is not always *just* a plastic pop-up seat.

Motherwell take the lead. Bizarrely it's a goal from a set-piece and fickle fingers of blame are being pointed at Steven Pressley. The old lion is looking more and more vulnerable yet still demands the right to start Hearts moves, launching high balls forward.

Lee Miller struggles to turn them into anything positive. 'Whit aboot the passing game, Hearts?' is the cry from the row behind. Whit indeed. 'Well are tight, tough and sparky and deserve their half-time lead.

Ricky's on the pie run. 'What do you think,' I say, 'best of the season?' 'Huh, suppose so.' They're a glum lot as they munch, though, so I tell them it will be OK in the second half when the Jambos are shooting down the metaphorical slope.

But Jamie McAllister – Dine-Out was a winner of this cup the previous season – hasn't been reading the script. He gives away a penalty and 'Well go into a seemingly unassailable 2–0 lead. For the second match running some fans head early for the exits despite there still being 20 minutes to go. Now normally I would be perfectly happy with this state of affairs. Hibs have won a mere two trophies in my fantime, Hearts one less. If Hibs cannot win this competition, then Hearts must go out, *now*.

But I was there on a deathless night in Dunfermline, I saw Hearts blunder through the previous round and forced down a steak bridie on their behalf . . . I've invested something in this team and want some reward. ' 'Mon the Hearts!' I bellow, apeing Billy's legendary battle-cry.

The other guys stir, the fans round about us join in our chant, and soon the whole stand is roaring for another famous Jambo fightback. There are five minutes left . . . Goal! Then Pressley takes a tumble and the free-kick produces the equaliser. Bloody hell, did I cause that to happen?

Part of me wants to qualify my exhortation: 'Only kidding!' But I'm already on my feet, cheering. Ricky is shouting himself hoarse. Billy has already lost his voice. The guy on my left won't stop hugging me. Yeah, fantastic, mate, now could you please put me down? 'We must win it now,' says Peter. Then . . . injury time . . . We'll get the winner, the Jambos snatch defeat from the jaws of victory in the cruellest of ways. As the actress said to the bishop, seconds after revealing that she was a he – what a way to lose a semi.

There's no point suggesting a post-mortem pint or four, this lot just want to get home, to a part of the city they know. There's not a crowd that scatters quicker than the one denied a cup final. For a few really unlucky Jambos, there's more Hibee Water Torture. The drookit victims peer up at blackened windows, cops shine their torches, but they aren't making much of a fuss. They just want to get the hell out of here.

In normal circumstances, once safely round a street corner, I would be grinning under my parka hood after a Jambo defeat like that. But not tonight.

## 2 February

My new best Jambo mates – and Billy and Ricky in particular – have been standing by me. Rather, they've *sat* by me during renditions of 'Stand up, if you hate Hibees' and all the rest and I owe them for that, big-time. I am trying to love their club, I really am, but know I should be doing more than simply turning up, paying my £20-odd quid, sitting impassively through an hour and a half of stramash-bang-wallop – ears permanently pricked for a *Sportsound* update about Hibs – then patronising my friends over a pint post-match about how Dr Ruth is at least *trying* to get Hearts to play more football, but he'll only succeed at this when he can truly call the team his own.

So what should I do, apart from venture inside the terror-pub Robertson's, I mean? Sing more Hearts songs? Well, I've never been much of a singer at Easter Road, and anyway my Jambo lot don't really join in the chants either. Charlie, a Hearts fan and an old friend from school who I bumped into at the Ferencvaros match, admits that of the Edinburgh clubs, Hibs have the better songs.

Should I wear more maroon? I don't wear colours to Hibs games and neither do Billy and Ricky and the gang. Strips are poor quality, over-priced and, cynically, they change with the wind. A five-year-old sweatshop urchin in Honduras could tell you right now that in season 2009–10, footballers will mostly be wearing tops based on the tent-dimensioned T-shirts of the 1980s popularised by Wham!. She starts work on her 10,000-a-day quota soon.

There is, however, one way I can empathise with Jambos right now and that is by sharing their concern over the fact Hearts' best player, Paul Hartley, has become a transfer target of Celtic. That's bad enough in itself, but what must be especially galling to the Tynecastle faithful is that Pauline is being sought as a remedy for a previous Martin O'Neill cock-up in the transfer market. If O'Neill had got it right with the Brazilian superflop, Juninho, he would not be going after Hartley mid-season.

The Old Firm want it every way. They buy up the available talent in the SPL, weakening the league, then complain it's un-competitive and that we're holding them back and demand to be allowed to move to a bigger set-up. They like buying from outwith Scotland, to show off to the rest of us that they can, and that their ultimate ambitions lie beyond these shores . . . but when the foreign goods prove faulty, they still demand the right to use the SPL as a handy corner-shop for replacements.

Really, Celtic and Rangers are like fat tourists who waddle home from trips abroad with sacred-temple relics and shrunken-head paperweights and giant furry toy donkeys, only to discover after they've unpacked that their souvenirs clash with the decor.

I write a column in *The Scotsman* demanding that the Old Firm be banned from using the SPL as a branch of Alldays and it gets pinned up on Kickback and praised by Jambos, such as Tamus Flogel: 'Well said, ya Hibby bastard.'


**3 February**
'It's Hearts Of Midlithuanian' is the headline in the *Daily Record*. The winds of change are gusting through Gorgie, according to the paper, and Vladimir Romanov – Vlad The Xpelair – is building a team to blow away the Old Firm.

Romanov buys out Chris Robinson to become the major shareholder with a total stake of just under 30 per cent and says that, short term, he wants to bring stability to the club and ensure the long-term future at Tynecastle. In four years, he vows, Hearts will be challenging Celtic and Rangers.

He's joined on board by two compatriots, and one of them, Liutaurus Varanavicius, who possesses the lank, curtained hairstyle favoured by young guitar bands, stresses that the Jambos are no short-term venture for Romanov. The challenge they're mounting to Celtic and Rangers is a real one. He says: 'It's like coming to a swamp. Once you leave football, you never go away.' Hmm, interesting choice of words . . .

## 4 February

Romanov, it emerges, used to sell bootleg Elvis Presley records from the back of a taxi in Kaunas in the early 1960s – a daring debut as an entrepreneur in the Communist Bloc. We dismiss the release of this scrap of personal info as Vlad's attempt to endear himself to major Elvis fan Ricky.

## 5 February. Hearts 2, Kilmarnock 2

Fourth-round day in the Scottish Cup and Hearts are playing Kilmarnock for the fourth time this season. Next week in the league, it's Hearts vs . . . Kilmarnock. Ho-bloody-hum. There's a lot of repetition in Scottish football, the same ugly faces re-appear with deadening regularity. *It's like coming to a swamp.* And here once again, rising out of the sludge, it will be Killie captain Gary Locke, with his team-mates following his sizeable arse onto a field this ex-Jambo knows so well.

Like wild animals in a zoo, lolloping around a cramped pen, tedious, unvaried behaviour is a psychologically-damaging feature of the SPL. The 12-team set-up is too small; the league should be expanded to 16, with clubs only playing each other twice a season. But that would mean a 50 per cent reduction in Old Firm games and Celtic and Rangers would never go for that. Their worldwide brands depend on these regular slug-outs, and all the hype and hatred they can possibly stoke up.

If Celtic and Rangers were animals what would they be? Not

sleek jaguars, that's for sure. Old Firm matches are more tyranno-saurus rex versus triceratops, two gnarled combatants desperate to shed the armour-like skin they believe is necessary for life in the SPL and evolve and grow in some other league, some other age. But for now they're trapped in Scotland for these ritualistic skirmishes, while the rest of us prop up the fight-bill and the food-chain.

Today, it's me, Ricky and his usual match-day pals, Peter and the latter's son Lewis. We meet in a new Jambo pub for me, the Ardmillan, which is a hotel and so permits straw-haired scamps like Lewis to sip coke in the corner and spin beermats at the fag-machine. 'So who's your favourite player, Lewis?' 'Miko,' he says without a moment's hesitation.

At eight years old, you're allowed to be callously here-at-kickoff, gone-by-halftime in your choice of heroes. At eight, I had yet to become a football fan. But Lewis is not alone in his admiration for Saulius Mikoliunas. Most of Gorgie is clamouring to hail the 20-year-old Lithuanian winger as the greatest thing since a co-operative pan loaf. And there's an extra urgency to the claims because across the city Hibs have been hogging all the headlines about superbrats and boy wonders.

Lewis's dad Peter drives a meat van and is very friendly, very interested in the book, and I also meet Ricky's mates Dave and Paul, two brothers, and their pal Gerry. Everyone is still depressed by the Motherwell defeat. 'To lose in the last minute of a semi-final, that was a sore one,' says Dave. 'And especially having to watch from green seats.' Paul reckons Hearts' slide this season has caused Jambos to modify their ambitions. 'Before, when we were doing well, and Hibs were rubbish, we didn't bother about them. Now I'm sorry to say we get more of a kick if they lose.'

Still, another cup quest resumes today. The SPL title pretty much belongs to the Old Firm, and how chilling it is to have to acknowledge that. But the 'Scottish' offers the rest of us a chance of glory, even though no club apart from Celtic and Rangers has won it since 1998 when some mob from Gorgie triumphed.

We head across to Tynie on a bright afternoon and there's time to grab a quick one in Robertson's, the doom-pub, but the sign outside says 'Village People Lookylikey Contest' so I give it a miss. Killie have brought more fans than if this had been the bread-and-dripping of the league but the size of the Hearts turnout is disappointing, the Motherwell hangover is a real thumper, and Hibs will attract a bigger crowd for their tie against Second Division Brechin City.

Hearts make a better start and score early through Dennis Wyness with assistance from Miko, and the hawk-eyed Lewis is first to spot a small red, yellow and blue Lithuanian flag fluttering in the Wheatfield. But then Kilmarnock equalise, with a goal that Hearts would never have conceded earlier in the season, when the Craig Levein-organised defence was, in the words of the club song, 'as strong as the old Castle Rock'. Dr Ruth is placing less emphasis on it, not a bad thing in principle, but you've got to make sure you score more than the opposition and Hearts have hardly been Brazilianesque recently.

Unlike Hibs. When Hibs beat Killie 3–0 in the league the other week, the *Sunday Times* acclaimed them as 'the green Brazil'. This is the ultimate compliment you can pay my team and I've waited 37 years to hear it. And where am I when it finally comes? At Tynecastle, watching Hearts' version of Socrates – Neil MacFarlane – who doesn't so much play with the ball tied to his feet as with a ball-and-chain.

I shouldn't single out MacFarlane for ridicule because there are many in maroon who exasperate me, and at least he tries, won't hide, and doesn't labour under the illusion he's any more than a mere hod-carrier. And, really, it's not Hearts' fault that Hibs are turning on the samba style; just my rotten luck that they chose this season to do it.

The only time I get to see Hibs is in telly-highlight form on *Scotsport SPL*. Fans don't ask much of TV; just that it gives us the football. But here we are forced to endure longer, sustained exposure to Sarah O's breasts, Julyan Sinclair's hair and Jim Delahunt's shirts, all of them ridiculous.

Maybe I'm wrong. Maybe a Scottish football show which avoids screening very much Scottish football is TV at its most ingenious.

The original *Scotsport*, presented by Arthur Montford, was the wonky, wooden-tripoded football round-up of my youth and his TV testcard jackets were indeed the stuff of Arthurian legend. In Montford's pomp, the football was great. It seems to me that in the successor to his finest hour, *Scotsport SPL*, we get the kind of gimmicky, desperate coverage our game now deserves.

But in the highlights of that Hibs-Killie match I did notice that all three goals were scored by Deek Riordaninho, the string-and-bone strike sensation from the *favela* of Drylaw, the imp imperial of the Easter Road youth club, and, according to *The Scotsman*'s Mike Aitken, the best Hibs prodigy since Peter Marinello left Leith for The Arse as 'Scotland's George Best'.

It's not fair. You wade through season after season of slime and swill – Liutauras Varanavicius is right, it is a swamp – in the hope that every now and then, every three decades in Hibs' case, and only for one year, because we're not greedy people, your team just *shimmers*.

Riordaninho, because he grew up in Drylaw, will have almost certainly, as a boy, have made a sandbox out of the bunker at the 17th green on Silverknowes Golf Course, and as he's demonstrating every week, didn't suffer from the fact it wasn't the Copacabana he was feeling between his toes. After being forced to watch Ally Brazil, the most inappropriately-named player in the history of football, blunder about in the Hibs midfield of the 1980s, I deserve to see the real thing.

Hibs win again today, and fans will be fantasising about a cup triumph at last, I just know it. But Hearts concede a last-minute equaliser and must replay. This makes Dr Ruth very grumpy indeed. The ref, John Rowbotham, has become something of a baldy nemesis for the Hearts manager and after their latest barney, Dr Ruth accuses the SFA of having a vendetta against the Jambos. 'It's unfair, they are big and I am small,' as Calimero would say. 'Nobody loves me, it's an injustice.'

**12 February. Hearts 3, Kilmarnock 0**

I don't go; I'm saving myself for, um, Kilmarnock on Wednesday. Meanwhile, at Ibrox, Hibs lose 3–0. So they're not Brazil, eh? Yes they are. Both teams have an Achilles heel. Brazil rarely win the World Cup in Europe, Hibs hardly ever come back from Glasgow with three points.

**16 February. Kilmarnock 1, Hearts 3**

Who are the real Jambos around here? I can't get Billy or Ricky or Peter or anyone to go to Rugby Park for the Scottish Cup replay. There had been wild talk of us blagging our way onto a supporters' bus, which would have been a new experience for me, but at the last minute, and despite Saturday's win against the same opposition, none of them fancy it.

I tell Billy I might still try and go to the game, but from the other end of the phone I can detect a feeling of mild hurt. These guys are protective towards me, but also possessive. They're probably thinking their Jamboness is as good as anyone's, and of course they're right. Anyway, I don't feel I can desert them, so we're all watching the tie on TV.

Da-Da-Da! is a newish bar in Edinburgh's West End opposite the Habitat store and, appropriately for Jambos these days, it's supposed to have an East European theme. The walls are painted red and it sells Russian and Czech beer, and if that amounts to a theme, fair enough. At least the theme isn't oppressive, like those Oirish bars with dressers, road-signs, literary quotes and other tat Superglued to the walls, all in the name of ambience.

Billy tells me that the guys who run it helped introduce Hearts to Vladimir Romanov so if his revolution really does happen, and Hearts become Scotland's top club, then Da-Da-Da! will deserve at least a footnote in the story, maybe even a plaque on the wall as part of a heritage trail of places of special Jambo interest as hundreds of Japanese girls declare undying love for Neil Mac-Farlane.

The lads were all at Tynecastle on Saturday and, like most in the Jambo Village, they seem to be turning Japanese in their fan-love for Miko. And tonight Miko has brought along a pal, Deividas Cesnauskis. Both sport moptop haircuts and they look like Lithuania's answer to Oasis' Noel and Liam Gallagher. All of a sudden, Hearts are in serious danger of becoming a sexy football team. Carol in the club shop must be anticipating a big, unseasonal upsurge in demand for replica shirts, all of them requiring extra Lithuanian lettering and earning more for the club than a 'WEIR' or a 'TUBE'.

The mad-for-it, Vlad-for-it Jambos get off to a cracking start with a goal from Lee Wallace, the teenage left-back who made his debut on Saturday. Lee Miller gets a second and Hearts are cruising, all the way into the next round of the cup where, you never know, they could yet play Hibs.

Ricky introduces a cautionary note when he bellows at the screen during a typical piece of fuddery from his least favourite Jambo. 'Fuck off, Simmons! What a niggly, sneaky wee shite, eh? He kicks the cunt and then runs off. Doesn't finish what he started.' Remembering Ricky's description of the carpet-fitter's walk, another reliable indicator of the pseudo hard-man, I think I've found a nickname for Simmons – General George.

Peter expresses the hope that Romanov and Co are serious about their intentions. He'd hate to think they viewed one great Edinburgh institution (Hearts) as a subterfuge? – through which they can ingratiate themselves with other great Edinburgh institutions (the banks).

'The Scottish football public is rightly cynical about big-shots who say they want to invest in our game,' he says. 'I mean, I don't think any of us would do it if we won 20 million on the Lottery and we're here every week.

'I just don't get it. What's in it for Romanov? Were we his favourite Scottish club when he was a laddie back in the days of the Soviet Union? Has he [in the simpering, eager-to-please voice of players from provincial clubs who reveal previously dormant affections for the Old Firm on the day they sign for Celtic or

Rangers] *always wanted to own Hearts*? Did he even know of our existence last year? I'm sorry, but for me it doesn't stack up.'

Miko and his countryman, soon to be nicknamed Chesney by the faithful, are definitely a cut above everyone else tonight. We speculate on whether the former has a Lithuanian National Haircut No 1 and the latter a Lithuanian National Haircut No 2. We order yet more beer and now Da-Da-Da! seems like the real thing, a bona fide boozer transplanted lock, stock and foaming barrel from somewhere swinging and downtown in Vlad The Imbiber's hameland. Tonight, we've all become a little bit more Czech, a little bit more Russian, and a big bit more Lithuanian.

That is, with the exception of Peter. He remains the Jambo conscience, the still beating heart of Gorgie traditionalism, and good for him. Billy is the opposite and welcomes intervention from a part of the world he knows well. You could say he embraces it, but 'grapples' might be more accurate.

I don't know how we end up talking about women but we do. Billy has had a few Eastern European girlfriends in his time as a Jambo, but only one amounted to a 'fling' in every meaning of the word.

Matter-of-factly, but with a keen understanding of the dynamics of great theatre, he tells us about the night he paid for a swanky hotel room, then paid for a woman to wrestle him.

'You *what?*'

'I found her on the internet.'

Billy chose Ivana the Terrible because she had trained competitors in the festive telly stocking-filler, *World's Strongest Woman*, although he says there are a lot of sites offering similar services.

'So what's your favourite, chuckmeroundtheroom.yahoo! or harderharderharder.aarrgh!?'

I wish we hadn't teased Billy about Ivana because he went in the huff after that. Still, every single one of us left Da-Da-Da! trying to picture the scene, and imagine what kind of racket a Jambo makes as he crashes into the trouser-press, knocks the minibar door off its hinges, rips the valance and sends the Teasmade flying across the bed.

And to think that this is the same Billy who, earlier in my Jambo journey, caused me to mark him down as safe, old-fashioned and ever so slightly dull for never leaving the house for a night game without first turning on the lights and closing the curtains, thereby giving the impression he had both his feet snugly tucked into a big slipper, teacake by his side, waiting for another thrilling episode of *Emmerdale*.

### 18 February

There's a debate on Kickback about a chant heard a few games ago, up at Dundee. 'Can we please stop the "Edinburgh is wonderful" song before it becomes a disgrace?' writes Captain. 'Edinburgh is indeed wonderful because it is a vibrant, cosmopolitan city, and I'm including Jews and Pakistanis in that.' Sounds as if the chant, and the singing of it, is already a disgrace. Whatever it is.

### 19 February. Motherwell 2, Hearts 0

When was the last time I was in Motherwell? It must have been back when it seemed the entire male population of Lanarkshire worked at Ravenscraig, one of those big, grunting, hellzapoppin' places that was emblematic of Scotland's industrial past. The five towers of the steelworks spewed their last in 1992, so where do the men of Lanarkshire work now? In call-centres probably, or maybe they clean call-centres. Sights Of Contemporary Scotland That Faither, The Socialist, Would Not Believe, Were He Still Getting A Kick At The Ball, No 138: offices at dusk, silhouettes in the windows, men grappling with vacuum cleaners.

Not for the first time this season, I'm travelling to an away game on a route that does not correspond to the classic text: the Texaco routemasters' guide that served the old man and I so well. Billy is taking Ricky and I on the scenic path and we're bumping through Motherwell's hinterlands: sad, samey places which lie down and open themselves up to cars heading for the relative metropolis.

They aren't even one-horse places, the mangy steeds bolted long ago. The through road seems the villages' only purpose. Lads in shellsuits sit on the pavements outside shuttered-up shops, their feet in the gutter, and spin their baseball caps at each other between the traffic and contemplate a game of 'chicken'. The shops that aren't closed are offering kebabs for lunch to these tykes and after that, for a change of scene, they might hang around a garage forecourt until they get chased. 'How fuckin' depressing must it be, growing up through here?' says Ricky.

Neds have been much in the news this week. The Scottish Parliament's Justice Minister, Cathy Jamieson, was pictured in every paper delivering a sermon on the menace posed by what used to be called juvenile delinquency while a Tacchini-clad toerag flicked the vikkies behind her back.

But why aren't his soul brothers, one of whom gives us the same two-fingered welcome to Lanarkshire, getting off the streets for a day and going to a game? They almost certainly can't afford it – the SPL is ridiculously expensive. When Sky TV took their money out of oor fitba, and the foreigners removed their exotic colognes from the dressing-rooms, we were entitled to expect a reduction in admission prices because suddenly our teams were mostly made up of kids, but this hasn't happened.

The Heathrow Express, the train route linking the airport to the centre of London, is supposed to be the most expensive in the world given the distance travelled and the mere 15 minutes you spend on board. Is Motherwell vs Hearts, then, the costliest 90 minutes of 'entertainment', considering the predictable tapioca-like texture of the match, the threat of snow and the mounting anxiety that at any minute Ramon Pereira – Ferrero Roche – could prance on the field and attempt a comeback for the Jambos?

In Motherwell, we find ourselves walking behind a local lad with a jumbo chain stretching from the waistband of his jeans to his back pocket, presumably to keep his wallet safe. He has another one, even chunkier, round his neck, and this amuses Ricky. 'What's that aw' aboot?' he says. This is a town that used to be synonymous with steel, the football team are nicknamed the Steelmen; now a steel substitute – steelette? – provides hip-hop stylings for local youths, much the same as it does for white-wannabe-black kids the world over. The town, like so many, has lost its identity, but then I'm a fine one to talk about that, being as I am Guy Ritchie, the film director and middle-class prat, hanging around with rough boys and getting a thrill out of it.

We're looking for a pub and eventually Jack Daniels hoves into view. It's a brick outhouse and instead of 'Bar' and 'Lounge' the dual entrance reads 'Home' and 'Away'. The 'Away' part is already heaving; it's hard to believe some Jambos have beaten The Human Map here. We try to fight our way through the crowd. 'Check the barman,' says Billy. He's wearing an England top and yet when we eventually get served it's clear he's Scottish and a Lanarkshire native. From goodness knows where, I summon up the faintly ludicrous idea that I'm bold enough to challenge this tube about his choice of casualwear, until Ricky calms me down.

It doesn't take long for this vague bluster to disappear completely. The Jambos are singing. They're showcasing a new version of one of their favourite songs, and it goes something like this:

> *Tony Mowbray's got a fuckin' monkey's heid*
> *A fuckin' monkey's heid*
> *And his wife is deid*

Mowbray's first wife Bernadette died of cancer. At the time there was a lot of sympathy for him. But obviously it wasn't universal. Nothing is, in the hard, hard world of Scottish football. And the atmosphere in Jack Daniels is really intimidating. Does Motherwell have a boozer called Tia Maria or Babycham? Unlikely, but I'd love a complimentary shuttle-bus to take me there. *Now.* This is hardcore, this is ultra, and before long a familiar little drama unfolds. Everyone is singing – it's the Derry Boys song – apart from Billy, Ricky and me. These two don't dance to anyone's tune. Billy is too well respected. He has one cry, the kick-off exortation of "MON THE HEARTS!' Ricky? Well, no-one *dares* tell him what to do.

Which leaves me, and I don't have an explanation for the fact I'm not singing. Well, I do, but the Jambos here won't want to hear it. Correction, the Jambo now standing right in front of me, close enough for me to smell his beery breath, close enough for me to be hit by his spittle, he's singing *at* me and in a manner that suggests he wants to know *exactly* why I'm not joining in.

I stand out, I know I do. Like a sore thumb. I'm Michael Douglas down the disco in *Basic Instinct*, desperately hoping that Sharon Stone doesn't notice he's wearing a classic auntie-present V-neck pullover the colour of a sore thumb.

'You Hibby bastard!' he roars in my face. 'You Hibby bastard!' No-one else in the immediate vicinity seems to have noticed this grand unmasking. They're too busy with a chant of their own: 'Vladimir Romanov! Vladimir Romanov!' But it's only a matter of time before I'm rumbled by the entire 'Away' bar. This is it, I'm thinking, this is the moment I've been dreading all season . . .

But Ricky, who seems to have ESP for when trouble is about to kick off, pulls off a brilliant manoeuvre, swapping positions with me so now he's standing closest to my accuser and, almost inevitably, the Jambo pipes down and slumps back into the Lanarkshire leatherette of Jack Daniels. Ricky effects this with all the elegance of Christopher Dean readying Jayne Torville for a swooning lunge on the ice, though I don't think he'd like the analogy too much. Even if the fact-freak could tell me the duo's marks for artistic expression when they won gold.

I was grateful for my safe middle-class upbringing but maybe it was too protected. That's my excuse and I'm sticking to it. But I know my dad despaired of me when, coming out of Easter Road after a game, eager to avoid the splurge of away fans, I'd quicken my pace after spotting my mother parked up in the Saab Estate, and would run the last few yards towards it. 'You had your tail between your legs there,' he would say, disappointedly. (The wild 'n' crazy opposition that day? Partick Thistle).

This was his eldest son, the same one who pestered his mother to buy him Doc Martens then only wore them in the house, because to do so outside was to invite a square-go, even first thing in the morning, on the way to the newsagent's for your copy of *Shoot!*, or on the journey to school. And they stayed firmly under the bed, my safe middle-class bed, on the few occasions I left the New Town and dared to venture into parts of Edinburgh that were livelier than my own.

The first two rounds of my Subbuteo competition with Jim, Norman and Kenny were in the Edinburgh scheme of Clermiston, which I only knew of as the home of the Young Clery Jungle, one of the rampaging Edinburgh street-gangs of the 1970s, and had therefore built up in my head as being completely lawless. I wimped out of both nights.

And when I finally braved a bus ride to Silverknowes for the next round of matches, and Kenny wasn't at the terminus to meet me like he promised, I stood on a spotless pavement of this immaculately-tended suburb and burst into tears. What a sap I was, and not much better now.

So after all these years of scrupulously avoiding bovver, maybe I'm quite enjoying hanging out with fans who are not my usual type, who take me to pubs I'd normally shun, and experience the sort of extreme behaviour that would shock many in my genteel city. I find Billy and Ricky's company pretty seductive, and I bet it's the first time *that* word has been used in the context of Motherwell's Jack Daniels.

I'm hardly the first to show such voyeuristic tendencies. In 1968, Arthur Hopcraft published his book *The Football Man*, a classic text on the game, in which he wrote: 'I am not going to be popular in some quarters by saying that I believe more people than are prepared to admit it take a surreptitious pleasure in the display of oafish anarchy on the terraces.'

But why am I behaving like this now? Maybe I'm trying to break out of my comfort zone. Maybe my new habit of turning down the offer of a cardboard sleeve for my takeaway caramel latte is another indicator that this is to be the season of living dangerously.

It could be an age thing, this need to challenge myself, or it could be guilt at having come this far in life without requiring a visit to the local Casualty Department. Can I blame Faither here? I'll try. He taught me about football and great television programmes but not how to look after myself. He never bought me the boxing gloves I wanted. When the judo craze arrived in Scotland, he wouldn't send me to lessons. In all the snaps he took of me as a wee boy, I'm sniffing flowers. He wanted to take me out of the education mainstream and send me to choir school. He wanted to call me *Tarquin*, for goodness sake.

It's inevitable that Hearts will lose. Against Motherwell, they always do. The Jambos in Fir Park taunt the home fans with chants of 'Ravenscraig, Ravenscraig' but neither they nor their team can force a break with tradition, and after their heroics in the past couple of games, Lithuanian National Haircuts Nos 1 and 2 are extremely disappointing. The snow that's been looming overhead all day finally falls.

On the walk out of the ground, I spot the moron from the pub and now he's haranguing a group of 'Well fans. 'What are you lot smiling at? You just got jobs or something?' But the 'Well boys just keep on grinning. You just know they get this kind of taunt from big-city swankers all the time.

Today Hearts were 'embarrassing' – this is Dr Ruth's frank assessment, post-match. Despite all the hype and hullabaloo whipped up by the Romanov revolution, the Jambos are still just that: talk, nothing more. Before they ever cause fear and alarm to the Old Firm, they are going to have to start lording it over bogey teams like Motherwell where it really matters, out on the pitch. Already, the third spot they regarded as theirs by right looks beyond them. Hibs, who always seem to net four goals against Dundee, repeat the feat again, and one word from the *Sunday Times* sums it up for them, too – 'mesmerising'.

## 27 February. Hearts 2, Livingston 1

I'm in the Ardmillan with Ricky and Peter, we're talking about Vlad the Injector's big £30 million promise – the cash would be spread over three years – and both of them are highly sceptical. They have painful memories of the last time a lot of money was thrown around Tynecastle, and how it was frittered away.

But no man, however large his pockets, is bigger than the club and its traditions, and Romanov soon pales into insignificance next to *the* hot topic of the afternoon: the prospect of an all-Edinburgh Scottish Cup Final. Recently I dreamed that Hibs played Hearts in the quarter-finals (and naturally a last-minute Deek Riordaninho overhead kick won it). In reality, the last-eight draw paired Hibs with St Mirren and they came through yesterday.

Ricky says that every time in rehearsals for the draw, Hibs and Hearts came out of the hat together. Then he adds: 'Of course we'd do yez.' I laugh, but inside I think he's probably right. Hearts are rubbish just now and Hibs are scoring goals for fun, but the Jambos probably still retain most of the psychological trump-cards. This is a fair-sized admission for me which proves that if nothing else I've been paying attention.

Hearts duly dispose of Livi and later on that night are the first name to be pulled out of the bunnet in the semi draw. *And Hearts will play . . . Celtic.* That means it's Hibs vs Dundee United. A text comes in from Billy: 'Lucky bastards!'

# MARCH

## 2 March. Hearts 1, Rangers 2

You can't beat night games. In fact, you cannae whack 'em. The seductive glow of the floodlights in the night sky, drawing you away from *What Not To Wear For Celebrity Wife Swap On Vacation In Miami* on the telly, pulling you into the ground in a blizzard. And what could be more alluring than a visit from Rangers and especially an Ibrox team boosted by the return to the royal blue of Barry Ferguson?

Bazza has a nippy, gurning pus that finds its greatest expression when prodding – yes, that's the word – out of the top of a Rangers shirt. Eighteen months previously, he quit Govan for the English Premiership and Blackburn Rovers, complaining he was bored of the old, SPL routine of Dunf and Killie four times a season. Now he's back, and the Jambos are keen to help him with the re-adjustment process.

'Haw, Ferguson – back in the small time, eh?' The man sitting next to me in the Wheatfield is on Bazza's back straight from kick-off, and doesn't let up all game long. 'You lack ambition. You couldnae cut it. Back in the small time!'

The match is a stormer. Rangers start at 100mph and threaten to blow Hearts away. But the Jambos have a record four pairs of white boots out there on the greasy pitch tonight, and they battle their way back into the game with what you would have to call flair. Lithuanian National Haircut No 1 is dashing and brave, as is Lithuanian National Haircut No 2.

But Rangers get a penalty, a *last-minute* penalty. Sotirios Kyrgia-kos, their Greek central defender, goes down in the box like a pile of plates. In the long and grim history of at-the-death Rangers spot-kick winners, this one really takes the caramel wafer. I've never seen a more outrageous award, and it enables Bazza and Co to steal away from Tynie with a potentially season-defining three points tucked in the Burberry kit-bag.

The Hearts fans go spare. So does Calimero, and the entire Hearts team. Lithuanian National Haircut No 1 barges into the linesman who flagged for the spot-kick and gets himself sent off.

Like everyone else in the Wheatfield, I'm shouting and scream-ing at the linesman, the ref, the whooping Rangers fans, the Rangers players mobbing scorer Fernando Ricksen and the monu-mental unfairness of it all. On this pulsating, bonkers night, it's been a classic case of floodlit robbery. 'Fuckin' boo! Fuckin' boo!' At long last, my inner Jambo reveals itself.


## 4 March
Every club in Scotland has suffered what happened to Hearts against one of the Old Firm. The traditional response is to grumble a bit, then take your medicine – your cod-liver oil, your Dr Gregory's Powder – and slope off to bed. Not the Jambos: they're demanding the match be re-played.

So let's recap: the previous Hearts manager has an affair with the girl from promotions . . . the current one blasts and fumes at officialdom and kicks rival coaches . . . the new team pin-up, a Liam Gallagher lookylikey, starts behaving like the Oasis star when confronted by a paparazzo or a bouncer or some boy-band twat . . .

Who on earth said that Hearts were safe, boring and authority-loving? They're the most rock 'n' roll club around.


## 5 March. Dunfermline 1, Hearts 1
We're now getting into that seen-it-done-it-pass-the-luger phase of the season where not just the same teams come round again but also the same grounds. Today, David, the solicitor, has joined Ricky

and I for another demonstration of free-jazz driving from Billy. 'Don't ask The Human Map to tell you how he works out his routes coz he cannae,' says Ricky.

We're discussing what many football fans have been talking about non-stop since about 9.35pm on Wednesday and that's The Penalty That Never Was. Billy tends to stay quiet during these in-car debates, then when we're in full flow, he'll demand our attention about some road matter or other, say the indecisiveness of another vehicle, or a route quandary. I call it free-jazz driving, but there's a possibility Billy has worked out the entire route beforehand, right down to the last cattle-track short-cut, like the one we're bumping along today.

'On ye go, Human Map,' says Ricky, who then brings David up to speed with the stories of the journeys to recent games he's missed. They're much more exciting than the actual matches and David is engrossed.

'And in Dundee, Billy, did you park in Graham Street as usual?'

'Yup,' comes the reply from the driver's seat. The Human Map looks straight ahead, only averting his eyes to glance in his rear-view mirror, though of course there are no other vehicles on this road. With an obviously well-practised technique, he unwraps a Curly Wurly.

This is my life now. I go to see the Hearts with these guys. I still think I should be spreading myself around, trying to meet new and different Jambos, but I know this lot wouldn't let me. I'm not complaining: they're good fun. It's a different life to my one as a Hibs fan. With my Hibby mates, I would be having a spot of lunch in some over-priced gastro-pub, and the fact I'm sweepingly calling them all 'over-priced' suggests how far I've come down the Jambo route. This is pure Ricky. He scrutinises food prices in pubs, then expresses astonishment that anyone would pay £4.95 for a burger (without chips) when McDonalds would only charge you half that and chuck in fries as well. He will not be conned like this, no way, and it's yet another assertion of his uncompromising, independent spirit. 'Is this [adopts gastro-sneer] *made on the premises*? Is it fuck. It'll have come from a frozen pack, 20p each.'

With my Hibs pals, I would be talking about that day's game, but mostly old games, our misty, watercolour memories of them, and asking the rhetorical question: 'Paddy Stanton, what a player, what a *man* – did anyone look better with the ball being prodded forward on the outside of the right foot . . . commanding, upright posture, chest puffed, hair decisively parted in the style of a knitting-pattern model, never falling out of place as he ran at the heart of the Rangers defence?' Now, I do this with my Hearts mates, and although the chat is mainly about Jambo personnel, and I therefore do more polite listening than talking, Billy is old enough to have seen Stanton play, and honourable enough to acknowledge his brilliance. Then Ricky reveals he's related to the great 1970s Easter Road captain.

'*Really?*'

'Dinnae get excited, only fuckin' distantly.'

We talk about cars. Or rather the rest of us talk. Billy is concentrating on the road, ever wary of the potential flying-pigs hazard in rural Fife. Ricky says he doesn't drive. He's been behind a wheel once, but that was while under the influence of LSD and so doesn't really count. Surely the unluckiest motorised-transport passenger in the world, he's been involved in a total of eight accidents. 'Five write-offs, one rollover,' he says, ever ready with the stats. 'So maybe that's why I've no' been in a hurry to learn.'

In Dunf's East Port Bar, the atmosphere is subdued; the Rangers penalty travesty seems to have knocked the stuffing out of the Jambos. Celtic are blocking the route to the Scottish Cup Final, and Hearts are almost certain to be without Lithuanian National Haircut No 1 because the beaks at the SFA will want to make an example of him with a lengthy ban.

It's impossible not to feel gloomy and some are probably already looking forward to the season's end so they can file it away under 'tempestuous, transitional'. We count down the next few weeks, Caley Thistle at home, Livi at home (what, *again?*), Celtic away . . . no, says Billy, the Tartan Army foot-soldier, who's proud to be a Jambo and a Jock, Scotland play Italy before then.

Ricky asks Billy if he's going to the – from a Scottish perspective – futile World Cup qualifier, but the rest of us already know the answer. 'Four nights in Milan,' he beams.

'Fuck Scotland, fuck that shite,' says Ricky.

Billy looks hurt.

'They're no' ma nation.'

'Who's your nation then?'

'Germany!' Then he removes his jacket. Underneath he's wearing the familiar white shirt of the gobbing Rudi Voller, the goose-stepping Andreas Moller, the goal-terror Gerd Muller, the goes-down-like-he's-been-shot Jurgen Klinsman and of course the god-like Franz Beckenbauer. 'Brand new, guys, you like it?' Billy groans. Ricky ruffles his hair and says it's only a wind-up.

'What you going to do in Milan for all that time anyway?'

'You'll just laugh.'

'No we won't, eh no' guys?'

'Well, there's this really good bookshop and all it sells is motorsport . . . ach, fuck off the lot of you.'

It's ten to three and we're still in pub. I'm reminded of that 1970s government-sponsored anti-booze telly commercial in which an alky-fan sells his Scotland ticket just before kick-off for the price of a nip and one more pint of Double Diamond. 'If drink's become the most important thing in your life,' went the chilling reproach, '*think again*.' Its shock value was immense: thirty years ago, you had to be really desperate, completely beyond salvation, to put bevvy before *the geme*. The ad wouldn't be anything like as effective today, not with this Scotland team, and even the most patriotic like Billy would have to agree with that.

I ask Ricky more about his obsession with Germany, and where it comes from. 'I *love* efficiency,' he says. He's too young to have seen Beckenbauer and Co in their pomp, but is extremely knowledgeable about the current scene. We chat about the strutting midfielder Michael Ballack and the strutting disco frequenter Oliver Khan. We discuss great German fightbacks, Ricky confirming the times of the goals. 'Gunter Netzer was great, aye?' Aye, he was. And suddenly I realise I love Teutonic soccer almost as much as he does.

So did Ricky not approve of Berti Vogts becoming Scotland coach? Did he not support the national team when he was in charge? 'Course I did. And when everyone started to slag him off, I was for giving him more time. In the end he had to go but there were aye these jokes about no' mentioning the war and I felt a bit sorry for him.' Who said Ricky was intolerant towards other cultures?

In my column in *The Scotsman*, I was as guilty of crass national stereotyping as any member of the fans-with-typewriters brigade, especially after a dismal defeat featuring five more dark-blue debuts by players I didn't even know were Scottish. Once, shamefully, I actually wanted Berti's Vogtsland to lose. When we were 2–0 down to the puffin-eaters and whale-murderers from the Faroe Islands in a Euro 2004 qualifier, the masochistic streak that's in every Scottish fan threatened to burst out of my guts like the *Alien*.

Ricky says he tries not to overdo the Teutonic taunting when Billy's around because he's a sensitive, serious Scotland fan and Ricky respects that. But he can't stand 'jockery': professional Scots, plastic Scots and the porridge-packet posers who 'kid oan they're warriors' and glory too much in the best-behaved-losers accolades.

Sensing this could be the moment, I tell Ricky that if he likes German football he should try some 1970s krautrock. 'Can, Faust and Amon Duul II have got the same relentless rhythms as a Germany team with Beckenbauer or Netzer or your guy Ballack running the midfield,' I say.

He laughs, and it would be once again resorting to cliché to describe the snigger as 'Obergrupenfuhrer'. Ricky would have hated the 1970s and all that chin-scratching about rock; he's a pop man. Actually, he wouldn't hate it at all. I can just picture him provoking a riot in a growly pub by putting his beloved Abba on the jukebox.

It's almost kick-off and there's nothing else for it: we're going to have to finish our drinks and trudge across Dunf's fine parkland to East End Park. Ricky, in his Prada, takes the long way round to avoid getting them muddy. Billy, who probably phoned ahead to check the underfoot conditions, isn't wearing his. As a result we miss the start of the game and, more crucially, the Pars' run-on song, 'Into The Valley' by The Skids.

Obscure but still-lovely pop songs hang on for grim life, for one more spin, at grounds like East End Park. Scottish football's eco-system is fragile enough and the Pars, with their much-criticised plastic pitch, are more vulnerable than most. But this is culture, this is heritage, and it must not be allowed to die. The songs, I mean. Football can get stuffed.

The artificial surface hardly imbues the game with meaning. The sunshine gives it an end-of-season air. The chant of 'Oh the Hibees are gay . . .' is half-hearted. Even Sinky's rejoinder of 'Elton John, Elton John' dies after the first couple of blasts. Midway through the first half the man himself gets up out of his seat, never to return.

Dunf, fighting to avoid relegation, score just before half-time and it starts snowing. This is more like it. 'Fuck off, Simmons!' roars Grant. This is definitely more like it. In the absence of Steven Pressley, Andy Webster steadies things. 'Webster's a right dirty bastard,' says a fan behind us, approvingly. 'You need that in a centre-half, don't ye?' Ricky smiles, as if challenging me to disagree.

Hearts rally in the second half and – wouldn't you just know it? – they get a dodgy penalty. That's 13 so far this campaign, although not all of them have been dubious. Hibs, on the other hand, got their first spot-kick only last month. What is it football people always say? 'Them's the breaks . . . these things even themselves out over the season.'

Hearts, and particularly Calimero, obviously feel they don't. 'SFA, yer havin' a laff' is the most popular chant among the persecuted maroon tribe as it shuffles back over the Forth, still upset at that Rangers outrage. We, on the other hand, are back home before half-five.

The Human Map does it again – doubtless inspired by his forthcoming visit to Italy, a country that truly loves cars – and it's unimportant that he stays more or less silent during journeys: in fact, this cloak or racing-jacket of solemnity rather suits him.

You want your getaway driver to keep it zipped. All great car guys in the movies are men of few words. Think of Steve McQueen in *Bullitt* or Ryan O'Neal in *The Driver*. Or the great Dennis Wilson in *Two-Lane Blacktop*, which follows a trans-American drag-race. There's barely 20 pages of dialogue in the entire film. Go, Human Map, go.

**12 March. Hearts 0, Inverness Caley Thistle 2**
It's a rugby weekend in Edinburgh, with Scotland playing Wales, but Ricky has little time for the dragon-eating hordes from the valleys. 'They all think they can sing, don't they?' he says.

Ricky doesn't like rugby. Correction: he knows everything there is to know about it, watches any game beamed live into his living room from Down Under at 6am in the morning, but has no time for rugger-buggers.

'I ken you guys probably got rugby at school,' he says to Billy and I, 'but I've always thought it was rubbish. These boys are supposed to be hard; they're no'. Me and my mates used to fight rugby boys, Scotland Under-21s and that. There would be more of them than us but we'd destroy them. Rugby boys are always: "I drank 60 pints and shagged 12 women last night." I'm like: "Wow, you must be crazy!" They're just beer liars and women liars. And another reason I don't like rugby is there's this gay vibe going on.'

Ricky has out-there views, but at least he *has* views and is unafraid to air them. I'm used to more polite company on match-days, indeed in life, where never a provocative word is uttered. I've heard enough PC opinions to last me a long, long time, or all the way through to Neil MacFarlane's next wonder-goal, whichever comes first. Maybe that's why I find the big man so refreshing and entertaining. '*They're just beer liars and women liars.*' Brilliant.

I'm gorging on Gorgie at the moment. Three out of four games in March are at Tynecastle. But this one almost doesn't happen as

campaign nerve-centre before this game. Still contemplating the purchase of an SOH ruler, I'm killing time before I meet the guys when this shaven-headed man walks into the Gorgie Road HQ, approaches the shaven-headed man behind the counter, and right away an argument starts. 'Fuck ye then.' 'Naw fuck you. 'Ahm bouncin' ye right oot o' here.' And the man behind the counter, who has a scar on his neck, chases the other man out the door and down the street.

What was that all about? The SOH man gets back behind the counter, takes a sip from his mug of tea and tries to calm down. 'He wanted his money back. I've had this sort of 'hing since September. The fans are all "Christmas is coming, Romanov will save us now." I don't get paid for this, not for takin' shit off arseholes like that.'

He says a letter will be sent out soon to fans who've contributed to the fighting fund offering them two choices: leave your money where it is or walk away with a 90 per cent return. The SOH man says there are no certainties in football: not even rich Baltic bankers can offer that.

'You see this?' he says, holding up a poster, ripped off from the old 'Your country needs you' wartime call-to-arms. 'What Romanov is saying is this: "If only 9800 of you are going to be turning up at Tynie every other week, then fuck yez." One of the 'hings that pisses me off aboot Hearts fans is they're so fickle.' Then he checks himself. 'Present company excepted, pal.'

Five minutes later, on an afternoon which is prickly-polyester hot, I'm in the Ardmillan telling the boys about this full and frank exchange of views. Dave and Paul admit they didn't know of the existence of the SOH shop until a couple of days before. 'Shows what good Hearts fans *we* are,' says Paul.

Peter, the most placid redhead I've ever met, continues to be sceptical about the Romanov revolution. He's heard big talk before. He's been told the fans must pull together before. 'If the punters want to criticise a manager or a player and certainly if they slag off the chairman, that's fair enough. At 20 quid a week, that's our right.'

It's our right, today, to review and rate last week's match against Inverness as no-star and feel-bad and poorer value than three Colin Farrell films strung together – yes, that awful. Peter digs out the descriptive term he saves for such dire occasions. 'That was a holocaust o' a match,' he says.

Dave laments the lack of good young talent coming through at Tynecastle. 'Hibs have Derek Rearend but who have we got? Graeme Weir, Joe Hamill and Steven bloody Simmons.'

'Steven fuckin' Simmons,' corrects Ricky.

The brothers head off with Dave reminding us of his 40th birthday bash and, as a pneumatic blonde saunters by in a 'Tony Mowbray's Got a Fuckin' Monkey's Heid' T-shirt, Ricky, Peter and I flirt with the idea of giving the game a miss and spending the afternoon in the Ardmillan's beer garden.

The same Ricky who hates 'rugby boys' and also has ideological problems with the Tartan Army and freely admits to all sorts of prejudices is now discussing literature. He loves Irvine Welsh, despite the *Trainspotting* author's avowed Hibbyness, despite the anti-hero in *Filth* being the most disreputable policeman in the history of fiction: a racist, a rapist and a Jambo. 'Welsh is *quality*,' he confirms.

'Elize du Toit is in *Ecstasy*,' he reports, bang up-to-date with cast announcements on the new Welsh movie. Peter looks confused. 'You ken, Izzy in *Hollyoaks*, the posh barmaid with the great tits . . .'

We could talk about great fiction until the end of time or I pluck up the courage to have a drink in Robertson's, whichever comes first, but a game against Livi – the third in seven weeks – is calling us. It must be the extra couple of pints we had because today Hearts look surprisingly cool, the colour maroon definitely benefiting from the absence of rain, mud and general winter gloom and, slowly but surely, the ebbing away of the feeling that I don't belong here. To add to the disorientating air, Neil MacFarlane is cheered for every thick-thighed lunge. There's almost a poetry to them now. It seems ages since Ricky made fun of Socrates' accountant's haircut. It seems ages since I first got to know my Jambo mates.

Over in Dunfermline, Hibs win 4–1 and the *Sunday Times* reports them as playing football of 'real beauty'. Deek Rearend – sorry, Riordaninho – who was left out of Walter Smith's first Scotland squad, scores a stuff-you double which I catch on *Scotsport SPL*. For his second goal he turns a Pars defender so many directions the poor sap must have empathised with the victims of George Best's deedle-dawdle brilliance, the ones left with 'twisted blood'.

It's another blow. My uber-Jambo mates are great and they're really helping with the integration, but the team are not. It's like I'm at a party and stuck with the really boring guy and he'd been *talking about pensions* and over his shoulder I can see this stunning girl – Elize du Toit – holding court, throwing her head back and laughing, and all those blokes surrounding her are having a much better time than me. That's what I feel like as I long to be with Hibs; they're the stunning girl.


### 25 March

It's the night of Dave's party and beforehand I meet Ricky and his girlfriend Jill in the Tynecastle Arms. Ricky is suited and booted by Armani. Even his tie and socks bear the winged logo. Jill is blonde and pretty and part of me wants to reveal Ricky's terrible secret: that his favourite Elvis song is *Can't Help Falling In Love*. But I think better of it; even in his best clobber, he looks far too tough to mess with.

To the Gorgie Suite, and an upstairs function-room plastered with blown-up snaps of Dave as a kid. The toothy grins don't reveal the pain of being a Jambo on the wrong side of town.

I meet his brother Paul at the bar and he tells me how they felt like the loneliest boys in the world as maroon-clan scamps holed up in Leith.

'Our dad wasn't bothered about football when we were young but our grandfather was a big fan of the old Leith Athletic and when they disbanded, he went with the Hearts,' explains Paul. 'Grandad reckoned there was only ever one Leith team and Hibs were imposters.

'Dave and I were the only Jambos in our school. It was hell. Every day the Hibbys nicked our bags and hid them in the rubbish bins or stuffed them down the toilets.

'One Christmas Dave got a Hearts strip and because Donald Ford was his hero he asked our mum if she could get a "9" sewn onto the back. She took it to Thomson's Sports Shop in Great Junction Street but when Dave got it back the number was green. The guy who did it probably thought: "I might get the sack for this but it'll be well worth it." '

I ask Paul about the two most momentous Jambo events in our fantime and he says he regularly re-lives the 1998 Scottish Cup triumph on video, freeze-framing the footage of him in the crowd, stripped to the waist, flaunting his wee fat belly.

He has a tape of the 1986 Dundee debacle but can't bear to watch it. 'When we got back from Dens it was the worst feeling in the world,' he says. 'My mum tried to cheer us up. She said: "Never mind there'll be another time" and I swore at her.

'Now ordinarily my dad would never ever hear anything said against our mum. But when she told him to have a word with me, he said: "Well, dinnae be so bloody stupid woman, there will *never* be another time!" Dundee was *that* bad.'

The disco is in full swing and the sausage-roll buffet is going down a storm and, from the window, the Tynecastle stands are lit up. Then the DJ gets Dave and his family on the floor for a Two-Tone stomp-classic from their teens.

It's been a good night. Dave is blootered and gives me a big hug at the end. Paul has a confession to make: 'It's bad parenting, I know, but when my wee laddie Christopher was about five or six he said to me: "Dad, you know how Hearts were born in 1874?"

' "*Created*, yes."

' "And you know Hibs were *created* in 1875. Well, in 1874, who were the scum?"

'Half of me's thinking: "Oh no, what have I done?" But the other half is like: "That's my boy!" '

We agree, Paul and I, that the Hibs-Hearts rivalry is intense, but it's what makes football worth bothering about, and as long as it's there, football will always make life worth bothering about.

'Do you know,' he says, 'I think we'll be the last generation to get worked up by football to this extent. Among our contemporaries, the guys at our work, we're regarded as being a bit odd for liking nothing better than rolling up every week to watch football, and *Scottish* football at that. Sometimes I think the sport is cool everywhere in the world but here. We're the last of the cavemen, Aidan.'

He gives me a prehistoric handshake and I stagger out into Gorgie Road. I contemplate a nightcap with the Darwinian Study Group in Robertson's but change my mind and run all the way home.

# APRIL

**2 April. Celtic 0, Hearts 2**

On the train to Glasgow, with the forthcoming General Election in mind, we're talking politics. Or rather Ricky is talking and the rest of us are listening. 'Anyway,' he says finally, 'I'll only be voting if the BNP put up a boy roond ma bit.'

We're on our way to Parkhead and, as is traditional for such big away-dayers, Billy has stocked up. A four-pack of vanilla slices, a box of Quality Street, two Curly Wurlys, two Turkish Delights and a Milky Bar. 'That's what I call a scran!' says Ricky. 'This is for me – where's yours?' says Billy. Is he joking? Is Ricky joking about the BNP? Maybes aye, as Kenny Dalglish would put it, maybes naw.

The chat soon turns to Dr Ruth. His three-quarter-length quilted polyester dugout coat is on a shoogly peg. Billy has bought a selection of papers as well and the wee man is all over the back pages. With a little lemon smile for the cameras, he quips: 'I'll have to win the cup to avoid the sack.' Incredible, when you think about it: he's only been in the job five months. The lukewarm rumour is that Terry Venables is being lined up as his replacement but Ricky is not happy about that. 'What's he done since Euro 96? He's past it.'

This afternoon in the SPL, both Hearts and Hibs are playing warm-ups against Celtic and Dundee United, the teams who stand in the way of the first all-Edinburgh Scottish Cup Final since 1896. Hearts won that day, 3–1 in front of a crowd of 16,034 in the capital, in Logie Green. So the Hibee Nation and the Jambo Village are daring to dream.

And it promises to be an afternoon like no other in Glasgow's East End. Pope John Paul II is dying, he's been given the last rites, and the Catholics in a 60,000 crowd will carry with them an air of distractedness far higher than any you normally experience in this stadium, during a match against one of the SPL riff-raff.

The lads started early with a pint at Waverley Station, and they're in no way intimidated by facing the mighty Celts, who're leading the league and on course for yet another title. At Croy, half-a-dozen Hoops get on the train and the ever-alert Ricky counts the sovvy rings as they pass through our carriage. 'Aye, ye cannae hide class,' he quips.

It seems ages since we were at a game, the long build-up, and equally long post-mortem, surrounding a Scotland international being to blame. It's good to see the guys again. Billy, of course, was in Milan for the World Cup qualifier and we're keen to hear his stories. They're typically Billyesque. He checked if chuckme-roundtheroom.yahoo! had a branch in Italy's style capital, tragically not. On his first night, walking back to his hotel, he got talking to some ladies of the night. Real stunners, but on further investigation, these girls turned out to be guys.

Billy has brought along another mate, Phil, and he has the air of a man who would not make the same mistake – he knows his way around Europe. He certainly knew the quickest way out of Estonia when some right bad yins got released from jail determined to hunt down the man who put them there. These were the New Mafia hoods he shopped to the police after refusing to agree to a hike in protection money in Tallinn. Phil ran a number of bars there, one of which had maroon walls hanselled by an autograph from Jim Jeffries, the ex-Jambo player, manager and gurner. He tells us a funny yarn about the night Jeffries was required to hide in a hotel wardrobe in Elgin – think Basil Fawlty – before continuing with the story of his dash from Estonia, through Poland, back to Scotland where previously he'd been active in Scottish Nationalist politics.

Phil now has an involvement in the Da-Da-Da! bar at the West End, which specialises in Eastern European beers served by hooded-eyed beauties from the same part of the world. I didn't know the barmaids were from Eastern Europe; to me they just seemed as bored with lame male chat-ups as any others in town. A new girl from the Czech Republic is due to start within the next couple of weeks and Billy promises to look in to say hello to her.

As well as bar staff, Phil has played a tiny part in getting work in Edinburgh for one V. Romanov. He's something of a cheerleader for Vlad, and thinks the Lithuanian beaks can take Hearts to a 'new level', competing with the Old Firm. Phil reckons they should start right away: he's bet £140 on a Jambo victory today.

We're looking for somewhere to have lunch when Phil spots a beer cellar, the Republic, just off Glasgow's Buchanan Street. He knows his beer and is soon urging Ricky, the Becks man from way back, to cut loose and try something different, a bottle of Krucovice from Poland. This is a breakthrough, Ricky is stepping through the wardrobe. He tells us the last time he did this: 'I've taken every drug up to heroin, because I dinnae like needles and I don't want tae die. Charlie is a rich man's drug, Ecstasy is over-priced and basically shite, but acid is the best value for 50p there's ever been. Walls are crushing on you, the sofa's talking to you . . . and as for being in a car on acid, that's amazing. D'ye mind those coloured specs you'd get free with Hula Hoops? Me and a mate were wearing them in his motor and what a trip that was.'

I order a Quilmes, which I have been unable to find anywhere since a holiday in Argentina. 'Did you see any fitba when you were there?' asks Ricky. Yes, I say, River Plate. 'No, *River*, man, they're the rich man's team. You should've gone to *Boca* . . .' The beers encourage a mood of internationalism: we talk about the Champions' League, it's the quarter-finals next week, when the Hysel teams, Liverpool and Juventus, are reunited, before mention of the Pope brings the chat round to shopping in Rome: Ricky went to Armani and Prada on a recent trip to the Eternal City and was unimpressed, although he's sporting both labels today.

And sex. The conversation always comes back to that. Billy is intrigued by the existence of a sex-wrestling club in Amsterdam and this is Phil's cue to tell us about the time he submitted himself to the less-than-tender mercies of a dominatrix.

'You're put in this cage and she doesn't touch you, apart from when she attaches objects to your 'nads.'

What kind of objects, I'm wondering, a replica of the Scottish Cup? That would be a Hibby's ideal of heaven *and* hell. What with Phil's predilection for S&M, and Billy's for being at the eye of a hurricane of a hotel-room makeover, I'm thinking I'm going to have to revise my view of the sex position that best sums up Hearts – it's not the boring old missionary after all.

Ricky is feeling a bit left out of things, so offers up the story of his mate, the porn star. 'Totally hyper-sexed. At school he'd have to go home at lunchtimes for a wank.' The pal auditioned for a sex-reality show produced by the Fantasy Channel and made it through to the final stages.

Did Ricky watch his money-shot at fame? 'Nah, the programme's still being shown, but I dinnae want to see my mate's cock, you ken what I mean?' Anyway, they haven't spoken since the friend nicked Ricky's credit card while he was sleeping and spent £200 phoning a sex-chat line in Vanuatu.

'D'ye ken where Vanuatu is?'

What a multi-national afternoon. Next, Billy spits out a syrupy Belgian beer and substitutes it with one from China, which would be his nationality of choice for a wife. He was one of the few Scots fans who travelled to the Far East for Scotland's pre-2002 World Cup tour, a competition for which they were left on the outside, looking in. Ricky again, 'Have you seen Billy's fake business card for when he's on the pull?' It says "Fashion Photographer".'

We hit the streets, completely pissed. 'Look, a triple!' says Ricky, spotting the bejewelled hand of a ned. We taxi it to Parkhead where the match has already started and, miraculously, Hearts are holding Celtic. A Jambo is ejected from the away end, much to the delight of the Celtic hordes. 'Churry-o, churry-o!' This annoys a Hearts fan near us, 'Ya potato-muchin' tink fucks!' So a Hoops fan turns his back on us and points to the name on the back of his strip, only it's not that of his favourite player, it's the legend: 'God bless the Pope'.

Then Hearts score. Crikey. And then they do it again. We're –
Hearts, that is – for it now. But the Celtic onslaught never comes.
Or rather Andy Webster and Steven Pressley – the latter right back
on form – cope with all that's thrown at them. Some of their
thumping tackles are truly heroic. A third Lithuanian, Marius Kizys,
has come in and he's running the show. Ricky says Lithuanian
National Haircut Nos 1 and 2 have brought flair to the team – and
now No 3 looks pretty useful as well. This is something he admits
he did not view as a priority in the Craig Levein era, but he's since
revised his opinion of the 'fuckin' borin'' way Levein's team played.

'And these dudes look cool as well.'

This result is a small disaster for flag-chasing Celtic and the
Jambos, despite being modest in number, ram this point home.
'Fuck all! Yer gonnae win fuck all!' they sing, followed by,
'Champions – yer havin' a laugh!' Ricky takes a picture on his
phone of the fast-emptying home stands and pings it back to the
Jambo Village.

At the final whistle we're kept in our pen to avoid the potential
for bovver. The gulls are squawking over the stadium and we're still
there. *Sportscene*'s touchline twit Chick Young is prattling to the
managers and we're still not being allowed out. 'Chick Young! He
takes it up the arse!'

We want to celebrate, but where? All the pubs around here are
Celtic-oriented, and draped in green, white – and orange. We
won't be welcome. But Billy knows a place. It's Walkers at
Bridgeton Cross and, sure enough, the red, white and blue is flying
defiantly above the door.

An old Rangers chant comes to mind: 'We are the Bridgeton
Derry boys . . .' Then an old poem: 'Up in a tenement in Bridgeton
Cross/Of all the teddy boys he was the boss.' You could call the pub
an oasis of Protestantism and Loyalism, but that makes it sound
unique, special. Then again, this is almost certain to be a one-off,
never-to-be-repeated experience: I'm clapped in to the bar by the
Rangers regulars who then buy me drinks.

The place is almost windowless and virtually airless. Shilpit wee men and square-shaped, spray-tanned women scuttle about. On the walls, a giant flute-band flag – 'Bridgeton Chosen Few' – plus lots of pix of Gers greats, including Colin Stein, Derek Johnstone, Willie Henderson, Tam 'The Scythe' Forsyth and the late Davie Cooper.

'Well done ma bonnie boys!' says a man missing both his front teeth, slapping me and the rest of the guys on the back amid the sweltering, tattooed throng. 'We were through in Edinburgh this mornin' for the Apprentice Boys. Then your result came in. And now we're waitin' for the auld cunt tae snuff it. Whit a day! Now, whit you lot havin' . . . ?'

The next round is on Phil, his £140 bet on an unlikely Jambo victory having netted him a grand. I don't bet, ever. Far too cautious, so I am. But, happy though this scene is, I just don't know the songs. Are they going to ask me to sing one? Billy, sensitive soul that he is, notices my edginess and rounds everyone up. 'Thanks for the drinks, guys,' he says, although of course the gratitude really flows in the opposite direction. Rangers will go back to the top of the SPL tomorrow if they beat Motherwell. Ricky wishes our Hun hosts good luck: 'Hope yez dae the business the morn'.'

A couple of hours later we're safely back in Edinburgh, in the Haymarket, and it shows how far I've come this season when I feel snug and secure in a Jambo enclave. Traditionally at this time of night, the chat turns to music. Ricky has just discovered another 1970s soft-rock gem: 'Blinded By The Light', the Manfred Mann version. He's also getting into Hall & Oates. 'New music is pish,' he says, when I mention a current fave: LCD Soundsystem. 'The auld stuff's the best.'

Today, we spent a few hours in the company of two diametrically opposed factions who believe, truly, that the auld stuff is the best, that tradition – mutually deadly tradition – will never die. It would be a fine thing to see this internecine struggle relegated to the equivalent of a stairheid rammy in Scottish life. Who knows, maybe Hearts splitting the Old Firm could help bring that about.

But just as I'm thinking this, the pub telly flashes up the tickertape message 'Pope John Paul II Dead' and Ricky and Billy high-five each other.


## 3 April

I'm checking my emails after a couple of days and as usual it's all just so much junk. A Niagara of Viagra offers, inch after inch of tadger extension opportunities. But what's this? 'Dear Aidan, very long time no speak!'

I'd almost given up hope of hearing from Uncle Mike. It's quite possible, I reckoned, that he was dead. The family's jungle-drum network beats softly these days and we hadn't heard anything from Africa in yonks. In the event, he's had a few close shaves. 'Cancer of the kidney in '95, a heart attack in '97.' But he's hanging in there:

*I still follow Hearts, although I can't even pronounce most of the players' names now. Intellectually I know it's stupid and hard to explain, but Auntie Jo will tell you that I still have a dip in mood when they lose, and especially if Hibs win.*

And then, after bringing me up to date with the progress of his family – his eldest son Hamish is a father, to Bannock ('He didn't hate *Braveheart* as much as I did') – he drops the bombshell.

*Gordon* [his older brother, my dad, Faither] *was a fanatical Hearts supporter. I was going to write to you after reading something you wrote in* The Scotsman *about his affection for his namesake, the Famous Five winger Gordon Smith. It was so far from reality! I remember Gordon booing him every time he got the ball, which all Hearts fans did, of course. Gordon had to support Hearts. Our father was a Hibs fan for goodness sake!*

Pause for breath: Faither was a Jambo and his old man was a Hibby. Faither was a Jambo *because* Grandad Smith was a Hibby. This makes sense: my dad, sad for him, did not benefit from the same Faither-Laddie relationship that I had. In fact, he never had a good word to say for the auld bugger. It all makes sense, but my world has just been well and truly rocked.

*Gordon used to take me to Tynecastle, lifting me over the turnstile. We went to away games as well: Stirling Albion, Airdrie, Dunfermline by ferry*

*– there was no Forth Road Bridge then and I've still never seen it – Dundee United and even Aberdeen. I think we went to Brechin or Forfar for a cup match, too. And we both wore big maroon-and-white scarves and Christmas presents always seemed to be Hearts gloves and ties. We always lost them at New Year parties as well. In those days, fans didn't wear the sacred strip, that was unthinkable.*

*I particularly remember a day of delirium with Gordon and I and many other Jambos (the term didn't exist in the 1940s) skipping and hollering along Gorgie Road after Hearts had unexpectedly beaten East Fife – a good team then, dirty, rugged miners in ominous yellow-and-black striped shirts and nails sticking from their studs – and in fact we'd won 6–1. It was season '48–'49. The next week we beat Queen of the South 4–0, then Rangers 2–0 and Hearts were about to be a good team again.*

*The side (2–3–5 formation) was: Jimmy Brown; Bobby Parker, Tom McKenzie; Charlie Cox, Bobby Dougan and Davie Laing; Tommy Sloan, Alfie Conn, 'King' Willie Bauld, Jimmy Wardhaugh (with whom your dad later worked at the* Edinburgh Evening News*) and Archie Williams.*

*I think that East Fife game was the first time the Terrible Trio lined up together. I had been watching Willie Bauld play for Edinburgh City, Third Division, I think. I used to stoke up the boilers for the dressing-room baths at their ground in Ferry Road. Gordon had a couple of trial games for them as a goalkeeper, did you know that? I of course thought your dad was almost as good as Jimmy Brown, who was undoubtedly the planet's best goalie at the time. Anyway, hope this has helped you understand Gordon a bit more. Great to hear from you again, keep in touch.*

*Up the Hearts!*

*Mike*

Bloody hell. My brother, the advocate, who has been speculating about our dad's true football Heartsland for more than 30 years and has just been proved right, is wearing the expression of smug satisfaction he must reserve for court rulings in his clients' favour in civil cases worth six-figure sums concerning sludge (Sean's speciality). Me, I'm sure I must look like I've just been hit by £500,000 worth of sewage which, if you think about it, is a heck of a lot. *Bloody hell.*

I don't actually know what's worse: that my father was a Jambo, or that he apparently cared so little for football that he could change sides as effortlessly as he did his safari suits.

Did the Turnbull's Tornadoes team mean nothing to him when he watched them with me during the 1970s? Or did Hearts mean nothing to him? Now that they've been confirmed as his team, I think I'm more upset about the latter being true.

We travelled all over this dour land following that great Hibs side – Onion, Sloop, Nijinsky and the rest. As a boy, perfectly naturally, I loved the guys who got the goals – Alan Gordon and Jimmy O'Rourke. But Dad taught me how to tune into the dog-whistle-frequency required for proper appreciation of those classy providers in the middle of the park, Alex Edwards and Alex Cropley. Did he do all this through gritted falsers? Did he secretly wish he was somewhere else – Tynecastle?

I have to believe that while he might have been disappointed when I chose Hibs over Hearts, he went with it because he loved me, and ended up loving the Hibees, too. I have to believe this. But I also have to acknowledge that he was a Jambo and that I am, that old song again, 'Son Of My Father'.

Dot-bloody-dash, dot-dot-dot . . .


## 10 April. Celtic 2, Hearts 1

8.35am. Twenty-five to *nine* in the *morning*, that's when the first alcohol touches my lips, a new personal best. We're on our way to Hampden with the Orwell Lodge, and the £5 a pint-plus-scran offer is proving hugely popular with the Jambo Village. The air is thick with the irresistible combo of pork sausage and cup dreaming.

But it won't be the all-Embra final we fantasized about. The previous day at Hampden, Hibs surprisingly lost their semi-final 2–1 to Dundee United. I say surprisingly, but even though United are the worst team in the SPL, don't have a manager, and are helmed in midfield by the underachieving ex-Hibby Grant Brebner . . . and even though yesterday United should have been three–nil down at half-time, were completely useless for the first hour, really rank, and it seemed a foregone conclusion that Hibs would win . . . and even though Hibbys outnumbered United's fans by five to one, with all of them expecting a cup final appearance – at least – as reward for a much-raved-about season . . . we always knew they'd contrive to throw it away.

I'm not sure whether to tell the boys I went to the Hibs game. In the end I say I decided to go at the last minute, which is a bare-faced lie. Their reaction ranges from disinterest to Ricky's look of mild treachery. This might be the time to tell him about Uncle Mike's letter. His eyes light up as I describe the momentous news and he puts a thick Jambo arm round my shoulder. 'Uh knew ye'd been livin' a lie!'

We discuss the now-dead concept of a Leith-Gorgie showdown in the final and Billy says he wouldn't have minded the build-up, that would have been exciting, but the game itself would have been almost impossible to watch, and the result, if it had gone against Hearts, would have been cause for emigrating. 'Aye, tae Jupiter,' says Ricky.

As Peter buys another round of beers – it's now just gone 9am – I'm seriously thinking that the perennial cup crappers should withdraw from the tournament. Twenty-five thousand Hibbys were at Hampden yesterday and they must laugh when they're told about the Toon Army's mounting anxiety as Newcastle United's first FA Cup for half a century hoves tantalisingly into view. Fifty years? Try one hundred and flippin' three! The last Hibby alive who witnessed the 1902 triumph, and who was regularly wheeled out in his bathchair by the papers to summon up a dribbling reminisce, died some years ago. Jock Wilson, who was born 497 days *after* that win, is the next best thing and yesterday, the *Sunday Mail* 'bought' him up and laid on a limo for the trip along the M8 for the latest Hibby Hampden horror-show.

So it's come to this: a Hibs fan almost as old as that last triumph is viewed as something of a freak, and is asked questions like: 'Jock, we know you weren't actually born, but from inside your mother's womb, OK . . . inside your father's twinkling eye, could you tell us: When Hibs last won the Scottish Cup, how did you *feel*?' Then he's thrust into the emotional fast-spin of a semi-final. Win or lose, he'll probably keel over, and the paper will get a great exclusive.

Some Jambos at the Orwell are pointing at Jock's toothless expression in the paper and, cruel bastards, they're laughing. Then this chant starts up:

> We are Hibernian FC
> We ain't got no history
> O'Connor's fat
> Our fans are queer
> We ain't won the cup for 103 years.

These songs don't annoy me anymore, I find them funny. I think I've come to accept that my dad meant well when he tried to reassure me, in that birthday card, that Hibs would win the cup one day. But deep down he didn't believe it any more than I did.

A friend of Ricky's joins our company. This is Fergie, a joiner and Robbie Williams impersonator, a service he provides free, by showing off his chest hair at the windows of the Orwell, scaring locals as they fetch the rolls and papers and terrifying their little dogs.

Fergie is one of Ricky's oldest, maddest, baddest pals but they've both calmed down a fair bit, now that the latter has moved in with his girlfriend and the former has become a dad.

'There I was just yesterday, bouncing the wee yin on my knee, singing to her,' beams the proud father.

'What songs, Fergie?' asks Billy, anticipating 'Angels' or 'She's The One' or some other sweet ballads from the Robbie songbook.

'Naw, Orange wans!' The wean had to be rescued by Fergie's mum, a spin-doctor for Scotland's First Minister, Jack McConnell.

Not before time, because I'm half-pissed already, the Orwell Lodge charabanc sets off for Hampden. It's got a toilet on board – no need for slash-breaks on the M8 every 15 minutes; the middle-class-isation of football is indeed relentless – but disappointingly there is no sound-system. So, up the back of the bus, I read the reports of the Hibs game, about how the Hibees failure in the Scottish Cup is *getting beyond a joke*, and how their fans *surely can't take much more of this* and Ricky, bless him, doesn't interrupt, or take the piss, he just leaves me be.

I had hospitality for the Hibs game. Hospitality can give further cause to the old-skool football fan to utter the cry: 'And they call this progress?' I don't mean to sound ungrateful; the invite from Scott, my usual host on such occasions, was much appreciated. It's just funny being at a football match while dressed for a wedding, or a funeral, or a court appearance, or indeed a game 50 years ago when men always wore ties.

So anyway we're all looking forward to the second semi, all the more so after Hearts' win at Parkhead last week, and wondering if the Jambos can go one better than Hibs, when down the front of the bus this chant starts up, to the tune of 'When The Saints Go Marching In':

> *Oh Edinbra!*
> *Oh Edinbra!*
> *Oh Edinbra is wonderful!*
> *Apart from Hibs, Jews and Pakis*
> *Oh Edinbra is wonderful!*

This is the song that was sung at Dundee, that sparked a debate on the website, but I didn't know how offensive it was until now. A few sniggers from our section of the bus, then we're treated to this choice ditty:

> *Three Popes gone*
> *The Queen lives on*
> *Tooori-oori-ay*
> *Toori-oori-ay*
> *All Pakis are gay*
> *Ain't no black on the Union Jack*
> *Join the National Front*

This time, the singer is shouted down. It's Fergie. He stops when this order is issued by the transport convener: 'We'll have none o' that on this bus, pal.' Am I shocked? No, not really. No-one else joined in, and a ratio of one racist, sectarian, anti-semitic, homophobe per 50 fans is probably about average for the SPL.

Hampden is the national stadium, and a national disgrace. The redevelopment was botched and we've been left with a characterless coliseum. The stands were halved in size and left too shallow and too far from the pitch. Then, to compensate for the lack of atmosphere, the crap music on the sound-system was turned up to 11 on the dial and a nation which helped give football to the world was told: 'This is all you're fit for, deal with it.'

The one good thing about Hampden is the museum dedicated to oor fitba which, miraculously, is not foosty or po-faced. Instead, the beaks at the SFA have displayed a rare sense of humour by allowing a display dedicated to the huge part drink has played in the sport's culture. It contains old beer cans, Double Diamond and Bass Export, which pre-Criminal Justice (Scotland) Act 1980, served as refreshment receptacle, localised loo and missile. There's also a copy of the act itself and, even more thrillingly, a solitary Adidas Gazelle trainer left behind by a Hibs Casual, just about my team's only contribution to the hall of fame.

There was no danger of the Hibees winning the previous day. Deek Riordaninho actually scored the first goal, but his team-mates were constipated with nerves throughout. The feeling of impending doom was enhanced at half-time when my friend Simon and I hung around the concourse under the stand. This grim, grey, utterly soul-destroying space looks like it has been designed for mass state killings. But we were happier there than in our seats, having our ears pummelled by Tony Christie, whose journey from chicken-in-a-basket oblivion to No 1 in the pop charts is almost as improbable as Hibs ever lifting the cup.

'So how does it feel being back among your ain folk?' said Simon.
'Weird.'

'Aidan, are we losing you to the Jambos? I know these strange religious cults can seem appealing when you're impressionable and a bit lost, but fundamentally they're bad.'

Then Simon bumped into his cousin Vince, who he had not seen for years. Vince's mother died just before his 18th birthday and he was keen to pass on to Simon just about the last words she spoke. ' "Remember, Vincent," she said, "the Hibs, they'll always let you down." ' And as always, yesterday, they did.

But Hearts top that in their semi. They let down the club, Scottish football, the whole stunted nation, before a ball is kicked. There's a minute's silence for the Pope and the Jambos boo it, right out of the crappy national stadium, right onto front pages everywhere.

'Shamed across the world' is the *Sun*'s headline on a story rounding up international outrage, and the *New York Post*'s 'Soccer fans boo pontiff' is typical.

I am right in the middle of the angry mob. None of my lot boo but everyone else around us is jeering or flicking the Vs at the Celtic stands or twirling their Hearts scarves or waving their Union Jacks and the handful that are standing in silence are doing the Nazi salute.

It's bad, really bad. Some of the Jambos are going absolutely mental, veins are sticking out of necks. The referee decides to cut short the tribute after just 24 seconds and immediately the Celtic hordes start up a chant of 'Dirty orange bastards' and sing it repeatedly throughout the game. Recently, I've been pleasantly surprised to see Hearts reveal themselves to be rock 'n' roll. Now they're chucking TVs out of windows and stuffing groupies with red snappers.

The first riposte from the Celtic contingent has barely died on the Hampden swirl when their team score. Craig Gordon, The Young Count, is none too clever at a corner, and he's hardly blameless when Celtic double their advantage early in the second half. Then comes a spirited Hearts comeback, and a sensational volley from Lithuanian National Haircut No 2 of which Deek Riordaninho would have been proud. But it's not enough.

Normally in such circumstances, with Hibs going out of the cup the day before, I would not have wanted the Jambos to get to the final, no way. But all through the game I keep thinking of Uncle Mike's letter and I can't get an image out of my head: Faither in his Hearts tie and gloves.

The bus home is quiet. Fergie was last seen at half-time, stomping off in search of Celtic fans for a full and frank exchange of views. I ask the guys what they thought of the Jambo protest. 'It wisnae clever,' says Billy. 'But was it clever to try and hold the minute's silence in the first place?'

All week the debate will rage: in 2005, is Scotland not grown-up enough to acknowledge the death of a world figure in a dignified way, even though he was not all things to all men?

In deepest Zambia, for once, Uncle Mike won't have to search the worldwide web for too long for news of his dear, old, proud, romantic Heart of Midlothian. It's not on the back pages, it's on the front pages, and it's absolutely everywhere.


### 11 April

Just how mental are Hearts? Phil Anderton thinks 'very'. He's Tynecastle's new chief executive and he says: 'We are in the process of conducting a study which I think will demonstrate why many Hearts fans don't want to come to home games.'

He thinks home games are bad? He should have been at Hampden or Parkhead or Fir Park.

'They are uncomfortable with the atmosphere and frankly, if there is a perception that you are going to a ground where there will be obscene singing, the possibility that missiles will be thrown and violence erupting, I empathise 100 per cent with those parents who don't want to bring their children here. I wouldn't do it – and I have young kids – so I appreciate the concerns. Yes, the organisation has a proud history and heritage, but that doesn't mean we should simply let things carry on as they have done for the last 100 years.'

My Jambo friend Ricky is honest enough to admit to a number of prejudices. In the course of this season I've met other Jambos of like mind. One of them, Steve, scolded Billy in Dundee for buying his sweets supply from a 'Paki shop'. Here's the same Jambo looking forward to the day when he can pass on fatherly wisdom to his son: 'I'll tell him, no Paki shops, no Hibs and he better not turn out gay. If he does, I'll beat it out of him. It's a disease.'

Another Jambo, Chris, chanting 'BNP!' during the chorus of Franz Ferdinand's 'Take Me Out' during a game of pool when I met him, told me he planned to stand for the party at the next General Election. At this, his opponent put down his cue, shook his hand, offered to go halvers on the deposit and said: 'Are ye gonnae go canvassing in your soft-top with a loud-hailer and do you want me tae drive?'

These bampots are in the minority. Every club has an extremist element among its supporters. But they're unswervingly loyal and, what's more, season-ticket holders. Under a headline in *The Herald* dubbing him 'Scottish football's Blairite visionary', Phil Anderton says he wants to re-educate the bams. If that fails, presumably he will have to remove them from Tynecastle, reducing the Jambo contingent before the club can even start to grow to anything like Old Firm proportions, which is Vladimir Romanov's Big Idea.

Does Anderton really think there are lots of nice, polite, well-scrubbed family groups hiding round the corner from Tynecastle and waiting to take the places of those who are rather too committed to the cause? Anderton – nicknamed 'Fireworks Phil' after trying to brighten up rugby at Murrayfield with sparklers displays – has no football background and it shows. Of course he's right to condemn sectarianism, racism and the rest. But stadia devoid of colour, humour, edge and, yes, even bitterness and hatred, is a sure way to kill off football as well. You wish Anderton well, but some very harsh-thinking people are currently among his most loyal paying customers. In oor fitba right now, you takes what you get.

## 13 April. Hearts 1, Hibs 2

All season long I've painted Hibs as the artists and Hearts as the artisans. When Hearts beat Hibs in the first derby of the season, I consoled myself that they were the team who wanted to pass the ball, Hearts merely tried to burst it. And as Hibs smoothed their way past Hearts in the league, I nodded knowingly and told myself: 'Football always triumphs in the end.'

But tonight Hibs consolidate their grip on Hearts' favourite third spot by playing the Hearts way. We're not talking New Hearts or Porno Hearts, and anyway, I've yet to be convinced that Dr Ruth is the right man to direct *Debbie Does Dalry*. No, the clothes Hibs have nicked belonged to Old Hearts. They amount to a chastity belt, fastened tight round Brazil-type stylings.

Hibs were losing this game until they brought on a big, dithering striker from Mali, Amamdou Konte, pumped the high ball to him, and scored a couple of ugly goals out of the chaos he caused in the Hearts defence.

I think it was F. Scott Fitzgerald who said there is no such thing as an unsatisfying Edinburgh derby win. Well, he's wrong.

I should, of course, be happy. I'm still supposed to be a Hibby. Tonight Hibs triumphed at Tynecastle for the first time this century, and the win all but kills off Hearts' hopes of qualifying for Europe. But the way this was achieved simply wasn't the Hibs way.

All season long, I've watched cruiserweight-class football, and on good days – not dissimilar to very, very bad days – I've learned to appreciate its value and place in the world. So what's my problem? Probably that I now feel distanced from the mass of green and white jumping and whooping and thumping their stand's metal surrounds with their fists. Like everyone else in the ground tonight – like all the Jambos – I'm playing down this result. No, I'm completely dissing it.


## 16 April. Dundee Utd 2, Hearts 1

I hesitate to call Tannadice my 'Rosebud'. The elusive, last SPL stadium to be visited as a Jambo is not right up there with the elusive, last word uttered by the dying newspaper tycoon in *Citizen Kane*. But in its own way it has intrigued: by the end of this match, would the mystery of this season – the mystery of Jamboness – be revealed?

As a collectable, Dundee United's ground is George Cohen in my Esso 1970 World Cup Coins, derby County in my Esso Club Badges – the final one to be slotted into place. I didn't *have* to see Hearts strut their frumpy stuff at every ground, but being a bit of a completist, I wanted to. From my regular crew, Billy is on holiday at his villa in France – those Jambos, *so* decadent – but Ricky has kindly agreed to accompany me up the East Coast Main Line on a fine spring day, and good lad that he is, he buys the Greggs sausage-rolls for the journey.

He would not have gone to this game otherwise; Hearts are just not playing well enough. He's recently bought a DVD of *Crime Story*, collector's edition, and would have quite happily spent the afternoon watching that. So he's putting himself out for me and the least I can do is stick with these guys, not cheat on them with other Jambos, although I doubt I'd ever find another as fierce, and as funny, as Ricky.

Charles Forster Kane, the subject of *Citizen Kane*, was a man who couldn't love, which is inappropriate for Tannadice, where United take the field to John Paul Young's 1970s disco classic, 'Love Is In The Air'.

> *Love is in the air*
> *In the whisper of the trees*
> *Love is in the air*
> *In the thunder of the sea*

I love this song and it could also be an anthem for the city itself. Ricky and I struggle to get through the Wellgate shopping centre without being mown down by prams. They fly in formation, never less than three together at any one time. We glance over our shoulders as they trundle by: a riot of streaked hair extensions, pea-jackets, trousers with sponsors' messages written across the beam-ends. Dundee, you see, is a world-class centre of excellence for young mums.

We trudge the inexorable trudge to the Snug, the little bar overlooking Tannadice (and also Dens Park), but not to dream the impossible dream. Hearts' season is all but over. Robbo's tea is all but oot. Football is not gripping us so the conversation drifts into other areas, and before long we're resuming an earlier discussion about books.

Ricky, the unrelenting skinhead, has not only devoured the entire Irvine Welsh oeuvre, he's also read every Sherlock Holmes. In hushed but excited tones, he tells me: 'D'you know, I've been to 221B.' He means the museum in Baker Street, London, dedicated to the world's greatest detective. 'I bought a deerstalker, that was 24 quid. They also had an Inverness cape for 450 quid but you know, Aidan, while Basil Rathbone suited it, I'm just not sure it's a look that would work the day.'

Of course, I say, Sir Arthur Conan Doyle – Holmes' creator – was a Hibby.

'Was he shite!'

That's what Hibbys like to believe, although the evidence – Edinburgh-Irish roots, a birthplace not far from Hibs' old ground at Powderhall, a great love of football – would need some serious Holmesian scrutiny before it could be regarded as conclusive. Even then, I doubt Ricky would believe it.

To make him feel better, I tell him I've just discovered a new celebrity Jambo, Mark E Smith, the Philip Larkin of Punk, who really supports Manchester City, but told me that from boyhood, when City took full-back Arthur Mann from Tynie, Hearts have been his Scottish team. I don't think Ricky is impressed. He doesn't like The Fall. He'd prefer it if I could confirm to him that the Bee Gees or the bloke out of Boston with the biggest afro in the world or the King himself was a Jambo.

We rush back down the hill to get into our seats in time for 'Love Is In The Air'. Lithuanian National Haircut No 1 is back after his ban and some Casualettes down the front of the main stand chant 'Miko, Miko'. United, though, start better and score first to give them hope of avoiding relegation.

Lee Miller equalises but pretty soon for Hearts this match is going downhill, like a sled, which of course was the mystery of 'Rosebud'. The Jambo defence is a shadow of its former, impregnable, army-drilled self. Instead of 'Halt, who goes there?' there's a message pinned to the door: 'Help yourself, try not to wake anyone'.

Our minds wander and we're already looking forward to our *pehs* at half-time. This match is so tedious I'm even able to interest Ricky in a discussion about stadium architecture.

'Isn't it a pity,' I venture, 'that the most characterful part of Tannadice, the L-shaped stand down the far corner, is no longer used?'

'I ken,' replies Ricky, 'and you could say the same about the two corner areas across the pitch, where the old terrace wall rises up.'

Hibs are losing to Livi but Hearts, technically not yet out of contention for Europe, cannot raise their game. Then in the final minute the former Hibby Grant Brebner hits a thumping winner for United. He never did anything like that at Easter Road, not even in his wildest dreams. Still, at least we had a nice day out in Dundee, famous for jute, jam, journalism – and now – jailbait mums.

On this showing the mystery of Jamboness would baffle Sherlock Holmes. But maybe the 'Rosebud' connection is more useful, at least as regards this performance. *Citizen Kane* is, of course, a thinly-disguised biography of a real tycoon, William Randolph Hearst, and 'Rosebud' was his nickname for mistress Marion Davies.

It specifically referred to one body part. Hearts today were a bunch of fannies.


## 23 April. Hibs 2, Hearts 2

There are many highly individual quirks to the SPL, things you might call unique slagging points. One of them is the top six split, when the league halves in two for the run-in, in a bid to make it more exciting.

What is this like? I'll tell you: like an oil tanker spewing its sickly black cargo over the high seas, obliterating wildlife, wiping out entire species. Or, if you prefer, like a victim of the *Texas Chainsaw Massacre*, with blood and guts everywhere. And the sound, the terrible sound, of metal grinding on bone. You'll hear it in your sleep and you'll wake up screaming. It will haunt you forever.

But the worst thing is that by then the league is usually all over bar the gurning, so the split is a big anti-climax.

Not this year. For the first time since the split was introduced, nothing has been decided, all the prizes are still up for grabs, the dunce's cap of relegation, too. And for the first time in three years, Hibs have made the Top Six so here comes a fourth derby, a mere ten days after the third.

Derbies should have long build-ups, and equally long comedowns. There should be time and space for them to be discussed and dissected ad flippin' nauseum, and a long enough gap in between for a council-funded reception for the winners, counselling for the losers.

Maybe Hearts are keenest on a quick rematch, to make amends for a defeat when they had the previous derby in their sweaty grasp. Certainly Peter is confident when we meet up in Da-Da-Da! with Colin and Billy, refreshed after his hols, and anxious to learn of the latest prognosis on the stricken Dr Ruth.

It's not good, I say, he hasn't got long. A report in *The Scotsman* hints at a culture-clash with the Lithuanian beaks. They're smart-suited and courteous; he of course is a funny, wee, scruffy, shouty man. Peter, guardian of Jambo principles, says that for better or worse, this is what football people are like in Scotland and wherever the Lithuanians are going to take Hearts, they should not lose sight of that – 'because maybe that's how we prefer it'.

In the taxi-ride to the game I think back to what Paul said to me at his brother's party, about how football is changing, and how the old passions, the tribalism, seem out of place now. We pass a group of Hibs Casuals, late 30s or even older, with wrinkles round their eyes to compliment the dunts on their noses. They look absolutely knackered.

But in the stadium, in the Whyte & Mackay Stand, the Jambos are far from downcast after recent disappointments. They rip up a large chunk of the shelving between the two sections and dance and sing in monkey masks and probably they're showing too much of the kind of passion that Fireworks Phil says is scaring sensible-minded fans away from football.

The increase in the number of Union Jacks may have something to do with the fact it's St George's Day, or even the day when the BNP launch their General Election manifesto. If it's neither, this is possibly even more alarming for Fireworks Phil. How on earth is he going to keep the fans, change the philosophy and not crush the rumbustious atmosphere at games like this?

I have to say I love *everything* about this derby, including all the non-PC stuff. It's a cracking match which thrills a T-shirted crowd on a Sunshine On Leithy afternoon. I love the thundercrack goal from Deek 'I don't do tap-ins' Riordaninho which looks like giving Hibs another win. For Hibbys, after all Deek's endeavours, this must be a ho-hum howitzer; for me it's simply glorious. But I also love the bare-faced cheek with which Hearts nick a point through a late Andy Webster equaliser, leaving derby honours even over the whole season.

Gordon Smith, a hero to many in this ground – if not, I now learn, Faither – was one great football man to pass away this season. Another was Arthur Hopcraft, author of *The Football Man*, in which he wrote: 'If football were to consist only of delicate, imaginative distribution of the ball, without bodily contact at all, it would be short of a good half of its followers, as it would be if it were played only by the specialists in the tackles which can stun a man. There is no point in arguing about which set of spectators is best for the game; it is part of its greatness that it attracts them both.'

Hopcraft published *The Football Man* 37 years ago but these words could have been written about this derby. It's not just that I acknowledge Hearts' right to exist, I actually see the point of them now. Jambos are people too.

As we walk past the main gates, rival fans are screaming at each other through the railings and the polis are struggling to keep them apart. 'It's getting bad again,' says Billy, 'just like in the old days.' He should know; he was there. 'Aye,' says Colin, 'Hibs are violent and Hearts are sectarian, racist bigots – we should team up with each other!'

We dauner up Leith Walk. The pasta 'n' pizza joints have got their tables out, the waiters are jousting for custom, using their giant pepper-pots as lances, and the Champs d'Leithie is looking swish. It's a lovely afternoon for alfresco dining, but also for open-air fighting. Outside the Playhouse Theatre, Billy spots one of the oldest, hardest Hibs hooligans. He's stopped by the cops and questioned. Now he doesn't look so tough, trapped under a hoarding for *Starlight Express*, possibly the campest musical in the world.

Maybe, as a Football Man circa 2004–05, this tough-nut seems outmoded and faintly ludicrous. But he's been going to the game since long before it became middle-class and trendy and *safe* and he still looks well capable of, and interested in, hanging around for a while yet – no matter that he and his kind might not fit into the football worldview of a bunch of Lithuanian bankers.


### 30 April. Hearts 0, Motherwell 0

I've checked my scribbles. I've read them and re-read them and all I can find in my notepad relating to this game is 'Mr Prickles'.

Ricky is on holiday, in 'the Dominican', so he lends me his season ticket and I meet Peter, Dave, Paul and Gerry in the Ardmillan. 'Of all the seasons to try and be a Jambo,' says Paul. 'We're pretty shite and you guys are playing your best stuff for years.' This is the first Jambo acknowledgment that Hibs are the new third force in Scotland. A win for them at Parkhead today – improbable, I know – should clinch them the best-of-the-rest spot behind the Old Firm.

The Jambos have given up on catching their rivals and this is one of only two games today which has no bearing on anything. It's completely meaningless and is played out in a stupor. Motherwell probably deserve to make it five wins out of five against Hearts this season, but can't even summon up the effort to score the winner from the penalty-spot.

'Mr Prickles' is the toy hedgehog which Peter's son Lewis is looking after this weekend as part of a school project. 'I have to take him some place interesting and write about it,' he tells me. Interesting? And you've brought him *here*? Best of luck, Lewis.

If you think fluffy toys being able to discern the difference between 22 professional footballers and the extras list for *Die, Zombie, Die!* is a ludicrous notion, then get this: Hibs beat Celtic 3–1. Every goal is a 'minor masterpiece' according to the *Sunday Times*. In all my years as a Hibby, I've never seen them win at Parkhead. And to make matters worse, I miss them doing it in Brazilian yellow.

And I've just remembered something else about this game. Midway through the second half, a section of the Wheatfield start up a chant which, earlier this season, you would never have heard. It could be sympathetic. It could be ironic. It could be gratitude, for at least having a go. Or it could be an acknowledgment that, really, when all is said and done, we're pish and we know we are.

It goes like this: 'One Neil MacFarlane, there's only one Neil MacFarlane . . .'

A blush spreads across the face of football's most unlikely poster boy.

# *MAY*

### 7 May. Rangers 2, Hearts 1

These dispatches are getting shorter, for many reasons. This is the fag-end of the season. Also, Hearts more than most clubs are staggering to the finish-line. The repetitive nature of the SPL just wears you down, and even another visit to Castle Greyskull, even a glance up at the Rangers motto writ large on the red-brick Ibrox frontage – 'Abandon hope all ye who claim for a penalty here' – fails to provoke the usual, irresistible combo of fear and excitement.

But I'm no longer looking for Billy and Ricky to provide a revelation of the quintessence of Jamboism. Rather than me interrogate them under the cloak or replica shirt of conversation, we now just have the conversation. They are my mates, I see more of them than I do my wife, and I don't even have a wife.

If the trained-observer skills I'm supposed to possess as a journo have been dulled, however, then Ricky is still watchful, alert. For instance, it's him who spies this little vignette of Hun life, on the walk up to the stadium: 'Look at that van, it's called Burger Palace. Is that no' a contradiction in terms? And look at these girls in the queue, they're all wearing Rangers shellsuits. D'you know, there's nuthin' lovelier on a lassie.'

Before this game we sought out the beerhall from our previous trip to Glesca, but Billy's pizza was slow in arriving so he had to nip out for some Fruit Pastilles to keep him going. And Ricky had to tell him not to eat so fast although, thoughtful lad, he'd brought along some Gaviscon in case of just such an emergency. See, we're a real team now.

Which is more than can be said for Hearts, who are simply going through the motions on a sunny afternoon. Well, sunny apart from the little black cloud hovering over their little glum manager from first whistle to last.

Rangers, neck-and-neck with Celtic for the title, score two with ease and should be further ahead. The second comes from their Trinidadian central defender, Marvin Andrews, which is the cue for the Gers fans to start singing his name. A Jambo behind us says this is a bit rich, given that Andrews is black and they regularly boo other teams' black players. 'Aye,' says Ricky, 'but I think we're the really racist club. Long after other fans got bored of slagging off Mark Walters, we were still doing it. Remember that chant, "You'll never see a coon in maroon"? Of course, then we signed Justin Fashanu, who was black *and* gay.'

Compared to the last time we were at Ibrox, the Rangers beaks seem to have turned down the volume on the loyal, royal triumphalism rubbish. This doesn't amount to a complete rejection of creed, but there are Saltires flying in the Broomloan Stand now, and that's something. So when I spot a Hun in a red England shirt, I go a bit mental. He's too far away to hear me, but I shout and point at him at every available opportunity. Eventually, he gets lifted by the cops, and as he's carted off – with his wife and two kids forced to troop out behind him – I shout even louder. 'Hey you, calm down!' barks a steward. I look at Billy and Ricky. They're pretty shocked.

### 15 May. Hearts 1, Celtic 2
'So anyway,' I say, and of course the story has been embroidered a bit, 'there I was at Ibrox last week, shouting for Hearts, shouting so much for them that I almost got myself arrested.' I look at Rab and David and Ivan. They're pretty shocked.

We're in Tinelli, the Easter Road trat, where my Hibby mates have gathered all season, before feasting on beautiful football and barrie goals from Deek Riordaninho. My brother Sean has come along today, also Rab's girlfriend Mary. When Rab flitted to Shetland he didn't have a girlfriend. When we all last watched

Hibs together, David wasn't married. Now he is. There's been a few changes round here.

The most significant is that Hibs are playing like the team we know and love and our little gang has re-convened to see them clinch third place and a return to Europe. Rab and David have travelled from opposite ends of the country, Lerwick and London respectively, and me, well, as they like to say in *Hello!*, I've taken time out from my busy schedule as a Jambo to catch up with old friends.

They all want to know about my season in hell. It's not been like that, I say. It was difficult at the start because I was going to games on my own. Then I looked up an old Jambo mate, and he introduced me to his Jambo pals, and we've had a good laugh, especially on the road, and OK the football has been crap and you lot, by all accounts, have been watching Brazil . . . but I kind of knew the season was going to work out like that. Even when I want them to be rubbish, the Hibs, they always let you down.

'Well, *Judas*,' says Ivan, the Humanist minister, 'you'll see a show today.'

It's good to see these guys again, and I can't deny it's good to be back in Easter Road, not among the away fans, but in the East Stand, formerly the old terrace that stretched up to the heavens, where Dad and I used to stand, 15 steps up from the wall, 12ft to the south of the halfway line, at the exact spot where before every home game John Blackley of the great 1970s team superstitiously battered the ball against the trackside hoarding after running onto the pitch and exchanging passes with Erich Schaedler.

And with Tony Mowbray – Lord Shaftesbury – the newly-crowned Manager of the Year in his first season as a coach, confirming something many delirious Hibbys will have suspected – that the Brazil of the 1970 World Cup were his first, his last, his everything as a footballing ideology – I am intrigued and not a little excited at seeing the wonderful Riordaninho, this time unencumbered by maroon concerns.

But here's what happens: Hibs are crap. Nervy, needing only a point against Aberdeen to qualify for the UEFA Cup, they abandon their much-hyped passing game and go long-ball. Lord Shaftesbury must take some of the blame because he picked a big man up front, Amamdou Konte, the lolloping, novelty-act in the previous month's Tynecastle derby, requiring the readjustment of tactics. It's as if he lost faith in his grand design at the last gasp. Hibs lose 2-1.

So Hibs *aren't* Brazil. On this showing they more resembled Bobby Williamson's warped vision of what football should be like, or Craig Levein's Hearts. And the Hibs fans don't deserve them to be Brazil, not when they moan at Riordan, the 23-goal Young Player of the Year, accusing him of being lazy. The great Jarzinho never tackled back; when you're that good, you don't have to. I say goodbye to my old friends, not knowing when we'll next be at a match together. 'And remember, guys,' I shout after them, 'the Hibs, they always let you down.'

That was yesterday. Hibs will have one more chance to clinch third spot but today, for Hearts, it's the last home game, time to say goodbye to Tynie for another season. This could have been the last-ever, but the Lithuanians have ensured the club's immediate future will be in Gorgie, just like their famous past. The exact terms and conditions of Jambo life beyond that are still worryingly uncertain.

And, there's nothing else for it, I can't put this off any longer, today is my last-chance, my last-chance-saloon opportunity, for a wee, pre-game aperitif in the saloon that has lurked under the railway bridge and stared back at me all season long as if to say: 'Come ahead.'

Only Billy is brave enough to accompany me to Robertson's. We pass Gorgie City Farm, and bang off cue, the cock crows. At the door of the fright-pub, two burly, black-clad bouncers block our path. Billy shows them his season ticket to prove his Jamboness. I don't have this accreditation. I want them to turn me away. I want my mum. Then . . . we're both in.

I'm thinking of great pubs in fiction, of the Black Cross in Martin Amis's *London Fields*, as the heroine Nicola Six crosses the thresh-hold. 'She entered the pub and its murk. She felt the place skip a

beat as the door closed behind her, but she had been expecting that.'
Robertson's is everything I feared, and worse.

The bar is heaving. A mud-pool of maroon. And it's not my
imagination, my paranoia, my wimpish middle-class lack of bottle,
*everyone* is staring at me. And, bearing in mind today's opposition are
Celtic, this is the song the Jambos are singing . . .

> *Could you go a chicken supper, Bobby Sands?*
> *Could you go a chicken supper, Bobby Sands?*
> *Could you go a chicken supper*
> *Ya dirty fenian fucker*
> *Could you go a chicken supper, Bobby Sands?*

Many here weren't born when Sands, an imprisoned IRA
member, went on hunger-strike until he died. But they've learned
the song. And, with their narrow stares, in shadow under baseball
cap visors, they know precisely how to absolutely terrify me.

The assault on the ears delays adjustment of the eyes. Robertson's
is low-ceilinged . . . well, I can't actually remember if it is or not. It
could have been Rome's Pantheon or the Sistine Chapel, for all that
I noticed. Breathing heavy and fast, I stare at the floor until my eyes
started to water. Oh yes, I can tell you absolutely everything about
the scuffed wooden floor . . .

Naturally, Billy has met someone he knows. I come adrift from
him, but he keeps looking over his shoulder, to check I'm all right. I
need a drink and fight my way to the bar. No, I don't *fight*, I edge
through slowly, timidly: 'Thanks, sorry, thanks, sorry . . .'

What will I have? What's everyone else drinking? The trendy
Irish cider, Magners. Except when the lone, existential western hero
asks for one, it comes out as 'Marnier'. So am I about to take
possession of a liqueur, orange admittedly, in front of all these guys
chanting 'Fuck the Pope' and throwing Nazi salutes? Mercifully,
the barmaid realises my error.

Amisesque alehouse, Hogarthian howff. The Slug & Lettuce
(Hold The Salad), All Bar Fun. Robertson's is all of these things, if

you're not a regular, like the guys in the Chelsea caps, in tribute to the old-skool skins presumably, but also like the pensioners in their Sunday Best in the corner, old enough to have fought in the war, the ones who are laughing as the 'Who shagged all the boys?' chant booms out.

Not every Hearts fan is sectarian, not every Hearts fan in Robertson's this sunny afternoon is singing sectarian songs. I know many, like Peter, the meat-van driver, who hate that stuff. But this is just another slice of Jambo life, raw and cut (very) close to the bone.

After the game – Steven Pressley is sent off, Celtic grab a late winner – the thought of popping back into Robertson's to finish my abandoned drink strangely does not appeal. We're heading into town when Phil, mine host of our favourite Jambo watering-hole, but doing a shift in his other life at a city cab firm, swings by in a white stretch limo. 'Jump in,' he says.

'But it's only a few hundred yards to your pub,' we say.

Now we're feeling like soul divas. Well, wasn't it Mariah Carey who once famously declared: 'I don't do stairs and I don't do the last 400 yards to Da-Da-Da! in kitten heels either.'?

If I had been brave enough to retrieve my drink from Robertson's, I'd have raised my glass in tribute to the Jambo legend who gave the place its name. Dr Ruth, Calimero, Throbbo – no, he can go back to being Robbo now, for he quit Tynecastle before this game after refusing to accept a reduced post. I feel sorry for him. He tried to change the Hearts style of play – to endow them with actual style – but didn't have the players to achieve this, or the time. I'm thinking of the Hearts fans I met immediately after his appointment who were excited but also anxious: what if he failed and 'spoiled the legend'? Not just a pub, the man also has a Tynecastle stand named after him. I'm reckoning Bob, a SOH stalwart, must be one of those Jambos sorry to see him go when I bump into him in Mather's but, no, it was the right decision, he says. Robbo was turning up at the ground unshaven, without a shirt and tie. 'And that's not the Hearts way.'

Well, that remark is *very* Hearts.

## 22 May. Aberdeen 2, Hearts 0

Change is gonna come. Summer's almost here, and football fans have to skulk about. This isn't their time, there's too much brightness, they don't belong. Women want their men back: for a fortnight in Spain, to fit that bathroom shelf, to just be around. Princes Street is sunny and full of couples and it feels lumpily unreconstructed to be male and single and still in thrall to football, all the more so when it's not my team doing the thralling. The sun is only ever this fierce the first time you emerge from a blue-movie house following a matinee screening and the entire bus-stop queue glowers at you with disgust. It was *Mandingo*, starring a gloriously sluttish, slave-corrupting Susan George, and I remember that dead-eyed stare so well. You just feel *dirty*.

Metrosexual Man is here, too, the pink tee being the shirt à la mode for 2005. Back in 1955 or 1855 or whenever it was that this year's fashions were determined, designers must have had a great laugh speculating on how many neds and nyaffs from Northern Britain they could persuade to adopt a colour they would previously have outlawed as 'poofy'. I vowed never to join the pink revolution, not because I have an ideological problem with the shade, but for the simple reason of not wanting to be told what to wear. Inevitably, as sure as Andy Webster follows Steven Pressley onto the Tynecastle turf, I've succumbed and I'm in the pink today, too.

The day before the last game of the season, Billy, Ricky and I meet in Da-Da-Da! to watch the FA Cup Final on the box. Da-Da-Da! is changing as well. Posters in the windows advertise the fact it's going after a different kind of clientele and – while there's no mention of the fetishistic entertainment so desired by Charlie, yet another of those over-sexed Jambos – speed-daters will soon be welcome. I'm sorry about this for I've grown to like the place. At first I hated it, but, like Hearts, it has worn me down with its grim charms. We'll certainly miss Barbara, the Czech barmaid, and especially her Kournikova-esque pout.

Today the pink top is struggling to assert itself. Around 50 Arsenal fans in traditional red or away yellow are here for the showpiece against Man U and a flag on the wall proclaiming 'Scottish Gooners' confirms that our pub has been well and truly taken over.

At first we're respectful of this. Scotland and in particular Edinburgh has lots of English expats. But Ricky, ever-alert to football fuddery and especially phoneyness, soon starts to be suspicious of how the Capital came to have so many fans swearing allegiance to The Arse. 'Bet they never even liked fitba until *Fever Pitch*,' he says. 'Aye, that Nick Hornby has got a lot tae answer for.'

During the pre-match build-up the Gooners are singing their songs, which don't sound that much different from any other club's songs, but one fan dancing near us and chanting 'Thierry Henry, Thierry Henry' is really starting to annoy Ricky. 'Do you hear him?' he says. 'He's Scottish, right, but he's putting on a cockney accent. What's that aboot?'

This tube makes all the official announcements re the raffle etc and clearly reckons himself to be indispensable. He waves a ticket for the final above his head and I'm thinking: why's he not in Cardiff? 'Because he'd rather hang around a pub with his mates, showing off, playing the big shot,' mutters Billy. 'Any true fan would give anything to be at the match.'

Fans don't come more true than Billy and Ricky. Even when their team aren't playing well, such as right now, they still maintain a Jambo dialogue. They discuss Dave Mackay's autobiography and the book on the players wiped out in the First World War and the triple DVD box-set of Jambo goals down the years, and Ricky urges Billy to tell him another story about Drew Busby, the big, breenging 1970s centre-forward he knows he would have loved . . . and is it true that Busby towed monster trucks in training and instead of oranges at half-time he ate babies?

They're always down the club shop, checking out the Jambo accessories for a Jambo lifestyle. Billy, in fact, is a platinum-card peruser, and on first-name terms with all the girls there. But that does not mean they are dull and unthinking about their football, that they buy everything in team colours that's stamped 'Made In

Taiwan', or everything that's said by football people – the anodyne pundits, the players who've been media-trained to spout 'I love this club' right up to the day they sign for another one, and the mysterious money-men who ride to the rescue on a white charger which always begs the question: 'Is that a wooden horse?'

At first we aren't bothered who wins the Cup Final. Our only wish is that somehow Man U's Rio Ferdinand and The Arse's Ashley Cole, two supreme football chancers, both end up losers. But with Mockney and MacMockney accents dominating, we're starting to lean towards Man U. This preference is absolutely confirmed when a young lad in a United shirt, the only one in the pub, has to run a gauntlet of growling Gooners to sneak up the back. 'Pricks,' mutters Ricky.

These guys, my friends, have a clear idea of right and wrong in football. Don't be an arse – or an Arse – and above all don't be a fraud. I am obviously one, but Hearts for me this season have been an experiment. I've tried to be scientific about it, and the beagle required to smoke lots of cigarettes possibly had an easier time. So what am I now? Still a Hibby? Or a Jambo? I feel like the victim of another grim lab-test: the rat who wakes up and discovers it has grown a human ear.

Metrosexuality clearly hasn't hit Highbury, and in all probability, this lot haven't either. Billy nips out at half-time to Marks & Sparks and now he's wearing the shirt he bought in the sale: it's pink, too. Then the Cautious Managed Jambo Soft-Rock *Girls* stand together: against the English Premiership, the so-called 'best league in the world' which has only just expanded from a two-team contest to a three-team one, and against all its groupies. It's high time we claimed back a bit of *our* city, for *our* team.

> *Hullo, hullo*
> *We are the Gorgie Boys*
> *Hullo, hullo*
> *You'll know us by our noise . . .*

And I'm singing along, giving it total and absolute laldy.

The next morning, 9.50am, we're all hungover as we board the Portobello Hearts bus to Aberdeen. It's a miserable, damp day for a meaningless match – at least as far as the Jambos are concerned – and we're asleep until beyond Dundee. Then the clouds clear and Billy mentions the possibility of the 'six-goal swing'. If Hibs lose to Rangers and Aberdeen beat Hearts and the goal difference veers in the Dons' favour, Hibs will miss out on Europe. 'Aye,' says Ricky, 'we're making that midget Graeme Weir goalie today, just to be sure.'

So it's all come down to this: I want Hearts to win (or draw or not lose too heavily). For the first time since I started watching football 38 years ago, a Hearts result is going to have a direct impact on Hibs. I would be rooting for the Jambos anyway, even if I hadn't spent nine months trying to become a bona fide scarf-twirler, but here I am, among the season's fag-end hardcore, doing it in person.

How the world turns. I started 2004–05 hating Hearts, and yet no-one at Pittodrie today wants to see them win more than I do. Some, who believe in fair play, cheer for them as usual. Others, like Billy, munching on a Milky Bar, don't much care. And then there's Ricky, who never gives Hibs an inch, who in the 50th anniversary year of 'the vermin' being the first British club to compete on the continent, would like nothing better than to see them scuttle back to their rat-holes in Leith, having failed to qualify for the Uefa Cup at the last gasp.

' "Mon the Hearts!" ' I shout. 'MON THE HEARTS!' The Jambos near us are turning round to look at me and asking themselves: 'Why's he getting so excited?' I ignore them, and pump up the volume. 'IT'S THE ROUND WHITE THING! LOOK LIKE YOU'RE BLOODY INTERESTED!'

There's a moment, with Aberdeen two goals to the good and Hibs one down, when I'm absolutely screaming at the players, using the nicknames known only to me, and I'm thinking: this is like my very first match as a Jambo: same opposition, another blisteringly hot afternoon, and everyone else wondering: who's the Hibby in disguise?

I don't care. I tell Billy and Ricky that if the Dons score another, or Hibs lose another, then I'm going to run on the pitch and get this pathetic excuse for a game stopped. They laugh. 'You think I'm kidding?' I say. 'Wait until you see the T-shirt I'm wearing underneath this Metrosexual top. It says: "Never forget, we eased off in the second half and started Harlem Globetrotting around – it could have been much, much worse than 7–0." '

In the end the invasion isn't necessary. Once word comes through via radio that Hibs and Rangers are running, or rather walking, down the clock for a mutually beneficial 0–1 with shades of that notorious World Cup carve-up between Germany and Austria, the fight goes out of Aberdeen and this game dies on its arse.

I scan the field, focus on each Hearts player, freeze-frame a picture in my mind, for – unless a maroon-hued miracle happens over the summer – this is the last time I'll see them like this.

One by one, they shed the daft nicknames. They step out of the synthetic-fur clown-ensemble garb that they wore in my mind. Then off come the hard hats required for Jambo-style football, also invisible to all but my eyes.

Lisa-Marie goes back to being Elvis, Lumberjack to Robbie Neilson, Dine-Out to Jamie McAllister. All over the park slugs turn into butterflies, Hamsters into Hamills. Only one dissenting voice is heard, that of Neil MacFarlane: 'I like "Socrates" – can I keep it?'

The final whistle sounds and the Jambo contingent applaud the players, who acknowledge their support, sheepishly. Hearts aren't quite crap enough to stop Hibs qualifying for Europe, but there's some consolation for Billy and Ricky: Celtic, who pipped Hearts to the title in '86, lose the league in the final minute. Dundee, who party-pooped on Hearts that day, are relegated. And St Mirren, who maroon-clad conspiracy theorists accuse of lying down to Celtic, are threatened with going bust.

Small beer, but it's *Schadenfreude* all round in one of the golf clubhouses near Pittodrie, and as the seagulls swoop over the stadium, the three of us pick over the bones of the season. Ricky and I metaphorically arm-wrestle over the make-up of an Edinburgh 2004–05 Select, although I cannot nominate Hibs players with any authority, and the final selection ends up being Jambo-dominated and heavy on industry.

'I love efficiency, I fuckin' love efficiency. That's why I'm a Germany fan,' says Ricky.

'I admire Germany but I love Brazil.'

'Oh dinnae get me wrong, Brazil are *quality*.'

'So maybe this season I've learned to appreciate Germany more and you've learned to appreciate Brazil more?

'Aye, suppose so.'

'And I've learned to appreciate Hearts more and you've learned to appreciate Hibs more?'

'Fuck off!'

And so it continues like this, until the bus convener rounds us up for the journey home, and from nowhere, Billy pipes up: 'Hey, I've remembered the name of that song.'

Both of us: 'Which song?'

'The one I said I liked.'

'What, the one you said you liked in Dundee, in *January*?'

'Yes. It's "Afternoon Delight" by the Starland Vocal Band.'

In retrospect, without us knowing it, without The Human Map being able to plonk yet another soft-rock classic into the in-car sound-system, this has been the theme tune of our Saturdays together. Despite these Jambos having a Hibby in their midst, despite me choosing this season to watch Hearts when even two of their biggest fans admit they've been pretty dire, despite everything.

How do I feel about Hearts now? If nothing else my experiment proves that contempt breeds familiarity. But there *is* something else. Where once I saw a funny, wee, dour football team and a set of funny, wee, dour fans, now I see all of the aforementioned as attributes, along with sweat, grit, steel and fuckin' efficiency. I never thought I'd hear myself saying this, but there's a certain amount of truth in the unspoken Jambo motto: 'Beware flair'.

For this change of Hearts, little of the credit goes to the club. It's all down to the supporters I encountered during the season, and especially Billy and Ricky, who are now fast asleep on the bus and doubtless dreaming in Lithuanian.

Back in Edinburgh, I suggest one for the road in Da-Da-Da! but Ricky says he's having a quiet one. '*The Ultimate Fighter*'s on TV the night. That's boxing, kickboxing, wrestling, kickboxing and shoot-fighting.'

We shake hands.

'Anyway, next season, you ken where we'll be,' he says and his face – the one that never smiles – breaks into a huge grin.

We turn to say goodbye to Billy but he's already halfway across the road, shuffling in the direction of the sweet shop, quickening his pace to evade a tourist's rickshaw.

'He's got the afterburners on now,' says Ricky. 'Look at him go!'

# JUNE

## 26 June

It's funny, but all season long, I failed to spot that the Save Our Hearts Shop has a prime comedy location. I cannot believe I didn't notice that 106 Gorgie Road is next door to the offices of AKA Pest Control and opposite a knick-knack emporium, now closed, called Second Best.

Across Embra Toon, gloating Hibbys will argue that Hearts are in absolutely the right place, and that the natural capital-city football order has been restored with Hibs looking down on their great rivals, two places below in the final league table. I'd like to think that, despite the 1000 bad jokes I've cracked at the Jambos' expense, the fact I blew the chance for the 1001th – until now – proves that I took my task of trying to become one of them relatively seriously.

'The Save Our Hearts Shop is now closed – thanks for your support,' is the sign in the window. Nae bother, I say to myself, assuming the message to be a personal one, directed at me. Well, I did my bit. I saw Hearts play every SPL team, and at every SPL ground. I was there for every Inverness match, home and away, and every Livi match, including the cup-tie, including the game that never was. I followed them in Europe. Yes, I was in Rotterdam, and at lots of other rotten matches as well.

And now I'm in Gorgie Road, a goal-kick – or as I prefer, a Patrick Kisnorbo attempt at a two-yard pass – from the old ground and on this summery Sunday afternoon, as unfootbally a time of year as it's possible to locate in the calendar, I'm wondering when I'll be back.

A stout hymn – booms out of a wide-open first-floor tenement window as the net-curtains billow in the warm air. The Jambo Village has lost all of its fear now and I also can't believe I didn't lift my head from the pavement long enough before now to spot this shop, Gorgie Art.

Faither, the expert, wouldn't have fancied anything in the window but I could have told him, with some authority, that the garish guitar painting was of a Gibson Flying V, much favoured by Wishbone Ash, who were much favoured by dolts with inferior musical taste to mine, back in the tremendous 1970s.

I pass under the bridge . . . dare I even look? . . . a quick sideways glance into Robertson's, the dread-pub, its doors flung open, but the sunlight seems to have stopped short at the entrance and the interior is a black, gaping hole. One for the road? Hmm . . . all that stuff about this being the only gay pub in the Jambo Village? I was kidding. And today I'm wearing my sandals; they're white . . .

There's country-and-western singalong over at the Merchiston Hearts Social Club, and a maudlin you-done-me-wrong song is being belted out on the karaoke. Outside Carlton Bingo, a group of grey-haired women are making the most of their time, when they rool Gorgie, OK. But training has already resumed at Tynecastle – hey, let's call it Tynie – even though Hearts are still managerless. Big names like the German legend Lothar Matthaus (Ricky: 'I'd *love* him') pop into the frame, and just as quickly pop out again. A report in today's *Scotland On Sunday* casts yet more doubt on the Romanov revolution; his bank is under-performing, just like the team.

I think about stopping at the Ardmillan for a beer but decide to preserve it as my pre-match rendezvous with the guys. So can you really change horses in mid-stream . . . switch football teams in a mid-life crisis moment, *after* the tattoo and *before* the girlfriend who wasn't even born when your favourite bands were at their drum-solo apotheosis? I thought at the start of the season that for the turnaround to be validated, I would have to leap out of my maroon plastic pop-up seat during a derby and scream: 'Do it to Julia!'

Julia is not some Hearts player I've neglected to tell you about. She's the lover of Winston Smith, the hero of George Orwell's *1984*. As Winston is tortured in Room 101, as the rats are about to rip his face open, his cry of 'Do it to Julia!' confirms he has given up the last remaining kernel of himself and succumbed to The Party. For me, though, 2004–05 wasn't like that, not really.

Hearts, The Team, I know now, were the club of my father. There weren't many Hibs games in my youth where, at half-time or on the car journey home, the chat between Dad and I ran dry, but I wish I'd asked him more about his boyhood in this part of the city. Would he have owned up to all that *skipping* along Gorgie Road?

It's time, though, to move on. The past was great but eventually you tire of even your favourite triple concept albums. Guess what? I've got myself a pension now. The future's where it's at, and as Jon, my independent financial advisor, was telling me only the other day, you don't have to go down the Cautious Managed route, the one leading back to Tynie. You can tailor a SIPP – Self-Invested Personal Pension – so it's an expression of yourself, to illustrate to the world that if 'life is itself but a game of football', as the noted Jambo Sir Walter Scott once wrote, then you can be playing keepy-uppy all the way back to Leith and a happy and fulfilled second-half of your existence.

Today, I decide to wait for the No 25 bus. The shops at the stop are either boarded-up or stripped back to reveal old signs. I half-expect to find one reading: 'W. Smith – the only Hibs cobbler in Gorgie.' This was the grandfather I barely knew, the Hibby I never met.

The bus hurls me past an outlet called 'G-Spot – For all your personal preferences', further proof that the Jambo Village is not as buttoned-up as I first thought, then into the West End . . . past Da-Da-Da!, which Billy, Ricky and I kept in business through heroic drinking efforts . . . along Princes Street, past Wattie Scott's statue . . . and I jump off at John Lewis and dive upstairs for the best milkshake-bar panorama in the world: Leith.

To paraphrase the great 1970s disco troupers Odyssey, I am not a native Leith Walker. But I know the score by now. I know that Leith Walk is a superior thoroughfare to fat, complacent Princes Street. I know that no man who threatens to leave the 1970s behind can ever resist a peek in the window of Vinyl Villains, just to check how much his old Uriah Heep and Pink Fairies LPs would fetch now. I know that you should count your chickens; the hen statues at the top of Elm Row are always being nicked. I know that in this super-confident street, there is nowhere more sure of itself than Borlands – 'Established 1925 – Darts, Television'.

Is there more to life? Harburn Hobbies would tell you it's: 'Just in! New Hornby's 08–0–6–0 Shunter, BR Green, £54.99'. Everything a model train enthusiast could possibly want is in this shop ('Gravestones – £5.99'), and after a pre-match pint or three in the Windsor Buffet, my Hibby mates and I would always stop at the window display and remind ourselves that while we may be sad, there are some who are sadder still.

But these pals have gone. Hearts caught me at a weak moment, but Billy and Ricky have scudded into my life with all the intensity of a Jambo-style tackle and they're not about to leave it anytime soon. Where, then, do I go next season? I swing right towards Easter Road and . . . feeling like Bruce 'The Hulk' Banner, like the greenness is about to burst through my shirt . . . hang on, this is new . . . Utopia, a *style* bar. You won't believe me, but the older lad at my school with the momentous football boots, the Adidas 2000s . . . I've just spotted him in the corner. And I've just remembered his name as well, but I don't want to bore Phil with the story of what I've been doing for the last quarter of a century, now that the date on his fantastic footwear has finally come to pass.

Down into Albion Road, and for once the programme shop is open. I had a programme from my first-ever game but lost it. But here's a replacement: eight pages of Hibs-oriented facts, a squad photo, teams set out on a pitch drawing, adverts for Golden Export, the Army and Bandparts (suppliers of 'gramophone records' to the stadium), the crucial half-time scoreboard key – six old pennies way back when, but mine today for £1.50.

'My very first game,' I tell the man behind the counter.

'Really? How can you remember that far back?

'Don't get me started . . .'

But *now* what? If I carry on round the next corner, I will come to the home of the Hibee Nation. There, I could sit in the Famous Five Stand and gaze up at Arthur's Seat. Or I could sit in the West Stand and look down the Forth. Or I could sit in the East Stand and remember when I stood down at the wall, turning round every ten minutes to check on my dad's position in the surge and sway of the crowd, scanning the heads . . . ah, there he is.

But a 25 bus back to the Jambo Village leaves in a couple of minutes. Faither! Dot-dash, dot-dot-dot! Where the hell do I watch my football next season?

# INDEX

Aberdeen FC 2, 224, 231
Action Man 145
Adam, Stephane 150
Adidas 2000 football boots 29, 238
Albion Bar 162
Allen, Richard 48
*Amateur Photographer* 43
American Cream Soda 27
Amis, Martin 73, 80, 225, 228
Amon Duul II 94, 154, 185
Anderson, Alan 28, 147
Anderton, Phil 212–3
Andrews, Marvin 223
Anger, Kenneth 127
Arbroath FC, 141
Argent 13
Argentina, 1978 World Cup,
  horrors of 3, 126, 156
Armani, Giorgio 148, 195, 200
Arse, The (Arsenal) 20, 81, 228–30
Atlas, Charles 79
au pairs 163
Auld, Bertie 25
Aztec Bars 159

Bacharach, Burt 135
Balde, Bobo 64
Ball, Michael 111
Ballack, Michael 187
Banks, Gordon 107
Banks, Tyra 148
Banner, Bruce 'The Hulk' 238
Barker, Ronnie 163
Barnes, Chester 121

Basel FC 109
Bash Street Kids 23
Bauld, Willie 42, 68, 106, 205
Baxter, Stanley 27
Bay City Rollers 25
Beach Boys 152
Beckenbauer, Franz 163, 187
Beckham, Derek (né David) 24,
  54
Bellany, John 17
Ben Sherman shirts 48
Best, George 28, 172, 195
*Big Brother* 3, 16
Big Davie 37
Blackley, John 224
Blair, Tony 86, 213
Blane, David 157
Blue Oyster Cult 152
Boca Juniors 10, 200
Boco, Jimmy 7
Bodell, Jack 163
Bothwell Street Bridge 137
Bovril 2, 141
Bowie, David 12, 84
Brazil, 1970 World Cup-winning
  side 107, 108, 224
Brazil, Ally 172
Brazil (links to Hibs,
  notwithstanding Brazil, Ally)
  14, 30, 53, 107–8, 116, 124,
  171, 173, 221
Brazil (remoteness from Hearts)
  46, 110, 117
Brechin City FC 171

Bremner, Billy 115
British National Party 198, 213, 219

Beuzelin, Guillaume 57, 96
Buffalo Bill 141
Burns, Kenny 44
Busby, Drew 70, 93, 229
Busby, Matt 41
Butcher, Terry 92
Byshovets, Anatoly 109

CIS Cup 98, 162
Cala Homes 21
Camara, Henri 62
caramel wafers 180
Carpenter, Harry 163
Casuals 83–84, 114, 144–5, 217, 218
Celtic FC 35, 40, 61, 64, 168–70, 182, 186, 198, 201–2, 206, 211, 223, 227, 232
   chants 2, 50, 52, 63, 69–71, 77–8, 84, 93, 113, 132, 135, 140, 146, 155, 160, 178, 181, 189, 208–9, 221, 226, 230
Charles, Lord 78
Charles Buchan's *Football Monthly* 107
Charnley, Chic 'Chico' 7
Chelski (Chelsea) 20, 31
Chicory Tip 5, 12, 39, 84, 147
Child's Play 3, 136
Christie, Julie 2
Clark's Bar 37
Clearasil 38
Cleese, John 164
Clep, The 153
Clery Jungle 48, 180
*Clockwork Orange*, A 12, 55
Clydebank FC 142
Cockney Rebel 13
Cole, Ashley 230
*Commando* (comic) 163

Conn, Alfie 42, 205
Cooke, Charlie 153
Cooper, Alice 12
Cooper, Davie 203
Cooper, Henry 40
*coq au vin* 25
Corbett, Ronnie 15, 27, 29, 102, 164
Cormack, Peter 28
Cosgrove, Stuart 127–8
Cowan, Tam 128, 130
Coward, Noel 8, 132
Criminal Justice (Scotland) Act 36, 210
Cropley, Alex 28, 75, 206
Cruikshank, Geraldine 29, 95
Cruise, Tom 51
Curved Air 29

Da-Da-Da! 173, 175, 199, 218, 227, 228, 234, 237
Dalglish, Kenny 43, 115, 156, 198
Dalry Public Baths 54, 95
David, Hal 135
Depp, Johnny 192
Derrida, Jacques 60
District Bar 115–61,
Doc Marten boots 11, 117, 180
Doonican, Val 27
Double Diamond beer 36, 38, 187
Douglas, Michael 179, 192
Doyle, Sir Arthur Conan 141
Dr Gregory's Powder 184
Derrida, Jacques 40
Donovan 28
Dougan, Bobby 205
Douglas, Desmond 121
Doyle, Sir Arthur Conan 216
Du Toit, Elize 195
Duffy, Jim 7, 30
Dundee FC, 31, 81–82, 87–88, 117, 141, 151–5, 185, 196
Dundee Utd FC 31, 88, 147, 182, 198, 205–6, 215

Dunfermline FC 31, 98, 117, 118, 184, 189, 195
Dynamo Mince 191

Eardley, Joan 121
East Fife FC 141, 205
Eddie And The Hot Rods 52
Edgar Broughton Band 85
Edinburgh Festival 10, 20, 42
Edwards, Alex 206
Einstein, Albert 141
Essex, David 13
Etch-A-Sketch 14

*Face The Music* 129
Falkirk FC 141
Family 13
Famous Five 14, 16, 42, 55, 96, 107, 162, 204, 239
Fashanu, Justin 223
Faust 94, 188, 154
Ferdinand, Rio 230
Ferguson, Alex 43, 81
Ferguson, Barry 117, 183
Ferrell, Will 116
Ferencvaros 124–5, 127, 146, 167
Feyenoord 65, 92
Fireball XL5 143
Fitzgerald, F. Scott 214
Focus 13, 139
Ford, Donald 68, 196
Forres Mechanics 1
Forsyth, Tam 'The Scythe' 203
Foulkles, George 21
Fountain Brewery 149
Franz Beckenbauer Relaxed Ankle 163
Franz Ferdinand 213
Free 13
*Frost Report, The* 164

Galacticos 21
Gallumphicos 21, 45, 97
'Gardyloo!' 162

Gaviscon 222
Gemmell, Tommy 25, 41
Geordie 13
George, Susan 228
German football 93–4, 101, 187– 8, 233
Gerson 14
Gilzean, Alan 153
Gilzean, Harry 15
Glentoran 1
Glitter, Gary 13
Gold, Andrew 89
Goldberg's department store 163
Golden Export beer 238
Gordon, Alan 40, 74, 206
Gordon, Craig 45, 211
Gorgie City Farm 4, 119, 225
Gough, Richard 159
*Grandstand* 121, 163
'greatest game in history' 9, 10, 55, 73, 74, 75, 80, 232

Greggs sausage rolls 215
Greig, John 112

Haircuts
  bubble-perms 3, 126
  Hearts styles, crapness of, 23, 66
  Hibs styles, brilliance of, 58, 74–75, 85
  Lithuanian styles, 169, 175
Hall & Oates 203
Hamill, Joe 46, 79, 114, 136, 191, 194
Hampden Park, crapness of 210
Harburn Hobbies 238
Hart, Tom 112
Hartley, Paul 45, 49, 51, 113, 119, 134, 135, 154, 160, 168
Hartson, John 120
Hawkwind 13
Haymarket Bar 145, 203
Haynes, Johnny 66
Henderson, Willie 41, 203

Holmes, Sherlock 216
Hopcraft, Arthur 180, 219
Hornby, Nick 229
*Hornet, The* 18
Horseshoe Bar 72, 112
*Hotspur, The* 18
Houellebecq, Michael 60
Howson, Peter 80
Hughes, John 'Yogi' 7
Human Map, The, motoring
    excellence of, 102, 106, 128,
    158, 178, 185
Hunter, Russell 42

Ibrox 59, 62, 110–2, 114, 115,
    148, 222, 223
Inglis, Simon 148
Inverness Caley Thistle FC 50,
    51, 120, 190, 194, 235
IRA 16, 114, 148
Irn Bru 126

jacuzzis 125, 151, 153
Jairzinho 107, 225
Jefferies, Jim 74, 199
jockstraps 30
John, Elton 155, 189
Johnshaven Dauntless 121
Johnstone, Bobby 14
Johnstone, Derek 203
Jordan, Joe 115
*Joy Of Sex, The* 106

Kennedy, John F. 147
Khan, Oliver 187
*Kickback* 165, 168, 176
Kidd, Albert 88
Kilmarnock FC 20, 23, 91, 100,
    104, 169, 173
Kingston, Alex 36
Kisnorbo, Patrick 45, 52, 77, 95,
    96, 97, 143, 235
Klinsman, Jurgen 187
Kongos, John 29

Kubrick, Stanley 81
Kyrgiakos, Sotirios 183

Latapy, Russell 86
LCD Soundsystem 132
Led Zeppelin 5
Leicester City FC 81, 110, 135
Leitch, Archibald 148, 155
Leitch, Sam 41
Leith Athletic FC 195
Lennox, Bobby 41
Levein, Craig 5, 12, 15, 34, 38,
    81, 88, 89, 92, 95, 97, 99, 104,
    110, 113, 118, 138, 139, 143,
    151, 171, 202, 225
Levi Sta-Prest 165
Livingston FC 56, 58, 128, 159,
    161, 192, 235
Livingston new town, strangeness
    of 128, 159–60
Locke, Gary 169
London, Brian 163

McAllister, Jamie 46, 153, 159,
    166, 232
McCann, Neil 53
McConnell, Jack 208
McGregor, Ewan 15
McKenna, Kevin 45, 101
McLean, Lex 112
McLeish, Alex 110
McNeill, Billy 25, 40
McPherson, Dave 66
McQueen, Steve 123
macaroon bars 84, 108
MacDonald, Alex 112
MacFarlane, Neil 46, 100, 117,
    143, 171, 173, 190, 194, 221,
    232
MacKay, Dave 68, 229
MacLeod, Ally 43
*Magic Boomerang, The* 78, 97
Malcolm, Bob 111
*Man From U.N.C.L.E, The* 25

Manfred Mann 132
Manson, Shirley 15
Marinello, Peter 28, 172
Marx, Groucho 19, 34
Marx Brothers 51
mascots 15, 98, 118
mashie niblick 27
Mather's Bar 91, 124
Maybury, Alan 45, 77, 134
Medicine Head 13
Mercer, Wallace 18, 34–35, 74
Mikoliunas, Saulius 170
Milky Bar 198, 231, 236
Miller, Alex 85
Miller, Lee 153, 160, 165, 174,
    217
Moffat, Sandy 17, 44
Moller, Andreas 187
Monster Munch 59
Montford, Arthur 172
Morningside, aversion to knickers
    11
Moroder, Giorgio 147
Morton FC 141
Motherwell FC 30, 93, 162,
    165–6, 170, 176–7, 181, 203
Mott The Hoople 12
Mowbray, Tony 8, 15, 57, 81,
    89, 133, 160, 224
Mr Prickles 220
Muller, Gerd 187
Murdock, Colin 69
Murray, David 110
Murray, Ian 74
Murrayfield 22, 47–49, 77, 93,
    147

Narey, David 88
neds 177
Nedved, Pavel 6
Neilson, Robbie 45, 105, 109,
    155, 232
Netzer, Gunter 188
Nevin, Pat 127

Niddrie Terror 48
Norton, Ed 192

Odyssey 237
*Off The Ball* 99, 127, 129
Old Firm, tyranny of 36, 37–38,
    61–62, 64, 110–113, 114, 116,
    168, 183–4 (see also Celtic,
    Rangers)
O'Neill, Martin 168
Opal Lounge 100
O'Rourke, Jimmy 206
Ormond, Willie 14
Orwell, George 154

Pacino, Al 192
Parker, Dorothy 8
Parkhead 63, 64, 198, 201
Parlane, Derek 112
Partick Thistle FC, 1, 139–41,
    143, 148, 152, 179
Pele 14, 107
pensions 10, 102, 104, 106, 152,
    154, 195, 237
Pereira, Ramon 23, 46, 105, 177,
    191
Petric, Gordan 150
pies
    anti-climactic 154
    as alternative to sushi 151
    as missiles 132
    crummy 24
    Dundee variety (pehs) 151, 217
    half-time run 105, 158, 166
    importance of grease to taste 155
    lukewarm 16
    marketing slogans 105
    see also steak bridies
pigeon shite 7, 142
Pink Fairies 238
Pink Floyd 154
Pittodrie 50, 122, 231
Play-Doh 146
Play For Today 25

polyester 1, 22, 91, 193, 198
Pope John Paul II 211
Potter, Dennis 79
Prada 143, 188
Pressley, Steven 45, 79, 99, 105, 119, 136, 149, 153, 165, 202, 227, 228
Proclaimers, The 15, 34, 66, 86, 134
Psycho 16, 36
Python Lee Jackson 13

racism 64, 100, 114–5, 213, 223
randy monkeys 8
Rangers FC 35–38, 61, 62, 110–116, 168–70, 183, 184, 186, 203, 222
Rathbone, Basil 216
Ravenscraig 176, 181
Real Madrid 21
Red Hand of Ulster 38, 53
red snappers 211
Reilly, Lawrie 14
Republic Beer Cellar 200, 222
Ricksen, Fernando 184
Riordan, Derek (see Riordaninho, Deek)
Riordaninho, Deek 30, 58, 59, 77, 79, 116, 132, 133, 137, 157, 158, 172, 182, 195, 210, 219, 223, 224
Rivelino 14
River Plate 10, 200
Robbie's Bar 53, 54, 194, 197
Robertson, Fyfe 24
Robertson, John 50, 53, 87, 89; also Calimero 139, 172; Dr Ruth 106, 118, 127, 143, 160, 172, 181, 198, 214, 218, 227; Dr Sex 106; Throbbo, 106
Robertson's Bar, 4, 37, 67, 124, 167, 171, 191, 225, 226, 227, 236
Robinson, Chris 21–22, 165, 168

Rodd, Michael 73
Romanov, Vladimir, 31, 69, 117, 138, 139, 147, 150, 151, 168, 169, 173–4, 179, 193, 200, 213, 236
Ronaldo, Cristiano 6
Row Z 57
Rowbotham, John 86, 172
Roxy Music 12, 73, 80, 84, 152
rugby, hatred of 190

S&M 201
SC Braga 52
SFA, bampotery of, 50
safari suits 25, 44
St Mirren FC 88, 232
Saltoun Arms 122
Sands, Bobby 226
Sauzee, Franck 86
'Save Our Hearts' Campaign 21, 192–3, 227, 235
Scarf-twirling 24, 78, 157, 231
Schaedler, Erich 74, 75
Schalke 90, 93–5
Scotsport SPL 53, 79, 171–2
Scott, Dougray 66
Scott, Sir Walter 11, 154
Scottish Cup, Hibs' aversion to 140–2, 206, 209–11
Scottish League Cup 26
Scottish Premier League, crapness of 21, 59, 82, 97, 168, 170, 177, 217
Shankly, Bill 41
Shiels, Dean 58, 77
Shoot 180
Shorts
    baggy 14, 85
    skimpy 83, 85
Simmons, Steven 150, 159, 191, 194
Skids, The 98, 189
Slade 12, 21, 84
sly dunt 127

Smith, Gordon 14, 30, 219
Smith, Mark E. 216
Smith, W. Gordon (Faither) 2,
  25, 39–44, 48, 80, 88, 122,
  142, 151, 164, 176, 179, 180,
  181, 204–6, 236, 237, 239
Sneddon, Davie 105
Snug, The 216
soap-on-a-rope 40
Socrates 46, 108
'Son Of My Father' 12, 39, 147
Souness, Graeme 60–61, 68, 106,
  156
sovvy rings 199, 201
Spyrograph 50
Stamp, Phil 45, 51, 124
Stanton, Pat 43, 49, 186
Starland Vocal Band 233
Starlight Express 220
steak bridies 98, 166
Stein, Colin 203
Stein, Jock 41
Steps 109
Stone Island 54, 94
Strawbs, The 13
Subbuteo 63, 95, 96, 151, 180
Sunblest 132
Swinburne, Algernon Charles 8
Sweet, The 13

Take The Floor 43
Tartan Army, The 114, 126, 145,
  194
Tartan Special 131
Teasmade 175
Terrible Trio, The 42
Third Lanark FC 141
Thirty-Nine Steps, The 129
Tinelli trattoria 223
Tom of Finland 119
tomato soup 15
Tosh, Paul 7
Tostao 14
T.Rex 12

Trainspotting 15, 35, 194
Turnbull, Eddie 14, 43, 75
Turnbull's Tornadoes 29, 75, 84,
  206
Two-Lane Blacktop 190
Tynecastle Arms 195

UDA 16
UEFA Cup 40, 54, 224
Ujpest Doza 125
Ure, Ian 153
Uriah Heep 238

Van Der Graaf Generator 69
Van Der Valk 68
Viagra 104
viddy-printer 30, 140
Vogts, Berti 188
Voller, Rudi 187
de Vries, Mark 7, 33, 38, 46, 54,
  100, 114, 134, 135

Waddell, Willie 112
Waite, Terry 157
Walker, Billy 163
Wardhaugh, Jimmy 42, 205
Waring, Eddie 163
Webster, Andy 45, 51, 119, 189,
  202, 219, 228
Weir, Graeme 46, 64, 191, 194,
  231
Welsh, Irvine 15, 75, 194, 216
Wenger, Arsene 81
Whicker, Alan 25, 67
Wilde, Oscar 8
Williamson, Bobby (Mr Bobby)
  8, 15–16, 57, 110, 133, 225
Wilson, Dennis 190
Windsor Buffet, The 137, 165
Winchester, Ernie 28, 147
Wisdom, Norman 149
Wishbone Ash 236
Wiszniewski, Adrian 80
Wizzard 13

Wogga Wogga Wanderers 1
women (effect on football-
  watching) 23, 102
Wonderbras 57
Wyness, Dennis 46, 100, 105,
  118, 150

Yates, Ron 153
Yellow band fad 59, 66

Young, Chick 202
Young, John Paul 215
Young Leith Team 48
Young Mental Drylaw 48, 146,
  164

Zoff, Dino 58
*Zoolander* 28